To Dr. Shah,
helped so m

With admiration,
        Juliana McIntyre Fenn
                11/05/13

Wisdom at Play

JULIANA MCINTYRE FENN

WestBow Press books may be ordered through booksellers or by contacting:

WestBow Press
A Division of Thomas Nelson
1663 Liberty Drive
Bloomington, IN 47403
www.westbowpress.com
1-(866) 928-1240

ISBN: 978-1-4497-8922-0 (sc)
ISBN: 978-1-4497-8923-7 (hc)
ISBN: 978-1-4497-8921-3 (e)

Library of Congress Control Number: 2013906959

Printed in the United States of America.

WestBow Press rev. date: 06/14/2013

Oh, dearest, dearest child! My heart
For better lore would seldom yearn,
Could I but teach the hundredth part
Of what from thee I learn.

(William Wordsworth, The Period of Childhood, XII)

DEDICATION

I give thanks to children whose Wisdom released my spirit to grow.

I give thanks to Jim McIntyre whose Wisdom
enabled my school to grow.

I give thanks to Richard Fenn whose Wisdom
inspired my book to grow.

CONTENTS

PREFACE

I did not make it up. The Wisdom Tradition existed long before institutionalized religion. Throughout the ancient world, God's Wisdom was viewed as integral to the natural order of people, places and things—everywhere. Every human being, imbued with the divine image in a highly individual way, was essentially "I am." According to the Wisdom Tradition, the existence of God within the creation spiritually connected everything and everyone. Hence communities came into being. Formal religions eventually evolved as human beings tried to penetrate and understand Wisdom's mystery. I have drawn on the ancient Wisdom Tradition to find a way to describe what I believe to be the most transformative, creative life force—a force most easily seen in the early stages of our young. I have drawn heavily on a couple of sources, notably John Priest. There are different scholarly opinions about which ancient texts refer to God's Wisdom. Generally, it was widespread from Egypt to Mesopotamia long before the tribes became nations. The Wisdom Tradition takes us back to the childhood of our civilization—back to the essentials.

I have been around children all of my life, as a mother, a grandmother, a teacher and as a child myself. This book is a testimony to their inborn Wisdom that emerges so clearly during moments of transformation—such as play, connection, creativity or—most important—love. The Wisdom that surges through a child's solving of problems, healing of wounds and striving for justice transcends all reason. The Wisdom that enables a child to make a leap into imagination where time and space hold no authority transforms all logic. We often refer to a child's vital spirit without realizing that it is Wisdom we are dealing with—the language of the soul.

In this book, I focus on children with unique situations. The Wisdom Tradition is intensely personal. I write about how Wisdom comes into play within human relationships, relationships with creatures and works of art. I revere the Wisdom Tradition because it speaks of the search for God's Wisdom as a lifelong, loving devotion of the most personal kind.

God's Wisdom is not limited to children; it is in all of us, despite appearances otherwise. Wisdom is transformative and therefore redemptive. Children, because they are so young and inexperienced in life's many pathways, wear their Wisdom on their sleeves. I do not pretend to know Wisdom's whole story. I can only share with you my glimpses of its playful, surprising, and transforming power in the lives of children I have known. By their revelations I have been taught. It is no wonder that Jesus advised us two thousand years ago:

> Truly I tell you, unless you change and become like children, you will never enter the kingdom of heaven. Whoever becomes humble like this child is the greatest in the kingdom of heaven. Whoever welcomes one such child in my name welcomes me. If any of you put a stumbling block before one of these little ones who believe in me, it would be better for you if a great millstone were fastened around your neck and you were drowned in the depth of the sea.

> (Matthew 18:2-6, The New Oxford Annotated Bible, Third Ed., New Revised Standard Version with the Apocrypha, p. 34 NT)

The spirit of Wisdom breathes through children. It fills them with God's love, whether they know it or not. I hope that you will feel, as I have, the magnetic pull of this love—and that you will perceive what you can do to help children access their Wisdom as they grow. In their continuing transformation lies our own. If they stumble, so shall we.

INTRODUCTION

"Come and hear about our plans for a new school." The ad was no larger than a postage stamp.

The meeting took place in a church's basement on a hot evening in July, 1983. "How many chairs should we set up?" I asked Margaret as we surveyed the church's large, empty room. We pondered. If we set up fifty chairs and only five people came, the meeting would seem under-attended. If we set up five chairs and fifty people came, we would look ill-prepared. In the end, we set up fifteen chairs and twelve people came. After introducing ourselves and our colleague Alice Benson, we asked our guests to imagine a school for young children in this very space: a book corner here, an easel there, no walls, and three passionate teachers with a handful of homemade materials.

We shared a common goal: to nurture young children into academic excellence using every method imaginable to satisfy their hunger for learning. We had the blessing and support of two of Princeton's finest educators: T. Leslie Shear, a distinguished university professor, and Nancy Robins, a superb teacher and former school head.

That September, we made a leap of faith. Margaret soon became the head of the school's Board of Trustees and I became the head of the school. Together with Alice Benson, we taught our first tiny classes of children aged three, four, and five. In the following years, the school opened higher grade levels (nobody wanted to leave) and rented additional church facilities. These we alternated with a number of other tenants, from the Boy Scouts to the homeless. It took no small measure of confidence for parents to enroll their children in a school that was "struck" every Friday night and restaged every Monday morning, where teachers made their own educational materials stored in the trunks of their cars, and where children were asked to look inward for the wisdom that invigorates learning. Students' families caught their spirit of invention and helped in every way they could, building playground equipment, painting classrooms, cooking potluck dinners, responding immediately to our calls for help when the basement flooded or a funeral shut down classes for a few hours. The school evolved as a vital community, a way of life, a vocation. To this day, it dwells in the hearts of the alumni who travel the tortuous pathways of the adult world.

> Most of the memories of my early childhood involve swing sets and hide-and-seek, but considering that my teachers had me pegged for a writer at age four, I think I probably did a lot more than just run around the playground. Today, as an English and Studio Art double major, I think I have a lot of options as to how to spend the rest of my life, but all I can seem to imagine is fulfilling the prediction that was cast sixteen years ago. I can see myself writing and illustrating children's books. At a Teach for America meeting this fall, I was surprised and excited by the strong reaction I had to the program, and I am seriously considering teaching for them when I graduate. I've always had a desire to help people, and especially, a passion for working with children. I attribute this . . . to my experience at PJS. I can't imagine a more caring, open, and cultivating environment than the Junior School, and I'm looking forward to one day sending my children there.
>
> Alumna

> One of my fondest memories . . . is the time I spent with my fifth grade class . . . in Vermont—the final trip for a core group of us who had been together since kindergarten. [Mrs. McIntyre] took us with her forest manager at the break of dawn to a piece of land she owned, where we spent the day learning how to age trees, learning what a sick tree looks like, and learning how to cut down a tree with a two-person saw. This was a wonderful moment, but not a particularly unique one in my six years at PJS. Whether sculpting wooden birds with a piece of sandpaper, or on the beach at Cape May watching horseshoe crabs lay

eggs, or interviewing local artists about their careers, or on the playground looking through welding goggles at a total solar eclipse, I felt connected to what I was learning, clichéd as that may sound.

Alumnus

I would like to tell you about the school that launched these alumni. It is a school where we had to start from scratch, creating our own ways of organizing time and space. There children became teachers and the teachers became transformed by children. The lines separating work from play dissolved as children learned to connect themselves with the world far beyond their reach but never beyond their imagination. It was their courage, their willingness to be transformed, their surprising and often challenging questions that drew from the adults who served them a new spirit and a new hope. In telling you about these children and the school that they created with us, I will also tell you something about myself. Just as these alumni sense that their spark was kindled at Princeton Junior School, so do I believe that Princeton Junior School truly began when I was a child in a family that introduced me to myself—and to the surrounding community.

Returning again to the school's story: the town of Princeton became our campus. Within walking distance of our churches were ample resources for academic learning, community service and recreation. We frequented the public library and university museums. We explored the post office, municipal building and governor's mansion. We learned the town's history by visiting the historical society, the revolutionary war monument and the Princeton Battlefield where we flew kites among its gusts and ghosts. We sledded on the golf course, picnicked at the lake and bird-watched in the woods behind the Institute for Advanced Study. Our children planted a vegetable garden in a neighbor's backyard. They participated in a master class at the neighboring choir school. They performed plays in local nursing homes and 'went on the road' as Woodrow Wilson Declaimers. Photographs of those early years depict an exuberant fledgling school.

Where to fly? It eventually became apparent that without a permanent home, the school would not survive much longer. Occupying three facilities and living out of a suitcase might suffice for a short time, but we were flying in circles.

By 1990, the school enrolled about eighty students—preschool through Grade IV—in three separate locations. The faculty and staff amounted to fifteen. The Board had tried to buy or rent a property for the long term: a former schoolhouse, a deconsecrated church, a firehouse, a mansion, a warehouse. All efforts had failed for one reason or another. After searching unsuccessfully, the school found a beautiful site for sale—formerly a tomato farm—within easy range of several communities. To gain municipal approval for a school on the farm's back acres, to finance and finally to construct a permanent facility took several years. We moved to our permanent home in 1998.

The design for the new schoolhouse—a central commons surrounded by classrooms—was inspired by our conviction that children learn best when they are at the center of a loving community. The school's commons, built with barn timbers hauled down from a farm in Canada, provided a center for our gatherings.

Over the years we had become a community of hope—not only for a home we could call our own but also a home in which the Wisdom of children would flourish. This Wisdom, essential to the souls of children, had to be honored, encouraged, and shared *now* if they were to become creative and fulfilled in later life. Our hope was that the school—a microcosm of society—would have a positive impact upon our greater culture. Hence our interest in maintaining a diverse school family, a daily dialogue with the natural environment and a challenging curriculum at all levels. Looking back on those early years, I am convinced that when we focused upon what seemed most important to the education of children—their Wisdom—we were doing God's work. We were on sacred ground where Wisdom was at play.

"Children are an endangered species!" we hear from time to time. Despite current skepticism about education in America, I believe that children are born with the image of God etched into their individual souls—an image providing ample Wisdom to inspire a lifetime of transformation and growth. The presence of God expressed through the Wisdom of children is of infinite importance as we care for and educate them. Nothing should concern us more.

We do not always recognize a child's Wisdom at first, because when we ask, "What did you learn at school today?" the child's response is often little more than a shrug and a word: "stuff." Nevertheless, this "stuff" is the basic armature upon which a child shapes the clay of his or her life. This "stuff" can be quantified by testing and grades, but only in part—for it is born out of a Wisdom far beyond academic acquisition. The real test of early childhood education lies in the quality of life that it inspires. Children may not be conscious of their Wisdom at first, but certain experiences help them to access it. The freedom to *be*, to *believe*, to *become*, is their birthright, their buoyancy.

In this book, I shall describe some of the epiphanies that I have had with children over the years. The stories that I tell have been drawn from memories of my own childhood, from my children and grandchildren, and from the children of Princeton Junior School. Each story describes children who in one way or another have accessed their inner Wisdom so as to:

- start from scratch, plumb their depths, get back to essentials
- make friends with whom to work and play, respect all kinds of people, share what they know
- make connections with past and present, let the future begin
- kindle their imaginations, transform themselves in a creative process
- go beyond their immediate reach, take risks and learn from their mistakes
- create rituals to remember what they value, see beauty in ordinary things
- observe natural phenomena, note the ever-changing cycle of life
- get to the heart of the matter, exercise their passion for healing and justice
- reflect upon the experiences they have had
- learn who they are, learn how to give and receive love and how to cheer up the world.

A school's primary job is to honor childhood. Usually, young children long to learn about whatever interests them, whether or not it is prescribed by the curriculum. Hence the school must discern their Wisdom, encourage them to think, to question and to learn basic skills through the *experience* of subjects that truly interest them. In math, for example, they will learn to count, to compute and to calculate more readily if the process involves the head, the heart and the hand.

> I can't overstate how much Princeton Junior School shaped me as a person. Aside from my family, it was the most profound influence on my character during childhood. The Junior School fostered a deep love of learning that drove me to become a lifelong scholar. Our education was a hands-on experience; we were encouraged to approach it as an adventure. The spirit of creativity was everywhere. We wrote plays and performed them at other schools, we learned ornithology by carving wooden birds, we constructed our own playground equipment, we declaimed a series of Woodrow Wilson speeches, we published a newspaper.
>
> Alumna

Children should be encouraged to have a profound sense of their own abilities and those of others as well. They should be encouraged to communicate their growing knowledge consciously and generously. Therein lies a life that reflects the sanctity of the individual and his or her responsibility toward society.

You may be tempted, as I am, to think that the children of America are in danger of surrendering their childhoods to the distractions of our modern world. True, they may be sidetracked from the very Wisdom that moves them to seek justice, beauty, knowledge, and companionship as well as competence. However, their capacity for transformation is boundless. If their families and schools help them to recognize their inborn Wisdom, they will exercise their creativity and move ahead.

It is perhaps a far-fetched assumption that young children are knowledgeable, since they have not had much experience of this life. I grew up in a large family strewn with children, yet I was unaware that we "little ones" were teachers as well as learners. Later, as an adult, I acknowledged the truth of the matter. I had an enormous amount to find out from children about my God-given, inborn capacity to learn, to live, and to love. I have always wondered: what do children universally know and do that I—an adult—need to know and do?

Once, when I was walking around the school, I noticed a door that had been wedged open with a stick. I was about to remove the stick and close the door when I noticed a child's handwritten note taped to the door frame: "DO NOT shut the door. You will kill the baby." An arrow pointed upward. I looked up to find a tiny chrysalis nestled into the crack above the hinge. Days later, as I watched the children release their monarch butterflies into the air, I was glad I had done what I was told.

PART I: BEING

"May I?" I asked. I reached for the stethoscope and pressed it to my belly. I listened for a moment to my unborn infant's steady heartbeat. Its rhythm—dum, de-dum, de-dum, de-dum—pumped along with mine as we groped our way through the spiral of labor toward birth. It was a very slow process, for she was three weeks overdue, very large, and facing backward. For a few grueling moments during massive contractions, we suffered the doctor's attempts to rotate her body until it faced forward. After several attempts, she finally found her way down the birth canal toward the world, her heartbeat chiming wildly. A bevy of nurses flurried about the bed, chanting "Push! Push! Push!" One asked me whether I wanted to watch what was happening in a mirror. Was she kidding?

New form, new breath: a true miracle. I marveled at her slippery, separate body. This child who had dwelled for months in my womb was now flailing beneath a warm lamp on the other side of the room. Would we ever again know one another so intimately? The cry from Julie's tiny windpipe awakened in me an intense yearning for reconnection. "Julie!" I cried back. Finally, she was brought to me.

Julie gazed. Was she remembering her maiden voyage? Had she said all her good-byes before setting off? Did she know she was the bearer of a wisdom only God could give, one that existed before her and beyond her as well as within her, that longed to be revealed through creative work and play throughout her life, that flowed deeper and wider than the bounds of religion or social order? Her lips curled and quivered, but she never uttered a word. Creation remained her own mystery.

Birth is as great an awakening as anyone will make until experiencing death, when another incalculable labor and delivery will take place. To be sure, there are other awakenings in between, but nothing compares with one's first glimpse of a totally unique, live figure of God's imagination. When you tuck the covers around a sleeping infant, are you not awestruck by this slumbering miracle of being? This child has been conceived and received, not copied or imitated. If given the chance, she will awaken you to your own incarnation.

> For you yourself created my inmost parts;
>   You knit me together in my mother's womb.
> I will thank you because I am marvelously made;
>   Your works are wonderful, and I know it well.
> My body was not hidden from you,
>   while I was being made in secret
>   and woven in the depths of the earth.

Psalm 139:12-14, The Book of Common Prayer,
Church Publishing Inc., New York, pp. 794-95

As I gazed back into the face of my baby girl, I wondered where her wisdom would lead me and what lessons she would teach me within the circle of our life together.

Once upon a time, a school was born—not in the same manner as Julie, of course. However, in telling about the school's birth, I must acknowledge the same indescribable energy that pulsated through my soul at the time.

Someone once posed the question: "Who would be such a fool as to create a school such as this?" I have weighed that question often. It is time that I—the fool—try to answer it. When I was first offered the opportunity to found a new school, I visited the proposed site, a church's underground fellowship hall at the foot of a dimly lit cement stairway. With natural light and fresh air available only through small, high windows, the atmosphere was dispiriting. I imagined such a place would not inspire even the most motivated children and teachers. Nevertheless, on the day I visited the Bayard School which occupied the premises at the time, I was impressed by the cheerful demeanor of both the teachers and their small charges. Did they not notice the lack of light? I certainly did.

Despite the urging of several parents and colleagues, I turned the offer down. Little did I know then that within a year, the Bayard School would close and Princeton Junior School would be born in the same space. Nor did I know then that during the next fifteen years, the new school would expand into two additional churches, a public school and a theological seminary before creating its own permanent home.

What caused my change of heart? In the spring of 1983, I spent a weekend at a retreat center along the Hudson River. There I found the solitude I needed to explore new pathways for my restless soul. Aged forty-eight, married, and the mother of two children on the brink of leaving for boarding school, I prayed for guidance in my search for a new vocation. What did God want me to do next? My husband worked internationally and my children were leaving home. Should I return to my art studio? Should I teach? Despite having twenty years of teaching behind me, I feared I no longer had the stamina to weather the storms of educational change. The seventies had taken their toll on the American school system. Headwinds of anti-integration sentiment had blown schools into fragments across the country. As for me, I was comfortable in my own little corner, sculpting portraits of comfortable little people.

In contrast to some of the others at the retreat center, I received no inspiration during that weekend. Feeling as restless as I had when I arrived, I drove home in a gloom. Planning the perfect vocation was beyond me, a waste of time. I evidently had forgotten that a vocation is something to which one is *called*. In any case, I told God that He had disappointed me greatly. As I headed for home that Sunday afternoon, I grimly resolved to take any job that came my way, be it tutoring, typing, or washing dishes.

The following day, I received a telephone call from a former colleague who was now teaching music at the aforementioned Bayard School.

"Juliana, darling, how are you?"

"Fine," I fibbed. "What's going on?" Margaret never called unless something was going on.

"Well, I'm in a dither. The Bayard School is closing!" I could tell by the following singsong of details that she was narrowing in for the kill. "It's such a shame to let go of . . . well, to get to the point, will you agree to open a new school in September?"

3

"Me? I am a teacher, not an administrator!"

"Now, Juliana, I know you didn't want to do it when they asked you before, but I'll help! If there are two of us . . ." Her velvet voice crooned on and on.

I cringed. *Oh, God, is this what you want me to do?* Ruefully true to my resolve of the day before, I agreed to cofound a school. The gloom of that afternoon lifted to reveal a newborn me.

Princeton Junior School came into the world as the offspring of two teachers who—despite our long familiarity with children and our degrees in education from the Harvard Graduate School of Education and the Bank Street School of New York—had no prior experience starting or running a school. Two months before the new academic year, Margaret and I put an announcement in the local papers:

> Come hear about our plan to open a new school in September.
> Classes are offered to children aged three, four, and five.
> For further information, please attend a meeting at 8:00
> p.m. on Thursday . . .

The announcement was no larger than a postage stamp. The meeting took place at 8:00 p.m. in the basement of the church. We set out forty folding chairs but then thought better of it and put out fifteen instead. Twelve people showed up.

Margaret and I encouraged our audience to envision the school-to-be. "Have you ever thought about how much you can learn from children? How play—their most natural medium—enables them to learn academic subjects by heart? How best to let children be . . . believe . . . and become? We have both been trained to teach children the basics, but *how* they are taught is the key. They remember more when they learn something by experience. Yes, we have both taught in fine schools. Yes, we are both parents, too. True, we've never done this before. We want to start a school devoted to early childhood learning. Can you help us?" I don't remember what we said word-for-word, but the gist of it was, "We want to create a school family in which children love to learn and learn to love."

To our delight, twelve children were enrolled. They and the thousands who followed may not remember all the details of their time at Princeton Junior School, but the wisdom that transformed them then continues to flicker now.

—*w*—

Let us focus for a while on disruptions. I sometimes wonder whether people would ever have children if they knew in advance how much having children would change their plans. The arrival of a new, utterly original person requires our utmost attention. This is particularly true of one's first child. Uninterrupted sleep becomes a thing of the past. The breast becomes a reservoir. Laundry sets the table. A cry from the crib cancels conversation. Furthermore, the child grows and changes in the twinkling of an eye. The former babe now toddles with a will of iron to the foot of the parental bed, pleading admission. Privacy is out of the question. The bathroom wall is always wet. Graffiti garnishes the pages of books. Food falls from the spoon to the floor. Shouts tumble out. Words we have waited for finally come . . . but these? "No! More! Mine!" (My first words, I have been told, were like fire engines blaring in the Holland Tunnel.) We ask, "What is this child telling us? What has caused the alarm? Where is the fire?" Combustion threatens as we rush to cool the smoldering tyrant in the high chair.

Despite the chaos created by the arrival of children, there is wisdom to be gained: in and through this chaos their life begins to take form. Because they have not had much experience, they approach their challenges in the best way they know how: by following their intuition. How else would they have learned to stand, walk, and talk? When I was a very young child, my toes turned in and I often tripped and fell to the floor. I remember commanding myself to get back up and walk. After several years of exercises and special boots, I finally walked without tripping. I could not have done it without my insistent inner voice, plus the supervision of an expert podiatrist whose name—Dr. Stump—belied his devotion to his young charge. He played marbles with me—I had to shoot with my toes in order to strengthen them. I became good enough in time to beat the wise guys in the neighborhood.

—ᴧᴧ—

Haven't we all from time to time sailed into new waters, wide-eyed with a catch in our throats? The first day of school marks a new beginning: a time of hope, wonder and surprise. I watched children on that day leave behind the familiar good-byes and confront the rising wave of new faces. Had they been assured that they were loved, no matter what? Even now, after seventy-seven years of new beginnings, I occasionally feel uncomfortably shy. Overcoming timidity is no easy task. It requires trust. Only when I realize that transformation doesn't depend solely on *me*, but that God's energy moving through me is what changes me, do I have the courage to try new things. Young children may not think this way; they are more eager to leap into the unknown than we who have been stung a few times.

There is an inner dynamic of wisdom at play in our dreaming, our creative work, and our courage to reach beyond being to becoming. The wisdom of children is the expression of that inner dynamic. Our school, even in its earliest and skimpiest stage, invited children to call upon this extraordinary capacity of the soul. Their dreams permeated their play. Their play imbued their work with imagination. Imagination—the mind's eye—formed images, thoughts, and ideas that reached beyond the children's actual experiences. With sometimes reckless verve, they leapt from one stone to another to cross the shallow water between the known and the unknown. Our teachers were familiar with the life of the spirit, having lived it themselves, so they understood the seriousness of wisdom at play.

In a young child's world, play rather than language is often the best way to overcome shyness. Case in point: recently, my husband, Richard, and I visited his daughter's home in California. I was introduced to his two-year-old grandson, who silently stared me down. What was this little person, barely speaking my language but fully steeped in his own, wondering about me? After all, I was the newcomer in his short lifespan; I was the arrival, the interruption. His cool scrutiny quieted my impulse to hug and I waited to see what would happen next. He was scooped up by his father and asked to greet me nicely. Not yet. Head turned way, he squirmed. No matter. Rituals take time. To my relief, he was put down and allowed to dash out of sight.

So we older ones settled down for a cup of tea and conversation. O ho, what was that rolling toward me on the floor? A ball? From where? Over there, behind the chair. I picked it up and rolled it back. What? Here it was again. And so the game—or rather, the introduction— progressed. Before long, I could hide a block for him to find. He did. By the end of the day, this child had shown me everything, from his favorite books to a park where he exhausted himself. We tossed twigs into a trash can for fun. Was not action the natural medium of expression for this young man? Surely, such play would teach him the words he needed. Rolling a ball would give way to, "Hello, here I am!" Tossing a twig would give way to "Watch me get it in!" The sounds he uttered would give way to sentences, the scribbles to symbols, the stumbles to steps. At bedtime, when I bid my new friend good-night, he responded with a sleepy smile.

—∿∿—

In starting the new school, we were immediately conscious of our young children conveying a longing for connection as they entered this strange world away from home. They cared more about cuddling than curriculum. So cuddling came first until everyone relaxed into a school family and allowed such skills as sharing, taking turns, and forming a circle to follow. Their wisdom shone through in their eagerness to explore, discover and play with new subjects.

—∿∿—

One day, a boy arrived at school with misery written all over his young face. We waited for an explanation, but he said nothing. Later, I found him in the playground swinging merrily, his feet kicking at the shadows. I asked him why his mood had changed. With a flicker in his eyes, he shouted, "My teacher smiled at me . . . I swallowed her smile and my tummy stopped hurting." Later, when the Division of

Youth and Family Services (DYFS) inspector arrived and crawled on his belly beneath the jungle gym, looking for rot, cracks, and bees' nests, the same boy—now swinging upside down from a bar above the inspector's head—inquired, "What do you do for a living?" He got no smile from the inspector.

—◊—

No child could have progressed without the singular hospitality of my beloved cofounder. Margaret was no ordinary educator. Her empathy toward young children was legendary, as anyone whose little ones have ever sat on her lap can attest. She not only understood children; they understood her as if they had known her beyond the few years of their earthly lives. Between themselves and Margaret flew a spark of recognition that could kindle a bonfire. Her velvety voice, her smiles and her ageless white complexion projected an exotic beauty that was compelling—but what really transfixed them (and the rest of us as well) was her manner of dress. I often supposed that she arose in the morning anticipating a day of adventure and then created for herself a garment that would fit the adventure, whatever that might be. We all looked forward to seeing her float into school in a cloud of chiffon on May Day, or leathers and feathers for Thanksgiving, or cat's whiskers at Halloween. Occasionally, she would lead a procession of children around the playground, draped in the flowing remains of her living room curtains. Her exotic hats, embroidered wraps, lotus shoes and hair combs from China (her childhood home), in contrast to her demure demeanor, gave her a certain *je ne sais quoi*. Every morning, her vivid figure stood at the curbside waiting to greet each child who arrived by car. I often heard an excited voice cry out from the back seat: "Look, there she is, waiting for us! We're here!" With infinite tact, Margaret would open the car door, welcome the child with a hug, and dismiss the dazed driver with a wave of her gloved hand.

Nothing daunted this lady. One night, I borrowed a pickup truck to fetch some bookcases that I had bought for the school earlier that day at a yard sale in Kingston. The sellers had gone off to get pizza, leaving their ten-year-old son to help me load the heavy bookcases on to the truck. He scrambled into the truck's bed and tied them in with a length of clothesline. On the way home in the dark, the rope slipped and the whole load slid from the truck into a ditch. So much for knot-tying. I could barely make out the bookcases, none of which were lying on the road, fortunately. Leaving them behind, I drove to Margaret's house to call for help. She had just arrived home from a party, garbed in a cloud of gauze. Upon hearing of my dilemma, she exclaimed, "Darling, it's much too late to call anyone. We can't leave the bookcases there—someone will snitch them!" She trotted into her garage on her stiletto heels and returned a minute later waving a skateboard. "I knew I would find a use for this! I bought it today at the same sale." An hour later, anyone traveling along Route 27 between Kingston and Princeton would have sworn he had seen an apparition: a large diaphanous moth fluttering along the roadside, rolling a bookcase in the direction of a pickup truck.

Margaret played the recorder beautifully. Under the spell of its thin tunes, the children learned melodies that they hummed throughout the school day. Not only did her pipe evoke songs, it served as a chanter that stimulated the children to learn phonics or computation by heart. Chanting and clapping in rhythmic repetition brought meaning to memorization: it became a game.

———✵———

During the summers, I would retreat alone for a few days to our house in Vermont, a place apart from the bustle of life. There we were restoring a long-neglected farm. My retreats in June were always a time for solitary reflection as well as for airing the house, brushing cobwebs from the barn timbers and planting the vegetable garden. I would take with me a load of books, tapes, and a typewriter in hopes of discovering and shaping new ideas to guide the school's life, as well as my own.

On one such retreat a couple of years after we had opened the school, I was in the kitchen, ironing freshly washed white curtains. They had been hanging on the line outdoors all morning, billowing like sails in the wind. Now, indoors, as the steam iron smoothed out their fine wrinkles, I could smell the sunshine escaping from their cotton threads. All was silent save for the hissing of the steam and the occasional sigh from my dog asleep nearby. I decided while ironing that afternoon that I would listen to some lectures about the Benedictine way of life that my mother had recently given me. Listening to them as the hours flew by, I realized how closely some of Saint Benedict's advice, written in the sixth century by a layman for lay people, related to our school's brief life as a community. Many of Benedict's precepts harmonized with our secular school's simple, radical call to "start from scratch, plumb your depths, and get down to essentials." From Benedict I received support for much that we were already about: hospitality, diversity, equality, and most transformative of all, spirituality within the daily life of the school.

I am reminded of a vision my mother shared with me when she was very old. She dreamed that she had a conversation with God. He asked her to rake leaves into two piles: the first pile would represent things that she could let go of, that didn't matter. The second pile would represent things that truly mattered. My mother worked until every leaf was raked. The pile of things that didn't matter was large. The pile of things that truly mattered was small. When she was finished, God told her that she had done the job very well. Then He blew away her large pile and asked her to attend to the small pile for the rest of her life. How often do we attend to the few things that really matter and let go of those that do not?

> I look at all the colors,
> And I listen to the sound
> Of my grandma raking leaves
> Into piles upon the ground.

Student

This wise and holy man, Benedict, reminded me not to expect perfection of either the children or their parents or their teachers, but rather, to recognize their epiphanies as spiritual guidelines. Unexpected intuitive leaps of understanding were what I should watch for. These epiphanies would be glimpses into the wisdom within.

The following is an excerpt from my journal, written during the school's first year.

> Trust the spirit of God. Allow it to guide you. Trust that the child within you will grow and thrive regardless of outer hardships. Cooperate with your daily companions, young and old. Together you will bear fruit. Do not fear or make false judgments about the terrain which you tread. False judgment will prevent new life from emerging. Believe in transformation. Children do.
>
> J.

Princeton Junior School's mission statement, "We aim to provide academic excellence in a loving environment," was more evasive than persuasive, I thought. Its words could hardly define what was evolving. I believed that we were doing God's work within the secular routines of children's learning. How could I express my spiritual convictions in terms that were acceptable to our diverse school community? This became the challenge of my hours of reflection over the ironing board that summer. In a weekly update the following September, I made a stab at it.

> Princeton Junior School is a small, independent school that focuses exclusively on early childhood education. It is culturally diverse with no formal religious affiliation, although there is a deep sense of the spiritual within the process of learning, in which we develop the confidence to risk giving ourselves over to something beyond ourselves.
>
> J.

Looking back on these words, I wish I had added that the teaching of young children is a holy and creative process. That is what I believed. We had no endowment, we owned no property, we owed no money. We had no one but ourselves. No wonder we had to start from scratch, plumb our depths, and get down to essentials!

11

The sea rushes and waves blow. Fish toss. Now the sea is quiet and calm. It is nice and sunny and people are at the beach. Kids bury their dad's bellies in the sand. Seagulls make footprints in the sand. It is night and the beach is going to sleep. And tomorrow is waiting and there will be a new adventure.

Student

Early in the morning, while the rest of the family slept, my granddaughter and I tiptoed to the beach. Bread crusts in our pockets, a thermos of tea and beach towels in our backpacks, a bucket for shells swinging between us, we picked our way through the coarse dune grass and wild roses to the tide-striped sand. Together we settled and waited for the "sparkle" to appear on the eastern horizon. (She always referred to dawn as "the sparkle.") This ritual, which we practiced morning after morning, both wrapped and enraptured us. The gentle lapping of the waves along with our foggy voices wove a song of praise as the sparkle of light popped into sight. The waves reflected the dawn. We drank our tea and watched the sparkle stretch from rim to rim of the vast ocean. We searched for shells and sea glass—she the sandpiper darting to and fro, and I the tern. The wet sand was deeply etched and tidal pools gleamed with shells. As I watched my grandchild explore the beach, I shared her longing to search, to discover, and to learn the secrets that the sea alone knows.

After a while, we stopped to make a dribble castle in the wet sand. There it stood for a moment, its fragile form facing the approaching flow of the tide. I hastened to fill in the voids.

"Don't worry, Nana! If it falls down, we'll make another, higher up."

Here was the heartbeat! The child's words, spoken so casually, opened my ears to a truth so rooted in her nature that to let it fade would have been irreverent. She loved to make something out of nothing, whether her medium was sand, wood, paint, clay, stone, or flour. If it collapsed, she would begin again, for the joy was in the process more than in the product. My grandchild demonstrated that whatever form our wisdom chooses; whatever sight, sound, touch, flavor, or smell it evokes, whatever symbolic language it inspires—wisdom enables us to begin again. Our greatest challenge is to receive and live by it as well as we can, knowing that life will deal to us circumstances that obscure our wisdom. In the stories that follow, there are times when the handful of sand spills away and wisdom must struggle to overcome powers that threaten to thwart or abuse it.

Recently, my husband and I were walking on the beach in the late afternoon when we came upon an extraordinary sight. There, in the damp sand at our feet, lay a sandscape replete with two cone-shaped mounds surrounded by moats. Hollow straw posts formed perfect circles around the mounds. Dune grasses had been inserted into them and bent to make arches. Chips of driftwood formed bridges and portals. Dozens of white seashells formed pathways and ornamental sculptures. The creator? Nowhere in sight. The whole construction was a captivating example of what children do with free time, free space and free material. They enjoy making something new out of the discarded materials they discover as they travel from one place to another.

> Normally
> What you would throw away
> Make something out of it, please,
> Please save the day!

> Student

These children creating art on the beach are *in between* the inner world of their imagination and the world outside themselves. They connect the two in the forms that they create. Children live between two worlds—the natural and supernatural, the discarded and the new, the world of peanut butter and jelly and the world of dreams. Their wisdom lives in this in-between place, both here and beyond. Those of us who work and play with children have the opportunity to revisit those in-between places of our own. It is not too late to begin again. Children do.

Children love to create stories and games that express their feelings and ideas. When one of their creations breaks down of its own accord, they grieve briefly but begin again, "higher up." But when their constructions are deliberately broken down by others, the howl arising from such an affront can only be described as the cry of wisdom howling for justice.

———*ᴠᴠ*———

The inborn wisdom of children is too mysterious, too miraculous ever to be fully understood. Although they are just beginners, they know what questions to ask. One day, as I was walking hand-in-hand with a four-year-old toward the school, she asked, "Are we going to your school world? What will we do there?"

Immediately my mind began to spin: there, you will learn how to build a base for your future education, how to use materials that you love, how to make friends to work and play with, how to discover ways to grow deeper and higher, how to show others what you know, how to use your imagination, how to see beauty in ordinary things, how to observe nature's ever-changing cycle of life, how to respect all kinds of people, how to take risks and learn from your mistakes, how to learn who you are, how to become transformed, how to cheer up the world, how to rebuild when your castle is torn down, how to begin again and again. Remembering the small person who had posed the question, I bent down and whispered, "Come and see." Had she been a bit older, I might have told her that I had learned much from children such as she—not from photographs, reports, test scores, or theories about child development, but from their daily work and play. I might have told her that her inborn capacity for transformation was a resource she would draw from throughout her life, and also, that I prayed she would share her wisdom with me.

A later question changed the way I looked at things. A snowfall blanketed the school play yard with six inches of soggy white potential. I knew that before the day was done, we would build something important. During after-lunch recess, some children decided to build an igloo. They started by drawing a circle on the ground. Before long, they had built a two-foot-high wall. More builders, including me, joined the team.

Aware that our free time was limited, we worked ourselves into a frenzy. With drenched gloves, we scraped wider and wider swathes from the shallow snow of the play yard. Some builders raced over to the macadam to lift huge chunks from the snow plow's wake. Others staggered back and forth carrying snow-laden kitchen trays. One boy inspired others to roll the snow into balls toward the ever-growing igloo. Euphoria drove us to unprecedented cooperation.

At one point, I sank to my knees to pack snow into the chinks. All around me, children were offering armfuls of snowy mortar. One shrill voice cried into my ear, "Hey, Mrs. McIntyre, did you ever stop to think about what the world was like before humans were invented?" The question hung like a diamond in the air. Before I could gather my wits to reply, the questioner was gone—off to help haul a huge refrigerator carton from the recycling shed.

By now, our time was up. The igloo with its cardboard roof stood two and a half feet high off the ground: a triumph! Since everyone had built it, everyone wanted to go inside it, and they did, just to experience the feeling. Sure enough, its walls fell apart, leaving a great heap of laughter in the middle.

The building of that igloo outdoors, during recess, was play, yet it was an analogy for what went on indoors, all the time, everywhere in the school. Whatever we endeavored to build, be it a block construction, a math problem, a song, a map or a journal, the miracle we sought was a child's question that sprang from the creative act. Without creative activity, a child does not question. Without questions, there can be no new beginnings. Without new beginnings, there can be no education . . . no igloos . . . no laughter.

—◆◆◆—

As Princeton Junior School's early years went by, I begged God for "stuff". It seemed a little pushy to solicit God for snack food or a school car or furniture. So I didn't kneel; I leaned in prayer. People may have noticed a certain tilt to my walk in those days. I called it arthritis, but in truth, I was leaning. When we called an evening meeting of parents and teachers, the question would arise: "Shouldn't we serve refreshments?" It was as if the question hung in the air near the door during dismissal time and followed people home. On the evening of the meeting, several people would arrive early, unfold and drape cheerful fabrics over the squeaky church tables, set up chairs, uncork red wine, and bring in the refreshments—lasagna, salad, bread and cheese, fruit pies, coffee—a wonderful response to leaning.

Early on, our school developed a characteristic hum that never followed a particular melodic line. Descending the colorless stairway to the basement, a visitor would become aware of the hum issuing from the schoolroom. It was no ordinary sound, this symphony of learning. Generally, when children reach beyond familiar boundaries and enter unknown territory, they do so at risk. Letting go and allowing new growth to take place requires a leap of faith. They leap a lot. How else could they build forms out of sand or a house out of the big brown box or learn to read? No wonder they hum! Do children actually think this way? They don't have to. Transformation comes intuitively to them. Otherwise, they would never sit or stand, to walk or talk. They would never get up off the ground after a fall.

—∾—

When it looked as though we might not have enough space to accommodate our increasing enrollment, some parents offered their houses. When one teacher's husband died unexpectedly, we all grieved. When one of our teachers died, our hearts were broken. Princeton Junior School was a collection of newcomers bound together by children. Through them, we found our common humanity. Children put their faith in people before property or program. There was neither time, space, materials nor staff to stage a superficial show. We invited everyone to help form a school family in which no one would be overlooked, belittled, or exploited. Out of this union of children and adults emerged a school where materials and space were scarce, but faith was abundant. Faith in our capacity for transformation in both academic and social spheres is what formed the school then, and continues to do so now. In addition to faith, we harbored hope that our services to children would stand them in good stead for the rest of their lives. Above all, we loved our children, as I told parents in a letter in 1989.

At Princeton Junior School, our primary aim is to love and guide the children whom you have entrusted to us. Their instinct to learn is probably more powerful now than it will ever be again. To underestimate their passion for new experiences would be irresponsible.

Our authority derives from listening to and knowing your children, as well as from the curriculum we offer. We wish to enable them—in lively ways—to discover, absorb, and remember information. We find that children learn through experience that the security and discipline of simple routines and rules lead to greater freedom . . . and more learning.

We plan the content of our curriculum so that children take small, sequential steps: a process that combines both concrete and conceptual experiences. We encourage them to think, question, reflect, and evaluate as they go along. I highly recommend that you read aloud to your child(ren) *every single day*. Choose a book that you love, a time, and a quiet place, and go to it. Not only is it a pleasure for both of you, it also reaps benefits throughout life.

So much for our goals. I would like to hear more of yours.

J.

The more I heard from parents, the more deeply I understood their vulnerability. Their children were as precious to them as life. They were their creations, their dreams. Where they might treat any other subject objectively, when it came to their children they were passionate. Having been in the same place as a mother, I empathized with them and loved them, even when they were mad at me. In a note to teachers:

Parenting today is very difficult, as many of you know. Parents are anxious about parenting, and need a lot of support, even when their anxieties drive us crazy. We must remind ourselves of the many opportunities we have to educate, to nurture, and to help them make appropriate decisions for their children. They are our 'customers' and companions. Without them, there would be no Princeton Junior School.

I write this letter in hopes that our School environment will again become conducive to the kind of learning that we all espouse. Please take advantage of our conferences with our parents to reaffirm our faith in them."

J.

———⟋⟍⟍———

Any school in the making needs every child it can get, and ours was no exception. Within reason, we accepted every child who walked through the door and ventured down the stairs into our world. For us, "within reason" included all conditions of children: some securely settled into life, others for whom life was a kaleidoscope. Some had been born into Princeton's most traditional families, while others were unsure of where they lived. We collected families both rich and poor, educated and uneducated, foreign and domestic, urban and rural. Fortunately, most of them were looking for a school where children could build a firm academic foundation, and they opted for the extraordinary mixture that we accumulated. (One particular family brought a child to us for a week, but then vanished. A few days later, I spotted them trudging northward along the shoulder of State Highway 206, rucksacks on their backs. The child, who had missed his parents sorely during his week at school, now looked happy as a clam.)

In our efforts to expand our enrollment, we accepted several children whose parents could not pay even a modest tuition. Nevertheless, they were welcome. Margaret and I did without salaries for a while. Before long, our school boasted thirty-five fledglings aged three, four, and five, no two of whom were alike, but all of whom alighted each morning with a flourish. One was the son of a prolific author; another, the son of a chef; another, the daughter of a policeman; another, the son of a surgeon; another, the daughter of the town clerk. The mixture of parents, at first a bit spicy, became increasingly smooth and rich.

Gradually, through their common purpose, they came to know one another. When a field trip was planned, many of their cars, from Chevys to Cadillacs, were available. I bought an estate wagon from a friend for a dollar and turned it into a school minibus. In my effort to obtain a bus driver's license, I found that the state police were willing to cooperate: my art materials had erased my fingerprints and I couldn't attain the required bus driver's license. "You got plenty of deltas but no whorls, ma'am. The FBI won't tolerate that," I was told by Officer Ben. I understood how my bus driver's license might be withheld on the grounds of poor vision, but no whorls? Did they think children's lives would be endangered by a whorl-less woman behind the wheel? Officer Ben recommended lanolin. After three months, my whorls re-emerged and he gave me a bus driver's license.

Evening meetings took place in the church basement in the form of a delicious potluck dinner accompanied by wine and music. (Margaret never did anything by halves.) Despite the limited space, material and financial resources of the school, everyone was enthusiastic because their children were happy.

Countless parents helped us grow the school. Plumbers plumbed. Carpenters sawed. Lawyers advised. Doctors healed. Professors enlightened. Farmers brought baby lambs for the children to play with. Firemen, policemen, bankers, grocers—the list goes on and on—all took our school into their hearts and made it their own.

I, the director of education, learned from parents that the stranger at the door is someone to be welcomed and thanked. For this person brings us a child whose wisdom evens the playing field. What more can a democracy ask of us than this?

> Me, Uncle Sam, I'm your American bird!
> I fly high over your country—in my prime, a champion fisher.
> I'm a dark-headed youngster and a white-headed majesty.
> I'm not bald, you see; I'm a white-headed symbol of freedom.
>
> Student

Finding teachers who wanted to work in a new garden—a kindergarten full of fresh seedlings—was a challenge from the beginning. We had to look beneath the applicant's fingernails to see whether he or she was willing to start from scratch. We had to look around the eyes for laughter lines. We had to listen for a tone of voice that could melt or modulate, evoke or provoke a question. We had to discern a learner, and above all, a lover of children—someone who could engage a child's spirit and allow the wisdom of the child to emerge. How to do all of this within the grasp of a hand, or the reading of a resume, or the course of an interview? Intuition often led the way in these matters. The words of one teacher—"Juliana, thanks so much for believing that I could be a teacher. I'm still teaching, and I still love it!"—are still pinned in my scrapbook. That our intuition led us in the right direction can be confirmed by the words of one alumnus: "All my teachers were extraordinary people, and PJS was an extraordinary place. It was a blessing to be there."

Our way of discerning what a prospective teacher might contribute was successful: we observed each applicant interacting with a group of children. Our final evaluation depended largely upon whether or not the applicant kindled the children's spirits. If we saw a spark light the fire, we welcomed the person with open arms. Once I interviewed eight applicants, none of whom met the criteria for this very special occupation. I wrote to parents at the time, "A person who teaches your children every day must put his or her vulnerability, capacity to learn, and enthusiasm for life, *first*. He or she must teach from the heart. Nothing less is acceptable."

Call it what you will, the school was for me becoming a ministry. The people and the work struck chords deep within me, perhaps because I was to some extent reliving my past, but mostly because we were bringing a learning community to life. None of us could deny the children's huge hunger for information. We spent evenings and weekends exploring ways to capture their wisdom and put it to work. At the same time, we had to deal with our own fears regarding safety, sustainability, and accountability.

We did all we could to feed the children a balanced diet of work, play, rest and reflection—and to be free of past burdens or future worries. There simply wasn't time for "what if?" or "why bother?" There was a lot of laughter, as is often the case when people serve one another. As one child put it,

> To me PJS means that everyone is friendly and it builds confidence in everyone. You learn a lot but still have fun. You get to meet people from all over the world.
>
> Student

We focused on children's needs, not wants; we provided for them, but not to excess. We found value in the mundane and power in the simple. I can only describe the experience as radical engagement of our whole selves, all day, every day, with and for everybody in the school family, for the sake of the world.

The school now had thirty-five children. It was time to find a logo, a symbol for our educational process. Until now, my colleagues and I had searched for words to describe what we saw happening every day. Words came and went, some hitting, but more missing the mark. Somehow, we needed to find a symbol that would make sense to the children, an image that would appeal to their natural impulse to grow. Then one day, a close friend who understood my penchant for seashells gave me a beautiful half-shell of the chambered nautilus. I made a print of it using black ink on white paper. There it was: a symbol that children might adopt. I hastened to the nearest dictionary to learn more about the creature who created this extraordinary shelter for itself. I found that the nautilus is the sole survivor of a class of mollusks that flourished 200 million years ago. The shell, like a suit of armor, protects the soft animal. It has brown and white stripes on the outside and is beautiful and pearly on the inside. In the beginning, the tiny larva lives in one chamber. As it grows, it builds larger and larger chambers in a spiral formation, with a connecting canal that extends back through the walls to the core. The nautilus lives in the newest and largest chamber. When I broached to the children the idea of using the chambered nautilus as a logo, they responded as if they were greeting an old friend. They also made a print of the shell for themselves.

So, for Princeton Junior School, the chambered nautilus shell came to symbolize the child's spiraling quest for new knowledge in its multifarious forms. We invited parents to enroll their children during the dawn of their lives when their wisdom would shed its rays into successive chambers. The chambered nautilus reminded them of the journey outward from the core of their being. Unless they grew fearful and doubted their wisdom, they would never lose connection with it. We came to refer to our educational process as "spiral learning," or "learning from the inside out." When a child moved from one stage to another, whether gradually or by sudden epiphany, we hailed the transformation. The nautilus symbol was so clearly understood by the children that we designed many a lesson, both academic and communal, around it.

> What makes a baby want to crawl?
> What makes a toddler want to draw?
> What makes a child observe a rule?
> Or read, or write, or come to school?
> What makes us all so want to be
> A part of learning's mystery?
>
> What is this shining inner glow?
> What is this gnawing need to know?
> What can it be that makes us leap
> From shallow shores to waters deep?
> What makes us all so want to see
> The other side of "one, two, three"?
>
> The spiral form provides a clue
> For seekers such as me and you:
> Forever widening from the core,
> Outgrowing chambers more and more,
> It draws an everlasting line
> To show that learning frees the mind.

J.

Spiral learning took on a more than academic meaning. One day, when some of our older children seemed out of sorts and uncooperative, I gave them two-foot garden sticks and ribbon, and asked them to create a spiral in the grass outside the door. This they did, starting at a central pole and driving sticks into the ground in spiral fashion until the whole form was about twenty feet in diameter. Knotting the long red ribbon onto the upper tip of every stick was difficult for them, as the breeze wafted the ribbon's tail like a flag. After much huffing, puffing, and negotiating, they connected all the sticks with the ribbon and finally the spiral was steady. Everyone vied to be the first to walk round and round from its entrance to the center.

"Not now," I advised. "Only when you are ready."

"Ready for what?"

"Ready to let go of your problems, enter the center, and sit and think."

The weather prevailing, that fragile spiral in the grass lasted only a few days. Nevertheless, it made its mark as a guide to self-control. When a child felt angry or frustrated, he or she would ask to walk the spiral, enter its center, and sit for a while. No one was allowed to distract the child who was sitting there. (When I wasn't looking, someone placed a small chair in the center.) Whether problems were wholly shed in the process, I will never know, but more often than not, the traveler returned a calmer, steadier person. Years later, a labyrinth was created in the landscape of our permanent school, providing its visitors with an opportunity to enter, to center, and to begin again.

—◦◦◦—

Finding furniture for the school was a bother. In the early days, we foraged for furniture at yard sales, in basements and attics, and even on borough curbs during clean-up week. After a few years of such scavenging, I received an unexpected call from my former employer, Miss Morrison, whose extraordinary school for young children had closed in 1981.

"Juliana, good news! I have finally sold the building! The buyers have given me only a few days to clear the whole place out. It would

23

help me ever so much if you wanted any of the materials there. Would you be interested?" I was stunned. The four levels of Miss Morrison's schoolhouse were packed with furniture and colorful educational materials, many of which were homemade. The classrooms, kitchen and pantry, office, apartment, side porch, and play yard were loaded. To empty such a colossal treasure chest in two days would require nothing short of a Herculean effort. Nevertheless, I accepted Miss Morrison's invitation.

Word went out that afternoon. By nightfall, dozens of people had appeared to help with the removal. An unexpected parade of U-Haul trucks drew up outside Miss Morrison's building. Everyone swarmed throughout the dear old place, rummaging, sorting, packing fifty years' worth of things that children love—books, games, costumes, dolls, puzzles, hobby horses, paints, musical instruments—not to mention tables and chairs, typewriters, projectors, china, and kitchen utensils. Countless boxes slid down forty-foot planks from upper windows into the beds of the trucks below. We stashed everything away for future use in several storage units nearby. Believe it or not, two days later, Miss Morrison's school building was empty save for a few mice that had emerged to see what all the excitement was about.

A comment made recently by someone whose children attended the school in those early years rings true.

> In the old days, before you owned property and built a schoolhouse, everyone came for the learning program and the teachers. They didn't care about what you lacked in the way of space or equipment. It was the way that children were learning that counted. Everyone pitched in. My kids remember to this day their great teachers and the projects they did.
>
> Parent

As I look back over the first twenty-two years of the school family's life, I am deeply, deeply grateful for the devotion of parents—not only to their individual children, but to the school as a whole. Their spontaneous gifts of time and talent are as precious to me now as they were then. In the writing of this book I have reread dozens of letters from parents that reflect *their* transformation and growth.

As our school was housed in the basement of the church, we had to set up the space on Monday mornings and "strike" everything on Friday evenings so the church could carry out its weekend activities as if nothing had happened during the week. One newsletter in 1985 said it all.

SAVE, SAVE, SAVE, SAVE

The tools of our teachers are not just the paper, pencils, and books that we see. Our teachers are special because of their warmth, dedication, and creativity. That creativity does include tools that can be ordered from a catalogue. Careful scrutiny of the family trash may produce treasures for the classroom. Styrofoam meat trays, Leggs pantyhose containers, oatmeal boxes, coffee cans, old costume jewelry, packing materials, cardboard rolls from paper towels and toilet tissue, old catalogues, buttons, yarn . . . the list goes on and on. If it looks interesting, it may just be of value. If our teachers don't want it, they will be happy to throw it away for you!

J.

In our first church habitat, the forty-foot by sixty-foot basement was dimly lit by the light that came through well windows. At one end there was a kitchen; at the other, a stage that was off-limits. There were two small bathrooms around the corner at the bottom of the stairs. Tracks laid onto the ceiling allowed accordion-pleated wooden walls to be drawn, forming six separate enclosures.

We were apprehensive about the authorities who would determine our school's future. We had to create an early childhood education facility that would satisfy the Division of Youth and Family Services, whose license we sought. Were the toilets low enough? Were the curtain walls splintery? Was the stairway free of trash left behind by the occasional homeless sleeper? Or was the sleeper still on the premises? Was the playground enclosed? Eyebrows shot up when we enclosed the playground in bright ribbon rather than an expensive chain-link fence. At first, our examiners were not convinced by our defense: "Children respect the boundaries when they have strung the brightly colored ribbons themselves." Somehow, we won our case, and in the five years that we occupied that church, no one ever wandered beyond the playground's ribbon fence.

When beginning at the beginning, you have to be wise about how you use space and time. The basement itself posed the biggest challenge. When all the curtain walls were drawn—clackety-clack, clack, clack— six twelve-by-twelve roomlets appeared. When the curtain walls were returned to their original position—clackety clack, clack clack—the space yawned. We decided to start every day "open" so the children would see themselves as a school family, and then close the curtain walls to create separate spaces for art, music, math, reading, writing, science, and social studies. Children would rotate from space to space as they went from one activity to another. The total space would expand for play and rest. How to signal change? Margaret's gentle recorder tune would prompt the clackety clack, clack, clack of the curtain walls, and we would begin again in a new space.

It became increasingly difficult to squeeze everything into our small quarters. Each morning, the arrival of dozens of energetic children blew everything out of place. We had to find a way to keep the lid on enough for the curriculum to "cook." It was not long before a way of life developed in which responsibility and freedom synchronized. Everyone had a job: some had to do with safety, others with sanitation, others with maintenance. No job was considered too humble. Those of us in charge rolled up our sleeves, scrubbed floors, and put out trash as well as the rest. When everyone, great or small, was called upon to handle the ordinary disarray of school life, all work was dignified . . . at least by most people. In addition to DYFS, we suffered a church custodian who never failed to find fault: "You left traces of blue paint in the kitchen sink!" or, "Please wash the wall near the toilet!" (She signed her messages "Messiah.")

Once, during the first week of school, I was on lunch duty when a child accidentally overturned a pitcher of cherry juice. I had to scramble to prevent the crimson spill from staining the polished floor. I dove for a roll of paper towels and, skirt hiked up behind, sloshed around the floor on my knees, trying to wipe the mess up before it penetrated the floor. Andrea, the culprit, watched with keen interest. She was new to the school and inquired, "Do you work here?" Why yes, I thought, I do work here, if you can use such words to describe the endlessly fascinating process of creating a new school for children.

Andrea was waiting for an answer. "You're right, I work here. But so do we all. Would you like to have a turn?" I bundled the paper towels into her outstretched arms. "Find someone to help you." Before she could respond, three children leapt to her side and helped her finish the job. The floor gleamed. More to the point, Andrea gleamed, for in mopping up cherry juice she had made three new friends.

In this vignette, a child's simple question leveled the playing field. My rank was reversed, my chore became her challenge, and friendship was born.

—◦◦◦—

Everyone, old or young, strong or weak, was part of the staging process during those early years. Inevitably, when I arrived at the church early Monday morning, cars were already parked alongside, their passengers sipping coffee or munching the last tidbits of breakfast. An hour before the official opening of school, these families would greet me with a hearty, "Do you need any help?" All they needed to hear was my, "No . . . well . . . yes, in a way . . ." before dashing into the church like a band of brownies. In no time, closet doors were flung open, furniture was hauled into place, computers were plugged in, bookcases uncovered, materials situated, even the morning snack of fruit and cheese prepared. The stage was set! No sooner was the job done than the tall brownies faded away, leaving the small ones to enter the school that they had created only moments before. As one alumna recently remarked, "We were all part of it; we loved helping to put our school together every day."

Friday afternoons posed another challenge: We had three large wooden boxes and one closet below the stairs into which we had to jam all the school's materials. Needless to say, it was a feat that required extraordinary organization and patience. Only when a Chinese graduate student took on the challenge did we finally see every tidbit tidily tucked away. We concluded that he had been brought up on Chinese puzzles and therefore could conquer the confusion.

The Monday morning brownies came, year after year, in different cars and different attire, but their opening question was always the same: "Do you need any help?" No amount of skepticism about our facility deterred me. Despite predictions to the contrary, the little school grew. Children gathered in the playground every morning, followed the piper into the school at 8:15, threw off their outdoor clothes, and entered a world of playful learning.

———ᨏᨏᨏ———

Our students wanted to stay with us, so we looked around for an additional location to house a first grade class. It was summer and we had to find a place quickly. As I was looking for a new facility with the help of realtors, Margaret, while languidly swimming laps in the university pool, came up with the solution. Thanks to her efforts, we found available space in a church on Walnut Lane, just opposite Princeton High School. Another temporary habitat! This time we were above ground with conditional use of the church's sanctuary and full use of its kitchen. In contrast to our preschool, here we had five classrooms. They were very small—twelve feet by twelve—but they were big enough to grow in. They actually felt bigger than they really were because each room had a plate glass window that let in natural light.

The second location assumed the character of a village. Its classrooms, situated on either side of a hallway formed a neighborhood of sorts; the occupants of one "house" could look across the way into the "house" on the other side. Naturally curious, children peered into one another's classrooms, listened to one another's discussions, and appraised one another's projects.

Children from the preschool could now graduate to our elementary school! In a matter of five years, we added grades 1, 2 3, 4, and 5 successively. As new levels were added, so were new teachers, many of whom welcomed the chance to get away from the volume and bureaucracy of larger schools, and to practice our school's pedagogy which valued inquiry. How often I heard the words, "I just want to teach!" How often candidates gave up generous salaries and benefits, and state-of-the-art classrooms and materials in order to teach a small group of children in an atmosphere that encouraged children to question and teachers to explore with them.

One teacher wrote,

> It is early morning at Princeton Junior School. The teachers are chatting while setting up for the day. Tables are being dragged across rooms and desks rearranged. A feeling of camaraderie and a common caring infiltrate our little school . . .

> Yes, I suppose the space is small, but what we achieve here is beyond measure. The philosophy of the whole child allows us to incorporate the various disciplines while exploring topics that spark student interest. Through reading, writing, oral storytelling, mathematics, science, and movement, skills are enhanced and made relevant. Mathematics takes on much more meaning when we use it to measure and see just how big a fifty-foot whale is by tying our jump ropes together and stringing them between two trees, for instance.

> There is another aspect of learning. Of equal importance is learning who we are and how to get along. A child feels left out, a best friend turns away, another feels bullied— through children's literature and discussion we learn to identify the problem. By presenting imaginary yet relevant scenarios, we learn to list possible solutions and predict their outcomes before we pick the solution to try. Didn't work? Try another. In this way, we learn we are not helpless, but are able to take control of our lives. We discover we are not alone with our feelings, but share a common humanity.

The space seems small, but only to the untrained eye. Often, working to overcome our limitations results in our greatest achievements. We have no walls. Our world is huge.

Teacher

One of our parents, poet Paul Muldoon, reminded us to "make, make do, make believe." How wise. Children live according to this principle, as in the case of two sisters who created a "kitchen" among the shrubs along the driveway. In this sequestered space, they could play out the domestic altercations of their household with no greater interruption than the comments of birds nearby. In the schools of today, where are children allowed to help create their "scholastic kitchen?"

One alumna put it this way:

> At PJS, you never spent a lot of time seated or copying stuff off the blackboard. You *did* what you were learning. When I learned about the people of India, I dressed as they dressed, cooked as they cooked, danced as they danced. We had the Mayan unit out under the scrawny trees behind the Walnut Lane Church. We formed roads through the "mountains," created both rectangular and circular houses out of clay, ran water in the river grooves, modeled people, performed rituals, etc.

Alumna

The outdoor play space at Walnut Lane was small, but perfectly adequate for the purposes our children conjured up. The shrubbery became a series of "dens" in which stories were invented. The tall trees along the church's property line cast long, cool shadows for play on hot days. One child proposed that a sandbox be constructed in the shadows. No sooner did I agree than his mother arrived, lumber and toolbox in hand, to design and—with the help of several junior carpenters—build a magnificent sandbox large enough to accommodate ten children at once (not to mention nocturnal cats, who used it for their own purposes until they were repelled by chicken wire). Moreover, the sand in this sandbox was two feet deep—deep enough to make child-sized tunnels in.

Our preschool was now housed in the Unitarian Church. At three o'clock every afternoon, I would pile a few of our older students into the "school bus" and crawl through traffic from one church to another. There, children of all ages whose parents would be picking them up later would gather and play after school. "Backyard play" we called it in those days. It was play originating in the imaginations of children, play that produced games for hours, even days—recreation, pure and simple. I used to marvel at the rich variety of games these "unequals" devised. Their games, surprisingly, corresponded to many that I had observed on my trips abroad in Africa, Scandinavia, Asia, India, Latin America, and Alaska. (Might there be a universal games room in God's house that all children have visited and played in before birth? Often, observing two children facing one another, slapping their hands together and chanting, I would recall children doing exactly the same thing in other parts of the globe. Could it be that children share a memory of that playroom of the soul where hide-and-seek, marbles, hopscotch, cat's cradle, and tag are all examples of wisdom's methodology?) Any children who have been allowed to explore the family attic for leftover toys, clothing, letters, photographs, and artifacts will have an easy time making up plays that lead them across the boundaries of time and space.

It was during backyard play at the Unitarian Church that I witnessed the birth of a game. Autumn's golden light filtered through the trees, gilding the children in the play yard. From my perch on the steps nearby, I could see and hear their interactions clearly. One of the older boys, Nathaniel, called out to me, "Can we play ball outside the fence?"

The enchantment of the scene before my eyes called for a widening of the usual boundaries. At my nod, Nathaniel and two other third-graders opened the steel gate and raced into the grassy meadow beyond, tossing a ball back and forth.

No sooner had this departure been noticed than Will's shrill voice from within the fence wailed, "They took my ball away!" Immediately, a chorus of complaints swelled from the ranks of the younger children who—while still in possession of several balls—grieved loudly over the loss of the bright red one that now was soaring among the lofty maples out in the meadow.

Will's voice burst through the noise: "Why can't they throw the ball back over the fence to us?"

The older boys chanted, "You're too little, you're too little!"

"No I'm not! I'll throw it back!" Will's rash promise drew cheers from his boisterous playmates.

Nathaniel hesitated. He was not a mean lad, but he seemed reluctant to throw away his free moment in the meadow. Then, with a shrug toward his two glowering companions, he tossed the red ball back over the fence to the frantic group inside. Will retrieved the ball immediately, and with a bang of his fist, delivered it back.

"Well done," responded Nathaniel. I held my breath. Before long, the red ball was traveling back and forth between the meadow and the play yard. I watched and waited.

"You're throwing it too far!" shrilled a voice from inside the fence.

"You're throwing it too high!" cried another.

"At least we're throwing it! Isn't that what you asked for, Wee-wee Willie?" mocked a wild voice from the meadow.

The chain-link fence between them, children on both sides shot a tirade of verbal arrows through the holes at each other. I hesitated between ending the argument with a supervisory, "Give me the ball!" and waiting for them to solve the problem. Finally, a small peacemaker suggested that a line be drawn in the dirt across the play yard to mark a boundary beyond which the ball could not go legitimately. With a stick, the line was duly drawn and dutifully accepted.

Needless to say, the red ball now flew way off to the right and to the left, arousing more dismay among the younger players. This time, one of the older boys (not the long-suffering Nathaniel) proposed side lines on either side of the fence. Surprise, surprise . . .

In time, a court developed, with back lines, side lines, and mid-lines. When several younger ones complained that the older boys were hogging the ball, a rule was devised to ensure that players would alternate, each one having two turns to throw the ball over the fence into the front space. Shorter children took their places nearer the fence; taller ones hugged the back line. Even better, the older boys took turns playing on the younger children's side of the fence. A rule was devised allowing the ball to bounce once before being hit back, a helpful addition. The more they played, the greater their skill and strategy. After several afternoon sessions, a final design emerged victorious, much to everyone's great satisfaction. They had labored together. They had delivered their own fair game.

> Nobody likes a game that isn't fair, including us, so there are certain things we do to keep everybody having fun.
>
> #1: Sportsmanship is needed in games like bombardment, octopus, aggravation, and tag. If you've been gotten, you gotta go. Otherwise people get angry. It isn't fun anymore.
>
> #2: Teamwork is needed to make a game work. Everybody has to work together. Have the same strategy, otherwise everything goes wrong.
>
> These are two keys in our sports world. These two things make games fun and fair!
>
> Student

Nathaniel—who, by the way, suffered from Asperger's syndrome—found within this game a new way to relate to others and to be regarded as a leader. He was transformed. His companions, while initially unenthusiastic about returning the red ball to the "babies," could not resist the opportunity to invent something new. Just as when a bee enters a blossom, it does exactly what a bee is meant to do, when children enter play, they are doing exactly what they were born to do.

I believe that this game did a lot more than just pass the time or introduce youngsters to useful social skills and techniques. The game initiated transformation. The structure of play allowed for the loosening of boundaries, so that the red ball, the prized object, could move back and forth between children who were otherwise so different or even opposed to each other that they could not enter into each other's social or imaginative spaces. In longing for the red ball, Will's passion cried out and Nathaniel awakened. Was this not their wisdom pushing through? As I watched the children that October afternoon, I felt that I was glimpsing a timeless truth about children everywhere. Created in God's image—or call it what you will—children spontaneously, naturally, create form. Regardless of whether they do so to ward off chaos or to celebrate life, the creative process brings them boundless satisfaction. Otherwise, they would not create so passionately. These children wanted to play for the fun of it. They created a form, a game, which involved work: solving problems, experimenting, respecting one another, taking responsibility for their actions. They increased their skill and imagination through practice, and thus, readied themselves for the next challenge.

I once wrote,

> How can we as a school family nurture this extraordinary characteristic [creativity] of childhood so that it will grow and mature into adulthood? How can we make sure that curriculum, instruction, and assessment—crucial strands in our school's cloth—are interwoven with the weft of play?

J.

I felt that with faith, our school would become a loom on which such integration could take place.

Many a child has the capacity for leadership; a capacity that comes to life when a particular situation calls it forth. At such times, leadership takes various forms, often involving skill and know-how. But most of all, leadership involves qualities that our school fosters every day: integrity, courage, empathy, fairness, imagination, humility. Our students learned and led through experience. They had many opportunities to become leaders, both then and in the future. Take little Will, for example. There is a very old notion that even a small character has the capacity to change the world. In one of Aesop's fables, you learn that a mouse can help a lion.

This game encouraged children of all shapes and sizes to belong, to become whole. As is true for many games, the process of play recreated the players as integrated members of an imaginative community. Was not the child's inborn drive toward transformation at work here? Should we not consider this inner dynamic to be the very generator of learning? If we do so, then play—children's primary way of empowering their imaginations—becomes the pivotal learning tool in myriad situations, both sacred and secular. Should not the play principle be the *modus operandi* of early childhood education? If play stimulates a child's imagination, concentration, and sense of justice; if play challenges a child to reach beyond his or her boundaries and take the risks that learning requires; then why not allow the power of play to infuse academic subjects? Perhaps, by so transforming, we can preserve the sacred nature of learning throughout our lives. Play helps us to recreate the original image into which we were born.

Is it childish to avow that play flowed through the evolution of the school? Boundaries were stretched, relaxed, transcended, so that people could reach out, touch, and share the new world of learning. Play provided a court in which all could have their day, their voice, and their way of growing in love for one another. I remember a game called "Sick" created by three pre-school children: one, the son of an Indian doctor; another, the daughter of an American Christian Science practitioner; another, the daughter of an African American Episcopalian. The three played "Sick" during free time for several days. Plot: The African American girl pretended to be exceedingly sick, vomiting and writhing; the Indian boy performed emergency surgery on her and the Christian Scientist prayed over her from Mary Baker Eddy's book, *Science and Health*. Whether she was healed by medical or spiritual means didn't seem to matter to the children. What mattered: after much moaning and groaning, the patient recovered. Somehow, the game of "Sick" transcended the malaise in our society that is engendered by differences of color, race, gender or creed.

—∿∿—

But helping with all the work made us part of the school, not just customers at the school! PJS always made children part of the process. We were needed. We could not take anything for granted. We helped with setting up and cleaning up the school. When my Mom brought my brother and me over to PJS, he would beg her to allow him to enter the school early because "Mrs. McIntyre needs me!"

Alumna

Cramped quarters led to extraordinary collaboration among our teachers as well. They created a multiage class when it seemed best for a particular combination of children. It was there that they added to traditional book learning more experiential ways for children to obtain knowledge. In addition, we found great meaning in the work we did together to maintain the property. No job was considered unworthy of respect.

Working together to take care of the school was so much fun. Packing up the school on Fridays, setting up the Maypole, and painting furniture were only a few of the ways we learned to care for our surroundings Your love for beauty and creation of beauty has encouraged my own love for and creation of beauty.

Alumnus

At one point, a reporter from the *Trenton Times* spent a Friday with us in order to write a story about the school. She visited classes, talked to teachers and students, and took notes on everything about our educational program that she deemed important. When at 2:15 p.m. she prepared to leave, I suggested that she stay to watch the end-of-the-week ritual. For the next half hour, she might as well have been watching *The Sorcerer's Apprentice*, so goggle-eyed was she at the sight of dozens of children along with their teachers scrubbing blackboards, emptying wastebaskets, sweeping floors, piling chairs on desks, locking windows, not to mention tidying the play yard. The next day, an article in the *Times* described an unusual school in Princeton where housework as well as schoolwork was honored. The photo that accompanied the article showed a boy pushing a mop along the baseboard of his classroom.

Little did the reporter know that this boy was a hemophiliac who had insisted upon doing his job along with everyone else. He had been out of hospital a few days and only now was allowed to leave his wheelchair behind. The previous week, he had developed a bleed while on a train returning from a fifth grade field trip to Boston. We were approaching Hartford when he announced that his leg was having problems. I looked at the bruise and called his father on the conductor's telephone (no cell phones in those days) to see whether we should all get off at Hartford and take him to the hospital. No, that wouldn't be necessary, but for the rest of the trip he should keep his leg elevated high above his body. There was virtually no way to do this other than to "hang" the poor child from the luggage rack, upside down. He maintained this position from Hartford to Princeton Junction. Was he uncomfortable? Yes. Upset? No. Why? Because his friends supported his head and shoulders on the seat and played cards with him all the way home. The boy's spirits were restored and his bleed arrested. He could not have found finer therapy.

The pastor of the Walnut Lane church loved our children and went to great lengths to coordinate us with his other tenants. Somehow, we fit into his schedule as well as into his heart. Only once did I hear him raise his voice, when a curious child waded into the purification pool that he was filling for a baptismal ceremony to take place later that day.

Our elementary grades stayed in the church at Walnut Lane for ten years, every fall opening a new grade level, stopping short of sixth grade. The pastor and his Board allowed us the use of the sanctuary for all school events, and trustees' and parents' meetings. Once, we spent the night in the sanctuary in our sleeping bags while a thunder storm roared against the wall with the huge glass window. There was a smaller room with a wood-burning fireplace where we gathered for lunch, reading aloud, yoga, and games. We loved the fireplace room. Many a science project or really wet art project was completed in that space. We vacated the church only for baptisms, funerals, snowstorms, or floods.

—✑—

Word had it that in addition to a logo, every school needed a school song. As Margaret was the musician, I left it to her to come up with a good idea. Rather than waste time imploring her own muse, she went straight to the children and asked them to think about why they liked our school. One alumna remembers,

> The sense of everyone striving for the same feeling of the whole coming together for the celebration of learning . . . I remember having an assembly in the first church building off Nassau and writing the school song with everybody in the big basement room, and Mrs. _____ waving her arms as we tried out each new verse. That was pretty amazing, really. I completely remember people calling out what each line should be. "I like that one! 'All the teachers, nice as they can be.'"

Alumna

I called a songwriter friend and asked him to put the children's words to music. He took all their ideas and set to music those that most neatly expressed our school's spirit. The result is still sung today to a lively marching tune:

1. There's a school I go to every day.
   It's a school where I can work and play,
   Where I try to be all the best in me.
   At my school, my Princeton Junior School!

2. I like music, stories, 'Show and Tell,'
   And at quiet time I never yell.
   As I learn to care, so I learn to share,
   At my school, my Princeton Junior School!

3. All my teachers, nice as they can be,
   Say they like my curiosity,
   And the more I know, the more I grow
   At my school, my Princeton Junior School!

Additional comments by alumnae:

> I have kept in touch with [a fellow student] all these years and we are both pursuing extremely creative paths—with steady success. I like to believe a lot of it has to do with the years spent at PJS learning how to navigate and be in the world.

> The joy in waking up to go to school every day and not wanting to leave once the school day was done. PJS differed from all other schools by giving me the freedom to learn in my own way at my own pace—learning through real life experience outside the school.

My colleagues and I had little comfort, convenience, or security in those early years. We plumbed our depths to find new ways to understand and teach children. We valued them as unique, precious beginners who, with their inborn wisdom and the external conditions for learning, could transcend the approved academic norms. Indeed, they did.

We encouraged them to ask themselves certain questions: Who am I? What am I trying to do? Where am I going? Who are we together? These questions centered them. We asked the same questions of ourselves. We searched our souls and questioned our answers. Children readily trusted us when they felt that they were understood. For them, virtually everything was new—and playable.

An academic curriculum that includes the dynamic of play is as healthy as a plant that absorbs water and nutrients from rich soil. Play grows children. Play frees their spirits. For children, play is the soft, workable material in which they can stretch, shape, and satisfy their hunger for knowledge. Play shows them ways to take the risks that new learning entails and to pick themselves up when they fall short of their goals. We looked to the children for inspiration and their enthusiasm strengthened our resolve. All of us, both young and old, were learning from the inside out rather than the other way around. As one child put it, "Let's play school. You be the student. I'll be the teacher."

——*w*——

We discovered that our authority lay *with* rather than *over* children. They trusted our authority because it was born out of experience worthy of their respect: learning together, understanding each other, and serving one another. Consciously, they knew that we were acting on their behalf. Intuitively, they knew that they were coming into their own on our behalf.

> There was an understanding of how children learn, such as having cut-out paper squares of numbers so that youngsters could do arithmetic, including the rudiments of algebra in kindergarten, without needing the motor coordination needed to write the numbers. The children's first writing was phonetic, and for moms and dads not attuned to deciphering their early efforts, the kindergarten teachers would be at their sides to translate. Learning was fun . . . The students learned grammar and spelling and even letter-writing etiquette by corresponding with a bunny or with imaginary characters. (One incident that was both funny and touching was when the bunny rabbit died just before vacation. [The teacher] stored him in her freezer so that the children could have a proper funeral when they returned from vacation. Thereafter he was replaced by a stuffed toy rabbit, who was less interesting, but also less liable to traumatize the children.)
>
> Parent

——*w*——

One expository writing program (inherited from Miss Morrison) called for the children in Grade II to correspond with a gentleman who lived behind the blackboard. He would print messages on the blackboard for them such as: "I need to brush my teeth tonight but I don't know how. Would you kindly leave me a note telling me just how you do it?" In response, the children would write back to him, on the blackboard, exactly how he should go about brushing his teeth. Thus they learned how to write specific directions clearly and simply—as long as the question referred to something familiar. One child reported:

"Mr. Magargle is the guy we teach and why we teach him is because he does not know much. He is always confused. He lives behind the blackboard. We show him how to write sentences."

It is the responsibility of families and schools to give children the opportunity to learn in the way that comes most naturally to them. Transformation happens when the child can make a vital connection with at least one other person who receives the child's spirit, affirms the child's as yet hidden wisdom, and encourages the child's imagination to come into play. Transformation begins with a mother's response to her baby's first cry for reconnection. Transformation is a spiritual necessity.

For example: one morning in Vermont my youngest grandchild, Skye, peeked around the corner to see if we were awake. Detecting our pretense of sleep, she bounced across our room and onto our bed with a delighted cry. "It's time for you to come out and see our fort!"

"What fort?"

"The fort that we are making. Near the barn. Under the trees."

Five children between the ages of four and eleven had been working on something under the trees for the last three days. From our bedroom adjacent to the barn, we had heard muffled shouts along with the thumping and dragging of heavy planks from the ground floor of the barn. Kitchen cupboards had been robbed of cups and saucers, beds stripped of blankets, and the porch deprived of its swing. Furthermore, all planned activities that had been scrawled on the chalkboard in the kitchen were scrapped. Even swimming surrendered to the fort.

Finally, we adults were invited to enter the fort, sit down on the swing, have a meal, and listen to the story of its creation. A more splendid structure could not have been imagined. The entry, a post and lintel arrangement between two cedar trees, led to a foyer adorned with golden day lilies. Before us was spread a feast of nuts, berries, grasses, flower petals, and seeds. We watched with our hearts in our mouths as the children climbed a series of catwalks to branches eight feet high and swung down like monkeys into an enclosure woven together with sweet-smelling cedar boughs. Pine needles carpeted the earth. The children's creation was beautiful to behold. Who would have guessed that in the process of the fort's fabrication, five souls had been stretched to the limits of their vulnerability? Territorial squabbles between the girls and boys, exasperation over the disappearance of tools, greed over snacks, competition for the bamboo swing—all were somehow taken care of by the five children whose imaginations surpassed their aggravations in the end.

Through play, they had together created a world for themselves. Yet when I offered to photograph the fort, I was told by the children that I shouldn't—pictures would destroy the "magic." I hearkened back to some conversations we had had that week with the children at the kitchen table. One had told us that she sometimes had *déjà vu* and relived scenes from previous experiences. Another added that he sometimes dreamed about things that actually came true in real life. These comments at the table seemed to me to be directly related to the building of a fort from scraps. The magic was not sleight of hand, but rather, the effect of brilliant scavenging of the children's imaginations. "Fort" was hardly the word to describe such a feat.

For three days, the fort endured the weather of the souls who made it. Then it disappeared as mysteriously as it had been conceived. I grieved to discover that it was gone. "What happened to the fort?" I asked. "We tore it down," they answered. My guess is that they wore it down, exhausted it. In any case, the oncoming storm clouds would have washed it away. As it was, these young creators had made a mighty fortress that no giant could ever demolish.

On another occasion, several grandchildren invaded my studio. They poked their noses into everything: clay, paints, chalks, wire, wood scraps. For me to serve them brushes, water, tools, and paper at the pace they set required the panache of a head waiter. My eight-year-old granddaughter, Kenzie, produced an abstract drawing on a large sheet of white paper. When I asked her to take me into it, she told me to sit down. She explained that every color had meaning. The rosy color was the color of love. Various other colors gave hues to her longings. Certain colors were about places she wanted to go or things she wanted to do. Some colors stood for people she wanted to be with. Some were about particular people—me and my husband, for instance. When she was through telling me what every color in the drawing meant to her, she had described the feelings and hopes of a very big soul. Her inner world was full of plans for being with people and going to places. This vast capacity for making her presence known and felt had been there all along beneath the surface of her everyday life, and a very busy life it was. The only reason I discovered her inner spectrum was because I asked her to take me into the picture she had made—and she did.

My twelve-year-old granddaughter, Olivia, spent a lot of time drawing a detailed picture with colored pencils. When I looked over her shoulder, I saw a large circle filled with the sun and the waters of the heavens and the earth. There was an opening in the circle that allowed her to flow through to an outer world, a cosmos filled with galaxies and infinite space. When I asked her to take me into the drawing, she began within the circle and then spiraled freely through the opening as if she were flying.

"Do you ever dream about flying?" I asked.

"I do, a lot. It's fun, fun, fun." I remembered my childhood dreams of flying. Looking again at her drawing, I saw it as a dream of her soul's capacity to fly to—in her words—"beyond, to a world you can't really describe with colored pencils." She went on to explain that this drawing was indeed of a dream in which she had watched herself from a distance. Her claim to have watched herself in a dream was no sooner professed than it was echoed by every child in the room. All had experienced being beside themselves while dreaming. As her younger brother put it, "Dreams show you stories about what's inside yourself."

Eventually, the children left their drawings behind and raced away. As I watched them through the window, I speculated that it all boils down to whether or not you ask children to disclose the wisdom that is within them, and then, that you settle down to listen.

When I was a child, I often dreamt that I could fly. During the school's Halloween parades I dressed up as Mary Poppins, the flying nanny. In both dreaming and pretending, I sensed a soaring freedom that only the imagination can offer. From my new vantage point, I had an extensive view of the world that I usually occupied. I could choose to fly wherever I wished, to land wherever I wished. It seems to me that children who allow their imaginations to take them on such flights can enter into the lives of flora and fauna:

Whales

I see a pod of whales fly through the air and then dive toward the sea.
I see calves drink their mother's milk while the father sings nearby.
I see a mother whale pushing her calf to the surface for the first breath of air.

I see whales rise from the sea like angels rise from heaven.

I see the spirit of the sea whales.

Student

Douglas Fir Cones

Fat caterpillars with spiky fur,
Spikes on cotton plants,
Whiskers on a catfish,
All in our school playground
And in my imagination.

Student

Play naturally pervades children's learning, even that of autistic children, as in the case of my brother, Davie. Davie neither spoke nor related to anyone throughout his thirty-nine years of life. He lived in a different world. His play was entirely solitary: he rocked to his own rhythmic, guttural songs, he piled furniture into architectural hideouts, he shaped a network of pathways through the border shrubs of our backyard. At times, when frustrated or angry, his play became fiercely destructive as he ripped plaster off the wall or wooden boards from the floor of his room. Worse still, he would break through a door or window and run away. My mother would call the police—"Davie's gone again!"—and we would search everywhere from Edgehill Street to Carnegie Lake, calling his name. Whether he heard us or not, he kept on going. Once the police found him running alongside the traffic on Route 1.

I shared a room with Davie for a while. With the fervor that only a child can muster, I tried everything in my power to penetrate his absence of mind and coax him into my world. Since he liked to eat, I fed him. He liked to run; I ran with him. He rocked to music; I rocked with him. We sang (moaned) together. I discovered that if I turned the ceiling light on and off rhythmically, he would blink his eyes and laugh. I was determined to reach him in any way that I could. Nothing worked, until one day I found him tearing a batch of colored newspaper into hundreds of little pieces and placing them in a symmetrical design on the bedroom floor. When I gave him more paper, he continued his design until the entire floor was covered with a beautiful, perfectly balanced, oriental carpet of paper. Throughout the project, his concentration and satisfaction were supreme. This was the beginning of a series of colorful, complex designs. It dawned on me that in manifesting his own image of our Creator, he was transformed. This unknowable child taught me a valuable spiritual lesson: God shares with *every* one of us His power to create.

When I am asked to name a person who greatly influenced me during childhood, I reply, "Davie." When he was tested at Johns Hopkins Medical Center, Davie's aptitude for design was rated "off the charts." He was somehow connected to his wisdom—yet his creativity lay beyond my understanding. Even though I was unable to coax Davie into my world, I began to believe that "abnormal" people illuminate, in their own way, the image of God as they pierce their imaginations. At the same time, I wondered whether I, a "normal one," were not doing the same as I pierced through known boundaries and entered new territory.

Davie's influence on me reached far beyond my childhood to my teaching where I have found that with little coaxing and much encouragement, children create their own world—a world large enough for us all to explore and to become wise. The creativity of most children is not beyond a parent or teacher's loving and respectful reach. I began to see my own imagination as a pathway to God. In my 1986 journal, I wrote:

> The school is a closely knit, intimate group. People and program are more important to children than facilities. I should ask teachers, 'How can we make basic subjects, materials, and skills irresistible to children? Motivation is their key to learning. Do not hurry them. Understand their individual learning styles. Deal only with essentials. The rest will come naturally. The children will love to learn and learn to love.

J.

Above all, I wanted to bring to the children of Princeton Junior School the experience of learning that Davie had never had. My intense gratitude for the opportunity and the companionship that the school offered me is reflected in a letter I wrote to the school family when I retired in 2003.

> Children are fascinating. To provide them with an environment worthy of their desire to learn has been a great challenge. The whole point of starting the school was to get close to them, to help them become aware of their remarkable inner resources, and to encourage them to behave intelligently and compassionately. My vision has been clarified and blessed into action thousands of times by you during the past twenty-one years. No stage along my life's way has been happier. Thank you for your trust in me.

J.

There is an immediate connection between our inborn wisdom and the wisdom of the cosmos. As my friend, painter Tom George wrote in his ninety-fourth year:

> While painting these gouaches I, too, have found that, quite unexpectedly, an image can work itself up from the paper into sight and consciousness. Often when this occurs, the image is able to move from the particular to the universal. It is as though my marks—colors, lines, shapes and patterns—coalesce to form visual "meanings," much as letters make words or notes make songs.

Every once in a while, one gets a glimpse of a child's transformation in its purest form. Such a sacred moment occurred when my daughter, Julie, was about three years old. As always seems to be the case when a life-changing event occurs, we were just hanging out together, doing the usual stuff, I putting laundry into the dryer and Julie scribbling on pieces of paper on the cellar floor nearby. As I transferred an armload of wet sheets from one machine to the next, I listened to Julie's humming, her crayon traveling aimlessly over her white sheets of paper. Her purring indicated that she was happy and absorbed, and I looked forward to taping her scribbles alongside countless others on the walls of our kitchen art gallery. Just as I was adjusting the dryer's time dial, the humming stopped. "Mommy!" I looked over my shoulder to glimpse the astonishment on her face as she gazed at the paper before her on the floor. Peering more closely at the drawing she had made, I saw a circle lying there in the glare of the cellar's incandescent bulb. The end of her line had bumped into its beginning. My heart skipped a beat. Here, before our eyes, lay a newborn symbol that promised a lifetime of interpretations.

Thus, on that wash day, a scribble changed into a revelation. Whatever the circle conjured up in Julie's mind, it represented a *whole*. A face? A breast? A sun? Beyond what her small bank of words could express, the sudden circle rolled out a print for her to use in her search for connection. From that time forward, she was able to create visual symbols—shapes, numbers, letters—that would convey her innermost thoughts.

Julie raised her eyes to mine. What was she thinking? I could only imagine that, as happened with many first steps, this one would be overrun by others in the rush of discovery. I hugged her. "You have created something wonderful! Let's celebrate!" We turned on the dryer, and clutching the precious paper, mounted the cellar stairs for a cup of tea.

Symbols share the power of being of that which they symbolize, inviting us to journey beyond ourselves and relate to a world that we might not otherwise know. Symbols are necessary for us as we try to explore the infinite dimensions of the divine life.

> The scale is small but the task is large: to repeat and repeat the lines, shapes and colors I love until I am wholly myself in my art. When this transformation occurs, I sense that I am one with what I seek to reflect in the world around me. The drive to achieve this transformation is obsessive, but there is no other way.
>
> Tom George

Those of us who taught the little ones in Princeton Junior School were always on the lookout for a child's first symbol. Glimpses of these creations etched themselves on the plate of my memory forever: a circle, a triangle, a square. Tentative at first, the children's shapes gained strength and purpose; the circle became a sun, the triangle a roof, the square a house. Before long, lines were added to form a face or figure, a leaf or apple, a tree or bird. We called such transformations "shapes with names." I looked upon these early pictures not only as symbols of the child's world, but also as strokes by the hand of God in whose image every child was made. What more powerful way for God to make a mark than through the creative soul of a child?

As Princeton Junior School grew, the circle became more than a ball or a sun or a wheel. It depicted the school family. No sooner would young children settle into their classrooms in the morning than they would form a circle and sit cross-legged on the floor. "Circle time" was a time to show and tell about their experiences, both at and away from school. It was a time for sharing stories, feelings, hopes, and dreams. The children learned to wax and wane with one another. I watched as they made sure that each of their small bodies was equidistant from the center. Thus, everyone was a valuable member of the school family and no one was left out. Intuitively, the children came to know that the circle's center was the beginning point from which they would grow, just as when a pebble is thrown into the water, rings of ripples flow outward.

When, as a child, I danced around a Maypole, I was barely aware of its universal appeal or practice. Little did I know then how brilliantly the Maypole would express the circle of life. I learned that one could not dance around the Maypole by oneself; one needed dancers on either side to bring alive its beauty. One had to hold the streamers high, whirl and dip, trot and skip. Everyone was the same distance from the center, balancing, no one tugging too far. The central pole was the hub of the wheel from which all streamers flowed. The flowery straw bonnet that capped the pole bobbed and swayed, its ribbons gaily flying. Our feet hardly touched the ground. To the strains of English folk music, we children, like giddy spiders, wove the streamers into the most beautiful web in the world.

I made a Maypole for Julie's fifth birthday party. I attached a straw bonnet and twenty long streamers to the top of a pole that I drove into the soft soil of spring. Twenty little girls approached the Maypole in their party dresses, picked up the multicolored streamers, and began to prance in pace with the music. For many years, the Maypole spun its magic on the lawn on Julie's birthday, expressing beautifully the circle of friendship that she so cherished.

May 1st remains to this day a special moment in the school year. At first, we danced around the Maypole during our "Day on the Farm," a special spring celebration at the farm of one of our school families. Later, when we finally built our own schoolhouse, we celebrated May Day in the courtyard outside the Commons. According to tradition, early in the morning, children gathered to attach the straw bonnet and drive the Maypole into the ground. For the next several hours, children of all ages and stages danced around the pole to folk music. They probably knew as little as I did at their age about the unifying power of this whirling circle. Yet, in their desire to create beauty, they held the streamers high, pulled away from the pole in rhythm with one another, formed the circle, and spun, letting time and space set a merry pace. Even when the pole broke, as it did from time to time, the dancers raced to the center and bound it together with a streamer. After several rounds, the music bounced to conclusion and the dancers flopped down on the grass and looked at the sky. There they sprawled, their backs bathed in dew: a circle of panting performers who now, at rest, gazed into the deep space of the sky. This final pause to lie still and look completed the Maypole dance. I have come to think of this round ritual of spring as one of the most natural, unaffected ways to praise the Creator of life.

> My grandma Linda came. We had marigolds to plant. Then after that we read our cinquain poems to our grandparents and friends . . . After that, everyone gave their poems to their guests. Later, in the commons, we had a little snack . . . Later, our class danced around the Maypole. The we had to say goodbye to our guests and go to our classrooms. I enjoyed the day! My favorite part was the Maypole and planting the marigolds.
>
> Student

—~~—

Young children draw from their souls the power to connect with others and to love. According to their birthright, they do what they were born to do. A vital connection is one of the most obvious aims of children's wisdom. From the moment of birth onward, a child attaches—to the breast, to his mother's voice, to a teddy bear, to a pet.

One spring day, when my son, Jamie, was about four years old, he found a baby bird lying alone on the ground. It had fallen from its nest and was in danger of being devoured by Boomerang, the cat who lived next door. With great care, Jamie cupped his hands, lifted the pathetic, chirping bundle, and brought it into the house. For the next few days, he could think of little else. Using an eyedropper, he dribbled sugar water down the bird's cavernous throat. With pillow feathers, he made it a cozy bed. He named the bird "Tweet" and sang songs to it. I have no doubt that the tiny creature somehow felt his love. His daily routine revolved around the care of his foundling. We all watched and waited. The bird rallied for a while, but then one morning, it died suddenly. Jamie laid its little body in his lap and wept inconsolably. I could not bear to see him so heartbroken, and suggested that we bury the bird in the garden.

It was Sunday, so we had time to do something special. By noon, Jamie had pulled himself together enough to go ahead with a burial. He wandered outside to find a suitable place. I heard his voice calling out to a passerby, "My bird is dead! Could you come and help me bury him?" Looking out of the window, I saw that Jamie had hailed one of our neighbors: the president of the Princeton Theological Seminary. A man of considerable gravitas, he was in a hurry and looked as if he had very little time to chat with a small boy. However, he paused midflight to answer in his usual sonorous tone, "How very sad, my friend. Normally, I would join you, for I am very good at this sort of thing, but at present it is impossible. I am late for a luncheon at Lowry House." He nodded toward the house where the president of Princeton University lived, and continued to churn his way up the street. Jamie stood there and watched Dr. Miller's august backside pass through the entry gates to Lowry House.

Suddenly, a cry came from the upper window of the house next door. My mother was waving at Jamie. "Wait! Don't be discouraged! I'll help you! I have a prayer book. Go find a box for a coffin and we'll give your bird a proper funeral." Jamie pivoted and leapt up the steps into our house. We found a perfect little candy box, lined it with feathers, and placed the bird's body in it. My mother arrived with a prayer book and a candle. We formed a procession. After a few prayers, "Tweet" was laid to rest in a corner of the garden. Jamie placed a stone on the ground to mark the spot.

What causes a child to love a bird? Or a gerbil? Or a dog or cat? I believe that there is a spiritual connection that passes all understanding between a child and a creature. Could it simply be that they are both pure of heart and innocent of guile? Or is it that the child finds within this bond a unique way to love and care for another being, free from the fetters of human interaction? Whatever the cause, the effect is vast. Companionship, forgiveness, patience, humor, protection, play—all are possible when a child and a pet connect with one another. Somehow, time and space are exempted during their interaction; they simply *are*. Recently, I heard a veterinarian confirming that children and animals share a strong connection with something far beyond, and that this accounts for their empathy toward one another.

> Hot Dog was like a brother to me. He was a small yet long cat. He was only six months old when he died. He was always a hero in my eyes because he saved another cat's life. He was born on September 21, 1988, and died on April 20, 1989. And sometimes I go out to his grave and just burst out into tears. In 1989, my Mom didn't want me to watch Christmas shows because it always made me cry, because I couldn't go [through] Christmas without him. Others of my pets died but I didn't feel bad. With Hot Dog I have so much pain. If you have any ideas on how I could take the pain off you can write to me . . . or call me . . . Or maybe you can come over and you, my Mom, and I could discuss it.
>
> Student

I have often thought that children's fellow feeling for stuffed animals springs from the same source. The beloved security blanket, so often cast aside to engender independence, belongs in a child's sacred trust as well. For some children, a mere scrap of the cherished blanket becomes a relic.

At Princeton Junior School, there was a lovely, gentle dog called Jesse. Throughout her tenure, Jesse became the symbol of all that an animal can offer to a child. She seemed to know a child's thoughts without being told. Although she truly belonged to our school administrator, she was available to any child in need of a soul mate. When someone was upset or hurt, Jesse would heal with a nuzzle. When someone was shy or restrained, Jesse would offer a paw. When someone was fearful, Jesse waited. One boy was so terrified of dogs that he could not enter the area near the front entrance where Jesse always stood to greet children in the morning. We let him come in by the back door so as to avoid her gaze. We thought that, given a little time, he would allow himself to make her acquaintance. And so he did—or rather, they did—after several weeks. We found the boy kneeling on the ground, stroking the top of her head. This was the beginning of a friendship that lasted until the day the boy graduated.

Jesse had a way with children. Her extraordinary composure freed them to become their best selves. Sometimes, if a candidate for admissions arrived at the school looking starched and coached, we would refer him or her to Jesse for stress relief. It worked every time.

Sometimes connection is with a peer. Two boys of my acquaintance followed the ancient custom of pricking their fingers, rubbing the bloody tips together, and declaring themselves "blood brothers." I had the honor of documenting the ceremony on a piece of parchment to which they affixed their bright fingerprints. To this day the two are friends, sharing with one another their hopes and fears throughout the years of adulthood.

A child's journey requires playful interaction with companions. Shared play helps children to access their inner wisdom. When children's friendships falter, they want to rebuild. Bridge-building comes naturally to children in an environment where learning depends on linkage. The following words reflect three boys' experience of bonding:

I was a bridge once when two of my close friends got into an argument and I helped them bridge their friendship back together.

Student

When I was in third grade I acted as a bridge helping all of my classmates go from sad or angry to happy and cheerful.

Student

Charles formed a bridge between me having friends and me not having friends in first grade. He is now one of my best friends. Charles will always be my friend. You're the best, Charles.

Student

The connection between the young and the very old at times defies all understanding. My aging aunt, afflicted with severe dementia, spends most of her days in her own mysterious world. She resides in a nursing home alongside a nursery school. Whenever a child trots past my aunt on his or her way into the school, she straightens up, eyes twinkling, and addresses the little person with a hearty, "Hello, my friend! And how be it with you this fine day?" Inevitably, children respond to my aunt with a smile and a wave, not realizing that their very presence has momentarily freed my aunt from her mental captivity. Recently, I learned that she joins the children in the art room and takes a lively interest in their projects. Having spent her life as a ceramicist, she connects with them and communicates her delight. Art bridges the gap.

My question—"If you were given an entire day to do whatever you wanted, what would you choose to do?"—is often answered with, "I'd want to just play with somebody." By "just playing," children enter new homelands, bringing along with them whatever bundles from past experience they deem to be important. Their shared time off leads them to invent games that in originality and verve defy all forms of packaged recreation. During play, the clock on the wall is forgotten; game time allows children to dip into their wells of imagination and refresh themselves with the living water they find there. Once, in music class, when the children had learned a song by Margaret Jones called "Best Friends," they decided to make up two new verses.

If you were a door, I would be your handle.
If you were a jack-o-lantern, I would be your candle.
If you were a guitar, I would be your string.
If you were a finger, I would be your ring.

Grade I

If you were a xylophone, I would be your stick.
If you were a building, I would be your brick.
If you were a mouse, I would be your hole.
If you were a flag, I would be your pole.

Kindergarten

Sometimes a child and a stranger connect by chance. The connection often grows into friendship. When I was a child, I had one such connection with the disheveled old man who lived down the street. He would frequently take solitary walks around the block. As he passed our house with his tousled head down and his hands clasped behind his back, I wondered whether he was lonely. One day, I ventured to greet him. He stopped, turned and smiled at me, and then with a wink and a wave, continued on. So began a friendship that lasted for several years. I would walk along near him sometimes, hoping that he would speak to me with his unfamiliar accent. He seemed lost in thought much of the time, but if he noticed me or other children nearby, his eyes would light up and he would greet us heartily. As the years rolled by, we learned that his sister lived with him. We thought she was mean. Once, when neighborhood children gathered on his porch to sing Christmas carols, she opened the door and told us that he was too busy and we should go away. Despite her rebuff, he stood on tiptoe behind her, waving his violin high in the air, motioning us to go around to the back of the house. There we found him a few minutes later, shivering on the back porch in his long woolen sweater, tuning up his violin. We had a merry time together that evening, he with his fiddle and we with our voices. His sister remained inside, behind closed doors. Little did we know at the time that the endearing old man was none other than the world-renowned Albert Einstein. To us, he was simply a friend whose wisdom glowed through his love for children.

One of my friends, when she later found out who he was, asked Dr. Einstein to help her with math homework. In surprise, he answered, "I'm afraid I can't possibly help you. Your homework is too complex for me." I have been told that he eventually complied. The fee: two cookies.

—◦◦◦—

When children become friends, they often will go to extremes to advocate for one another—even in preschool. "That's not fair!" is a cry often heard on the playground as children sort out their rights and regulations. Once, as a teacher of three-year-olds, I admonished a little girl for interrupting me during a phonics lesson. Saki had repeatedly asked for a drink and I was tired and all too hasty in planting her on the time-out chair away from the others. She was embarrassed. No sooner had I turned my head to look for a book than another child quietly put her chair next to the guilty one and sat down. I continued to rummage through my pile of phonics lessons. By the time I was finished, six little people were sitting side by side in the time-out place, staring at me with tiny sparks in their eyes. How could I resist? I dragged my chair over and joined them. Justice won over strictness.

In a faraway school that I attended long ago, justice was carried out in a far less charming manner. If we second-graders failed to follow the rules, we were sent to the janitor to be swatted with a yardstick. Be it knuckles or buttocks, we endured the humiliation and returned to the classroom smarting.

Unfairness assumed other forms as well. There was a child in Princeton Junior School who, for medical reasons too unfair to describe, could not walk without braces and crutches. Despite his handicap, Daniel was a cheerful lad who lurched through life with a smile on his face and a good word for everyone. However, the steep cement steps down to the school tried his patience. He insisted upon navigating the stairs by himself, his face contorted as he lowered his legs one step at a time. When we offered to help him, he refused. Then one day, I heard shouts in the stairwell. I ran to see what was going on. There was Daniel, with a child at each side and two behind carrying his knapsack and crutches. They had worked out a method of descent whereby he plopped from step to step on his behind, merrily giving detailed instructions to his orderlies. By offering their services, his friends had created for him a chance for new independence. By sharing his struggle, Daniel was wise. He could trust his buddies to help him whether he was high or low.

In the cases of both Saki and Daniel, authority emerged from an unlikely source. The two "leaders" evoked the respect of their peers. Their friends may not have cried, "Unfair!" but they were acting out of a sense that things were not as they should be. Wisdom now connected their passion for justice and healing with everyday needs and hurts. We adults should not be surprised.

We often hear the words "peace on earth" intoned in the short days of winter—in places of worship, in malls and markets, in restaurants, on the radio. Pilgrims seek it. Philanthropists endow it. Politicians and pedagogues praise it. Children reveal it—not because they are peaceful by nature, but rather, because they are so passionate about justice. Foul play is anathema to them. They will do all they can to heal a breach of truth or trust.

Often, doing a friend justice is hard work. I remember well an occasion at another school when a young boy was dealt a punishment that far exceeded his crime during a physical education class. The coach, upon hearing the boy's flippant remark, demanded that he run around the track three times. The distance was too much for the boy and he began to flag after the first go-around. Nevertheless, the coach insisted that he continue. He stumbled to a halt at the end of the second round, flushed and gasping for breath. The coach was about to force a third round when, to his surprise, all the other boys left their team positions and joined the exhausted boy. With arms linked, they slowly walked abreast with him once more around the track. The class ended with the coach sitting by himself on the bench.

Why is justice so important to children? Because it upholds the wisdom that breathes within them. At times, however, they need to be reminded. A six year old boy of my acquaintance once teased his younger sister in front of several older children who found her pleas for attention tiresome. Her brother not only mocked her feeble attempts to keep up, he summarily discharged her with a smack. Astonished and distressed, she stood with chubby legs apart, yellow rivulets running down into her socks. Their father happened to be nearby and saw the whole thing. Immediately he picked up the distraught little girl and motioned his son over. Amid her cries, he hissed, "I saw the way you treated your sister in front of your friends. I understand your feelings, but what you said and did to her was unfair and unkind. How would you feel if someone you love more than anyone else squashed you like an insect? Yes, I know she was pestering you, but she's younger and she's your sister! You have no other sister in the whole world. You're the only brother she has. She trusts you. We're a family, so we need to protect one another and help one another to succeed. No matter what you feel, your job is to be kind to her. Do you understand?"

The boy looked at his smelly little sister for awhile. "Sorry . . . do you want a bath?" She nodded. He grasped her outstretched hand and they trotted off together toward the house. Their father blew his nose as he watched them go.

Four years later, this same boy sat on the school stage along with his classmates. The audience was packed with parents. The children were asked by the principal what they wanted to be when they reached adulthood. One replied, "Astronaut!" Another, "Baseball player!" Another, "Movie star!" and so on. Finally the question was put to the boy. He responded quietly, "I just want to help people." The applause was deafening. I thank this boy for these words—not just because he said them, but because he lives them every day. He needs no reminder. He watches out for his little sister.

―――

For some children, it takes years to draw out from the wilderness of their psyches a language that adequately expresses the treasure that lies within. Most will employ any means they can find, whether vocal, visual, or corporeal, to communicate their feelings and thoughts to others. If they are lucky, they encounter muses who will help them transmit their wisdom. With such support, they can achieve balance between the inner and outer worlds. Without it, they may experience an agonizing struggle behind closed doors.

Once, as a teacher in a school for children with communication impairments, I witnessed this struggle firsthand. Many of the children lived so fully in a world of fantasy that the very real demands of the school day daunted them. Our main objective was to ground them in the present, to help them acknowledge the here and now, and to connect linguistically with others. However, our understanding of children could not live on words alone. Since much of the children's language was nonverbal, I learned to decipher their gestures and actions in order to understand their needs. Like all children, they longed to know and to be known, to share their world within with the world outside themselves. During sessions with their speech therapists, the children would strain to mimic the sounds the therapist modeled. Sometimes their tears flowed when their attempts were in vain. More often, their determination broke the dam and words trickled forth. The tears were tears of relief.

A young child's developing speech may ease communication but at the same time increase our awareness of the unfathomable mystery beyond the child's vocabulary. Somewhere within this mystery lives a whole and holy spirit longing to connect.

—⁕—

Recently, I received a message on my answering machine from Skye, aged five. "Hi, Nana! Can you and Papa come here for my birthday?" She paused as if waiting for me to answer. Someone told her to continue. "Can you come to my birthday?" As I listened to her words, I sensed that she was simply unacquainted with answering machines and believed I was actually on the other end of the line. She had heard my taped request— "Please leave a message"—but when she received no response, she became agitated: "Nana? . . . *Nana?*" Then she hung up. Did Nana not care?

Young children need only to hear the sound of another's voice to feel a desire to connect. My first paid job was a summer stint looking after a blind child, Gail. I was fifteen years old at the time and ready to poke my nose into the affairs of other families. Gail's mother was a nurse whose morning shift gave me an opportunity to learn from a four-year-old blind child what connectedness was all about. When I arrived at Gail's house at 7:30 every morning, she would patter down the hall in the direction of my voice and hurl herself into my arms. Her cheerful mother followed with a few hasty instructions: "Bathe her eyes, remember the vitamins, watch out for the neighbor's dog—" Then suddenly she was gone, leaving her child folded lazily in my lap. For a while, I would gaze into Gail's glowing face as she told me of a dream or a wish. What colorful and lively images lay behind those eyes of glass! I could only imagine the world she described, for it was totally without reference to things I had seen and long taken for granted.

Gail relied heavily on her four senses of sound, touch, taste, and smell. When we took walks around the block, she would scamper ahead of me, her head tilted, her voice shrill with questions about the dog behind the gate, the car swishing by on the street, the birds and squirrels overhead. Her acuity kept her from bumping into things. But even more essential than her four senses was a fifth one that enabled her to proceed confidently: trust. On her tricycle, she would ride ahead of me with her head high, her tiny feet spinning the pedals as she rolled along. Her mother had taught me the signals she needed: "Slow down!" "Stop!" "Left!" "Right!" When I called to her, my heart in my mouth, Gail responded instantly and accurately, albeit on two wheels sometimes. I was amazed by her connection with her surroundings. Most of all, I was inspired by her trust in a fifteen-year-old whose eyes were only beginning to see.

———

To return to the story about children at the school: One day, I was in the Walnut Lane play yard retrieving toys that had been left behind. I came across a sheltered nook behind the storage shed. Carefully crawling on hands and knees, I entered its dappled chamber to discover a fully furnished hideaway replete with wooden table and chair, markers, and paper. On the earthen floor lay a rag rug. The only solid wall, the back of the shed, displayed a child's drawing, gilded by strands of light that came through the other walls and roof. These were woven out of feathery boughs that screened the refuge from the hubbub of the play yard. I marveled at the architect's wisdom in situating this sanctuary beneath the church's overhanging roof where it would remain dry, at least for a while. It did not take long to identify the person who created this nook. The following day, I saw her slip away from her playmates and disappear behind the shed. When she emerged, I motioned to her to come over to me.

"Lizzie, what an enchanting place you have made. I discovered it yesterday."

"What's enchanting mean?"

"It means a place that is delightful, beautiful."

"I made it so I could go there and be by myself. You're the only person besides my teacher who knows about it."

"Do you want to get away from your friends?"

"Sometimes. But that's not the main reason. I like to go someplace alone to be quiet and think about things. I have a place like it at home, too. Nobody knows where it is except my mom."

"Have you given your place a name?"

"I call it my Alone Place."

Weeks later, I had the honor of visiting Lizzie's family. After lunch, she shyly showed me her sanctuary, situated in a thicket at the far end of the meadow behind the house. I could imagine her visits there, where the ripple of the brook nearby would sing into the silence of her reveries.

I have thought a lot about Lizzie's two worlds: the one in the school's noisy play yard and her Alone Place behind the shed. While traveling, was she not wise to give herself occasional solitude? She needed time to reflect, to imagine, to dream. She needed to process the rich experiences of her association with others. Only then could she face with grace the turbulence of growth. Without moments of time off, children are deprived of their most important inner resource: creative imagination. They may lose sight of their inner world and grow increasingly dependent upon outside influences to stimulate their daily lives. Nothing deflates children's spirits as deceptively as the Super Schedule that drags them—often willingly—from one organized activity to another. Too much structured time can easily usurp the timelessness that one's soul needs to process everything that is happening in life. I sometimes wonder whether drugs administered to children to increase their concentration are not a Super Glue to hold their fragmented psyches together? Instead of educating children to think, are we are training them to work on an assembly line? Such supervision stretches them from dawn until dusk, when finally, in nocturnal dreams, their inner voices cry out.

For most children, moments of solitude—when both time and space are suspended—provide an opportunity to discover their true being. Places apart such as Lizzie's hideout or my studio replenish the soul. They are sacramental, outward, and visible signs of inward spiritual grace.

> My peaceful place is in my house. It is cozy and quiet and warm. And it is so nice and peaceful. It has a low ceiling. And it also has a couch and two tables. And it has one room that belongs to me. It has three windows and a ladder in case there is a fire. And it has one TV and two chairs and one green up-and-down chair. That's my peaceful place . . . I feel relaxed in my peaceful place.
>
> Student

—◦∿◦—

When I was a child, the Trinity choir sat in stalls facing one another in the chancel. The Holy Eucharist was always offered at the high altar beneath vivid stained glass windows. People came forward up through the chancel to receive bread and wine. As a young choir member, I sat in the front row on the right. Having yet to be confirmed, I was not allowed to participate in the Lord's Supper; yet I could watch the show from the nook of my choir stall. Sunday after Sunday, while the organ played softly, people walked past to receive the sacrament at the high altar rail. As they walked by, I wondered whether the Lord's table was not beckoning them, as my family's dining table beckoned me, to dwell in a space wherein presences both seen and unseen were welcome. I wondered whether my ancestors, who were buried in the graveyard outside the church's stone wall, could hear the music drifting out through the open apse windows. I knew, of course, that they were dead. But then, I had seen Thornton Wilder's play: *Our Town*. I believed in their presence and their continued connection with me in my daily life.

As my time in the choir lengthened, I began to do more than just watch these communicants. From their facial expressions and their movements, I drew my own conclusions about who they were, how they were, and why they were there. I made up stories about them, imagining their worlds, their preoccupations, their joys, and their sorrows. When the frail lady with the trembling lips missed the rim of the cup, I could feel her embarrassment. When the elderly gentleman started coming to the rail alone without his wife, I winced at his woebegone face. I became eager to see whether, from week to week, things had improved or deteriorated. If seeing was believing, prayer made its way into my chancel workroom as I watched my imaginary friends go by. Their souls whispered to me. The people who drank of that chalice long ago were transformed. And I, a child watching from my choir stall, was being turned by wisdom's lathe into a vessel myself.

One recent Sunday morning, my husband and I remained seated after a church service to listen to the organ postlude: Gaston Litaize's "Toccata." The whole sanctuary vibrated with the brilliant fantasia. Unexpectedly, a child came into view. She had wandered away from her mother and up the nave aisle into the transept. Her small frame swaying from one foot to the other, she moved gracefully into the embrace of the music. As the "Toccata" surged toward its climax, she stood still with her head back, her arms extended, and her eyes closed. Throughout the following thunderous crescendo, she seemed literally to float in space, enraptured by her muse. When the last note faded away, the child opened her eyes, turned and flew down the aisle to join her mother. We blinked at one another. Had we seen a vision? More likely, we had caught a glimpse of a child's wisdom.

I am reminded of a drawing of a tree—an outward and visible sign—made by a second-grader in the school. The tree in the picture is evergreen, tall, its feathery branches stretching from a slender trunk. This boy truly knew his tree! Superimposed on this drawing are the following lines, each corresponding to a bough of the tree.

High above the tree tops I tower
Where the wind shows all of its power.
No one shelters me
Because I am the tallest tree.
The ocean, rivers, and mountains I see.
Flying eagles, baby eaglets—it's a good place to be.
The sun, moon, and stars I see each day.
Puffy clouds and rain drops, a rainbow is on its way.

Student

The spiritual connection between mortals and trees is as old as the hills. Countless sacred songs, prayers, and rituals have been created to express such a bond.

I know a small boy who has a blueberry bush in a pot outside the kitchen door. He loves blueberries so much that his mother bought the bush for him at a farm market. All the way home in the car he hugged the bush. "You're mine, little tree! You're my friend. I'll take good care of you." Throughout the summer, the boy watered the "little tree" and talked to it. It responded by yielding a mass of berries. Every time the boy picked a berry, he patted the leaves. "Thank you for giving me such juicy berries." He shared some with his sisters and ate some along with his Cheerios. Then winter came. The blueberry bush, still outside the kitchen door, lost all its leaves and became dormant. The boy thought his friend was dead and cried for a long time. Finally spring arrived, and with it appeared tiny green leaves along the branches of the blueberry bush. "Oh, you're alive! You've come back to me! Thank you!" The boy hugged the bush hard and kissed the baby leaves.

I know a young girl who captured a grasshopper and placed it in a large Mason jar. She punched holes in the lid and placed some fresh leaves and grass inside. The grasshopper lived in the jar on the windowsill for a day or two. The girl worried that her grasshopper might be unhappy because it was born to hop and the jar was too confining. So on the third day, she took the jar outside, unscrewed the lid and watched the grasshopper crawl to the opening. "I waited for it to make a huge leap into the air but instead it came out and walked up my arm to my cheek. It gave me a kiss and then it hopped off into the grass."

Listening to these children, I am more convinced than ever that children are spiritually connected with the inhabitants of God's creation. They love and grieve with the rise and fall of them all.

I have marveled at a child's determination to maintain a connection when circumstances threaten to sever the ties that bind. John Fawcett's hymn echoes a child's hope:

When we asunder part,
It gives us inward pain;
But we shall still be joined in heart
And hope to meet again.

On one occasion, I overheard a child sobbing over the telephone. "Daddy, I miss you so much! Please come home! Won't you try to love Mommy again so that we can all be together?" He was torn asunder right along with the marriage. This child would have given anything to have his father come back to live at home. They were still joined in heart, but never again at home—at least, not home as he had known it. I still cry to think about it.

—⁂—

Hospitality is a path to diversity. As a very young child in a large family richly endowed with talent and opportunity, I learned from my parents that hospitality was one of the very best ways to connect with other people. My father was a lovable patriarch whose high standards were tempered by an irresistible sense of fun. His values were dealt as deftly as a pack of cards and I picked them up and played them accordingly. One of his comments about hospitality still rings in my ears: "Everything you do—no matter how big or small—to make people feel at home is important." I always respected, if not followed, his counsel. Both a model of responsibility and a *bon vivant*, my father personified a "way of life." I thank him for that to this very day.

My parents—initially dubbed "Bu" and "Maboo" by my older brother—invited people of all sizes and shapes to our hearth. "The Barracks"—the family's pre-revolutionary fieldstone house on Edgehill Street—lived up to its name in every sense of the word. In addition to billeting five children within its three storied frame, my parents sheltered relatives, friends and strangers (not to mention the ghost of a Hessian soldier who lived there until exorcized in 1952 by the rector of Trinity Church.) Granny lived in The Barracks during her final years. When Aunt Julie died at the age of forty-six, Uncle Tom attached a wing to The Barracks where he dwelt until he departed for England. It was exciting to have Uncle Tom attached because he was our introduction to the literary world. Such illustrious figures as James Thurber, Laurie Lee, Robert Graves and Adlai Stevenson were in his coterie. His four sons folded into the fabric of Barracks life for years to come. Then, when Cousin Cack became crippled by arthritis, my parents invited him to spend the rest of his life in Uncle Tom's vacated cabin. There he was no longer alone.

The Barracks was the perfect setting for such a large, diverse, and unconventional family. Life was hectic. As a young child, I was curious about a lot of things: the elves who dwelt behind the walls and ventured out at night, the bumblebees that nested beneath the porch and provided us with honey, the tooth fairy who left pennies under our pillows. These fancies were encouraged by my playful mother, who, at the drop of a hat, called upon imagination to put some sparkle into the sometimes strenuous task of raising so many children. Her daily batch of chocolate chip cookies drew us often into the kitchen, both then and even sixty years later.

> Hunger:
> I'm so hungry right now
> I taste my mom's sweet shrimp gumbo
> I hear popcorn popping
> I touch the lettuce when I cut it

I smell the chocolate chip cookies
I see jaws jumping
I'm so full now!

Student

Reunions on holidays were huge, with grandparents, uncles, aunts, and cousins filling every corner. We children were immensely curious about the characters who showed up. Our dining room table—a long, polished plank designed by the former owner for his academic seminars—was the sounding board for mellow conversation. Our friends used to sit in the deep windowsills to watch the show. Often at my father's urging we would break into song. Or Rosie, our ancient cook, would trot out from the kitchen and perform the cakewalk. The diversity of opinion around the dining room table both intrigued and baffled me. Clergymen, writers, artists, musicians, teachers, and bankers all had their say. This was the environment into which I was born and raised.

Was not God's presence in the lively conversations, songs, stories, and debates around that table where bread and wine were shared? I don't know exactly when I began to see what I had always known intuitively, that God was the host at these gatherings. We "little ones" were coming into being, and our young lives were the light of the people around us. Maboo had her hands and heart full. Left to our own devices, we entertained ourselves by making up and performing plays, creating forts out of sofa pillows, eavesdropping, exploring the passageways behind the walls and taming the squirrels under the roof. As in all large families, there were good and bad times that brought both heartwarming and heartbreaking experiences for us. The world of The Barracks was our primary education; the hospitality fostered by such a vibrant household taught us to give our best. Amid both the hopes and fears of my early years, I leaned upon my parents. Such a bond secured the kite of my imagination.

I cannot write about hospitality without mentioning the role played by beauty—"God's handwriting," as Ralph Waldo Emerson called it. The beauty of Princeton affected me deeply. In addition to the hearth at The Barracks, there was the radiance of autumn leaves, the chiming of the carillon bells in Cleveland Tower, the smell of spaded garden soil, the ripple of water between my toes in Frog Hollow. In these surroundings, I felt "found," as did a young writer in his poem about his more rural backyard.

> I know the sight of deer,
> Hawks soaring in the sky,
> Foxes with their young.
> I know the feeling of pinecones,
> The green trees, the muddy water,
> The dew on the grass.
>
> I know the sound of the neighbor talking,
> The children yelling of wild berries,
> The owls hooting.
>
> I feel free and cool, with family in my backyard.
> I know the familiar smell of the grass in my backyard
> While Luigi rumbles along on his lawnmower.

> Student

Moments spent over food and drink have special meaning for children, particularly when they initiate the occasion. Hospitality comes naturally to the very young. Have we not seen a baby remove a particle of food from his or her dish (or even mouth) and offer it to the person at the other end of the spoon?

The other morning, as Richard and I lay in bed listening to the dawn's chorus outside the window, a new, unexpected sound slid through the keyhole into our bedroom. No sooner had we raised ourselves upon our elbows than the procession arrived at the foot of the bed. One child held a teapot. Another, some cups; another, a plate laden with toast and almond butter; another, cream; another, lemon and honey. I recognized the dishes decorated with rosebuds as the ones that I had inherited from my mother's beloved friend, Henrietta Ricketts.

Our grandchildren carried the dishes very carefully. The youngest arranged the dishes on the coffee table and told us who was to sit where. For the next hour, we ate and drank and listened to dreams. What better way to start a day? To be sure, the aforementioned tea party was a moment during our vacation when time was available. Nevertheless, every day should allow for at least one such moment when time stands still enough for the soul to breathe.

—⁓—

During the early years of the school, the children began to share their learning with their families and friends by giving parties. For the youngest children, the Teddy Bear Breakfast became a tradition that combined food (B foods: bagels, bacon, bread, butter, blueberries), phonics (B guests: bears, bunnies, birds), and, needless to say, *fun.* The delicious fragrance of this popular event tantalized the older classes. For the kindergarten, a spring afternoon tea party became the tradition of choice. The party space, festooned with garlands, tablecloths, cookies, cakes, brownies, and iced tea, resembled an English garden. Five-year-old hosts and hostesses met dozens of guests at the door and ushered them to their places at table. Families and friends in attendance were served by the children. The tea party climaxed with a colorful rendition of "The Hungry Caterpillar," presented by the children.

> We had been instructed to serve cookies and juice to our families before serving ourselves, and I had so much fun with this role-reversal that I still remember it. I felt very old, though I was probably five years old and unable to tie my shoes tightly on the first try. PJS taught us how to act maturely and responsibly in spite of having none of our adult teeth. I also remember learning addition by hopping back and forth on a number line rolled across the floor. I wish math was still taught in this way.
>
> Alumna

One particular child invited me to lunch at her house at the beginning of her kindergarten year. Neither of us knew one another at the time, for she had just entered the school. When I arrived at her house, she invited me into her bedroom, where a small table had been beautifully set for two. Each flowered plate held a sandwich and salad. A full teapot, sugar, and cream completed the picture. Where was her mother? Oh, she was in the kitchen waiting for us to need dessert. During my hour alone with my five-year-old hostess, I became convinced that the school would be a success—because she was in it. When she graduated six years later, I was tempted to hand her an employment contract rather than a diploma.

Early on, when we were still in the preschool stage, we held a Christmas assembly prior to the two-week vacation. In preparation, I asked children to improvise the nativity story. This they did during the weeks prior to the assembly by dramatizing the story over and over again. Within each improvisation, the children could choose to play a different character: Mary, Joseph, baby Jesus, the innkeeper, a shepherd, a king, an angel, a donkey, or a sheep. A five-year-old boy, Isaac, wanted to be the innkeeper so often that as the day for the assembly grew nearer, we all assumed that he would play this particular character. But when the morning of the assembly finally arrived, Isaac stunned me. "Mrs. McIntyre, I'm not going to be the innkeeper ever again."

"What? Today is the play! You can't change your mind now. You'll be a powerful innkeeper. No one else knows him as well as you." His eyes clouded. "Why don't you want to play him anymore?" I asked.

"I used to like him, but now I don't. Nobody does. He puts good people in the barn."

"But it all turns out well in the end."

"No, it doesn't."

"The angels, and the star above? Have you forgotten that even kings came to the barn with gifts for baby Jesus?"

"They were pretending to be kings. They were just wise people."

"Wait a minute, we're talking about your part as the innkeeper. No one else can do it as well. Please, just one more time?"

"I don't want to. Nobody likes the innkeeper at any time in the story."

To my great relief, Isaac finally, albeit reluctantly, agreed to be the innkeeper one more time, and the improvisation took place in a small space, surrounded by enthusiastic school families. At first, a weary Joseph entered the scene, dragging a donkey who sagged beneath the bundle on his back. It was Mary wrapped in a blue blanket, muttering despondently about the distance, darkness, and danger of the journey. So far, so good, I thought, as I watched them slowly circle the scene. At last, they stumbled into Bethlehem and approached the door of the inn to beg for a room. Suddenly, the innkeeper—garbed in rich, full-length robes—threw open the door with his arms outstretched and cried, "Welcome, strangers! Come on in! I have a warm fire and lobster stew waiting for you." (Isaac's parents ran a summer camp on the coast of Maine.) Mary and Joseph, and even the donkey, were caught by surprise. The lodgers in the inn gasped as they were shooed offstage to spend the night in the stable. The innkeeper dragged the weary travelers in to warm themselves by the fire. After filling their stomachs with wine and lobster stew, he hustled Mary and Joseph to the inn's bridal suite. There, baby Jesus was born, wrapped in white linen, and laid in a cradle. The other players adjusted to the new situation and improvised the rest of the story: angels sang lustily, shepherds knelt by the baby's cradle, and gift-bearing kings bowed down before him. Although the innkeeper would not allow sheep, camels, or donkeys to enter the bedroom, they looked in through the windows and marveled at the sight.

In this nativity play, an age-old traditional story about the humble birth of the Prince of Peace was challenged—in fact, changed—by a five-year-old who wanted to be regarded as hospitable to strangers who came his way: not as a solitary, unpopular figure. Had Isaac's improvisation gone too far? No, his action was a paradox; his weakness challenged our strength. As I saw it, this child had unwittingly lived up to one of our school's life-giving principles: "Do unto others as you would have them do unto you." I could not fault him for that. In truth, I could not overlook his alteration of Holy Scripture; and yet, I *had* encouraged the children to improvise! I had empowered Isaac to follow his impulse by telling him that he knew the innkeeper better than anyone else.

So much for biblical authority! I could only wonder at how the "new" story expressed the Golden Rule that was so fundamental to our school from its conception. How could we be as good as our word if we disparaged this child's hospitality? He formed an effective, if surprising contrast with traditional points of view. Who is to say that his word contradicted the Word of Wisdom?

When the pastor, our landlord, later confessed to me that he had borrowed Isaac's version of the nativity story for his Christmas sermon, I was not surprised. This playing of that story took place very early in the school's life, when we had only thirty-five children in tow. Isaac's revision swept through my soul like wildfire. If welcoming strangers as members of one family was the pivotal point of the child's story, should it not become the pivotal point of ours as well? Were we not together in this school family to learn from one another?

I looked around me at the motley group that made up our school family. Without hospitality, diversity would fade and the school would lose its opportunity to foster paradoxes within its community. The school should enable everyone to live out his or her differences cooperatively. Differences complement each other in ways that we don't expect; we need them in order to find our common humanity. That is what *love* in education is all about: liberating one another to take the risks that learning requires.

—⁓—

Lest you think that it was easy to live up to our lesson in hospitality, there were times when we stumbled and had to be reminded—often by children—that diversity is more than skin deep. During a later chapter in the school's life, we rented a wing of a local public school. We accommodated nine grade levels, two-and-a-half-year-olds through Grade V. During that time, we adapted to public school regulations regarding transportation, arrival and dismissal, parking, security, the cafeteria, the gymnasium, and the library. Our landlord, the principal, was hospitable to a fault, the fault being that he tolerated us as long as we adhered to his standards. When we overstepped our bounds on the playground, whistles blew. When our children said a blessing before eating their homemade snacks, we were told to stop, for such a practice violated church and state separation. (Oh dear, I thought to myself as

I hastened away from the principal's office. Is God not allowed to be our guest? Do we have to muffle all those prayers for pets, parents, and plants that come so naturally to children? What about Muffie's "Dear God thank you for my mom who makes my life so fun and Dad who earns money for our food and Tom for teaching me to play "Twinkle Twinkle" on the piano," or Billy's "Dear God, in Sunday school they say you live inside me, but are you covered up with food?") I announced the principal's prohibition to the teachers and left it to them to figure out how to leave God out of snack time.

Two days had not passed before I received a telephone call from a parent whose daughter was in our kindergarten. "Hi, Juliana! Do I have your permission to address this issue of prayer that has come up in the school?"

"How did you hear about it?" I suspected that "addressing this issue" meant putting the story in one of the nation's leading newspapers, of which he was the editor.

"Well, tonight we were all about to have dinner and we asked Pattie to say the blessing. Instead of her usual 'Dear God,' she substituted 'Dear Lobster.' When we asked her why, she told us that God wasn't allowed in school any more. She said she would use the name 'Lobster' from now on because lobster is her next favorite thing."

The article that appeared in the paper the following day drew letters to the editor from all over the United States. A five-year-old had rattled the lion's cage.

———

Nothing, absolutely nothing could compare with the hospitality that our little school demonstrated when Thanksgiving rolled around. On the Wednesday before Thanksgiving Day, we had our own celebration that included an assembly followed by a splendid feast for all—prepared by the children. The threes made cranberry jelly; the fours, mashed potatoes; kindergarten, stuffing; Grade I, green beans; Grade II, pumpkin pies; Grade III, whipped cream; Grade IV, corn bread; Grade V, turkey. The preparations, including costumes, decorations, music, and stories, all took several days as they were integrated into the academic learning of the week.

> The paper placemats, paper bag vests, and black and white construction paper pilgrim clothes bring a smile to my face. We are still the humble, intensely creative school that lets imaginations run wild. We are excited today because the mayor of Princeton is joining us for the feast. Barbara Boggs Sigmund arrives and captures the attention of every child . . . She speaks to us of hope and thanks for the beautiful world we've been given. The children don't even notice the patch covering her right eye. We are infected with her love of life.
>
> Parent

It was exhausting, but fun. On one such occasion, I lost my car keys in all the excitement. After frantically searching through every pocket, drawer, trash basket, and briefcase, I finally found them tucked into the roasting pan with the turkey.

Even at Thanksgiving when public schools were allowed to include hymns and prayers in their holiday assemblies, and when the mayor and God could both attend, we encountered a challenge to our tradition of hospitality. We created a pageant replete with traditional songs and prayers to be performed in the huge gymnasium. On this particular occasion, the entire Thanksgiving assembly was almost aborted by one child who balked at the beginning of the procession. We had been granted the use of the gymnasium for one hour. The space was full of school families waiting for their children to perform. Margaret, all gussied up as Pocahontas, was playing "Come, Ye Faithful People, Come" over and over on the piano, and nodding wildly in my direction, obviously wanting us to *come* into the room. I was at the door with Mahmoud, a tall African-American lad whom I had chosen to lead the procession of eighty children. The elementary grades had all made their own pilgrim costumes. The "men" wore black paper hats, stiff white collars, long jackets, and buckled belts and shoes. The "women" were clad in pale paper hats and collars, with white aprons over drab, long skirts. In contrast to these grave figures, the preschoolers and kindergarteners were all dressed in homemade native-American costumes consisting of colorful feathers, beads, fringes, and a dab of face paint. Altogether, they were poised for a lively Thanksgiving pageant.

"Mrs. McIntyre, I need to have a word with you," Mahmoud's voice at my side was low, but insistent.

"Not now, Mahmoud. Look at Pocahontas: she's cueing us to start the procession!"

"Mrs. McIntyre," Mahmoud stood in the doorway with his feet apart, arms folded across his wide chest, eyes glowering under the brim of his floppy black paper hat, "I need to have a word with you here and now."

"Why? Is something wrong?"

"Yes. I refuse to go ahead with this. It's against my principles."

"What? Mahmoud, you must be joking! You're the leader of the whole—"

"I never asked to do this. You designated me to do it and didn't give me a chance to protest. I and my constituency all protest." I noticed for the first time that several African-American students had lined up behind Mahmoud. So this was his constituency! "Mrs. McIntyre, did the plain fact ever occur to you that there were no black pilgrims? Black folks didn't come to this country to be free. They came here as slaves—and you have us all dressed up like this, leading a parade, showing ourselves off as white Pilgrim Fathers? It's just not the way it was! Besides, I'm a Muslim."

I heard Margaret's frantic, "We gather together to ask the Lord's blessing; He chastens and hastens His will to make known . . ." Her feathery headdress had slipped over one eye while she bobbed and nodded in our direction. "Mahmoud, you have a point. Thank you. I never thought . . . I'm sorry, but it's too late to do anything about it, can't you see? You all have to go through with it this one time. We're depending on you!"

I waited while Mahmoud conferred with his constituency. It took forever. Finally, he returned to his place at the head of the procession. "We have reached a consensus. Just for you, we'll do it today, just this once." He then tilted his paper hat, straightened his shoulders, took a deep breath and strode forward. The procession followed, only now to the tune of "Oh Come, All Ye Faithful." Oh, Margaret! This was

Thanksgiving, not Christmas! Had Pocahontas lost track? If she had, it was not for long. The drumbeats of thirty-five small native-Americans helped her to recover the original theme.

When the celebration was over and I had time to reflect upon the whole affair, it seemed to me that Margaret's surprising digression to "Oh Come, All Ye Faithful" made a certain amount of sense in the larger picture. True, ten-year-old Mahmoud had come close to ruining his school's Thanksgiving assembly, and I had come close to admonishing him for that. Yet he was proud of his race and his faith and wanted them to be respected, especially within the theme of Thanksgiving. He had sharpened my awareness to a problem often overlooked in democratic life: the failure to acknowledge differences which, if they are not valued, can defy unity. I had to thank him for that. Later, when in a multicultural assembly, Mahmoud outlined the basic tenets of his faith as a Muslim, I was stirred by the breadth and depth of his insight.

Twelve years later, I responded to a knock on my door and found a tall, handsome African-American youth grinning at me. "Hi, Mrs. McIntyre! Do you remember me? I'm Mahmoud. I wonder whether you would consider giving me a job. I want to become a teacher." I gave him the only job that was available at the time and granted his one request: to take five minutes off every afternoon in order to withdraw to a private place, face Mecca, and pray.

Our occupancy of the public school space ended abruptly in August following our one year there because of an unexpected fluctuation in the public school's enrollment. We panicked, for opening day was only two weeks away, and we had no place to go. Margaret waved her wand. Miraculously, both the Unitarian Church and our former landlord at Walnut Lane had some space available. We moved the school into these two spaces a week before opening day. We took along with us a bunch of secular desks and chairs that the janitor of the public school said they couldn't use any more.

—⁓—

From the time I was born until I was fourteen, a nanny lived with us. My father would tenderly describe her as "a character who in no way matches your ideal of a baby nurse." She was thin, nervous, asthmatic, gloomy, and subject to harrowing homesickness. Although she adopted our family with a certain reluctance and greeted each successive newborn with guarded optimism, she responded to my autistic brother's growing demands with unexpected fervor, particularly when she took care of him during the several weeks that he was in quarantine as a tuberculosis carrier. From then on, she devoted herself to our family for the rest of her life. She was our advocate, our referee, our "Eeyore." It is no wonder that her death at the age of fifty was due to an enlarged heart. When, during her last year, she was bedridden at her sister's house, I would stop in on my way home from school to massage her cold, boney hands and trim her nails. How better could I tell her that I loved her?

When she first arrived, my older brother named her "Oo," as pronouncing "Ruth" was a task too complex for his toddler tongue. Our daily companion loved to stroll. Our afternoon excursions inevitably led us to her favorite checkpoints along the main street of Princeton. She called this stretch of sidewalk "my blue heaven." Our little procession— the baby in the stroller, my older brother and I grasping the shafts on either side, and Oo pushing and wheezing in the middle—would crawl along the bluestone sidewalk from Edgehill toward Nassau Street. First came Trinity Church. "That's where your grandfather lies in state," she murmured, casting a spectacled eye toward the graveyard. Occasionally we would wander in to gaze at his gravestone and try to connect Oo's description of our grandfather with our memories of the mischievous old rascal who sneaked into our bedrooms after we had been put to bed and buzzed like a bumblebee in the dark.

With Trinity behind us, we would cross at the top of Stockton and proceed down Nassau Street. This was Oo's fulfillment: stopping for a word or two with every other shopkeeper along the way. First it was Bamman's, a cozy grocery that offered Oo her first tidbit of gossip while we munched slices of sweet-smelling apple. Next, it was Lyon's Meat Market. We eagerly watched the butcher's blade attack a rack of lamb while Oo picked up her next tidbit. From there, we visited the mail room of the post office, where free lollipops were available. Then came Hill's Market on Witherspoon Street, where we were allowed to select two cookies from the big glass jars on the floor. Crossing the street again, we approached Nassau Hall's main entrance and climbed onto the great bronze tigers there. In summer, their broad metal backs, polished from years of tiger-riders, felt cool and smooth against our sweaty legs. Oo, having picked up a companion or two by this time, was perfectly willing to linger while we clambered on the tigers. From there, we visited the public library and borrowed a few books from the children's reading room at the top of the squeaky stairs. Our trip home an hour later included a climb on the Revolutionary War Monument. My brother and I could climb as far as the arched neck of Washington's horse before the figure of Liberty blocked any further ascent. It was just as well, as Oo could never have retrieved us without the help of one of her cronies on the police force. Our skinny nanny knew everyone in town, and they, in turn, welcomed her three little charges. We were "townies."

Needless to say, our afternoon walks taught us a lot about the world beyond our nest. They left an indelible mark upon my soul. I could not have imagined then what an impact such strolls would have on Princeton Junior School's future processions around the town. During the fifteen years that the school occupied church spaces, the entire town of Princeton became our campus. The churches were our first habitats. Their kitchens became our offices, their closets places for storage of chairs and cabinets, their ladies' rooms our laboratories. We were densely cramped and immensely restless. Their playgrounds provided the only perches from which our children could peer into the world beyond. When one caring neighbor offered us a corner of her yard in which to grow flowers and vegetables, we grabbed it. We ventured further into our surroundings and discovered parks nearby. As our students grew older, their curiosity prodded us to travel further. Walking hand-in-hand along the historic sidewalks, we poked everywhere.

Doors opened easily to such travelers as we. Our older students borrowed books from the public library, visited the university chapel and museums; they crawled through the secret passages of The Barracks, galloped in the grass of the battlefield and tiptoed through the governor's mansion; they gazed at displays in the historical society's museum, scaled fire engines in the firehouse, sledded on the golf course and dropped in at the police station and mayor's office; they watched the butcher at the supermarket, peeked into the vault at the bank and collected fabric scraps at a tailor's shop. They performed skits at senior centers and even sang carols at the governor's Christmas party. How much we all learned during those periodic escapes from the undercrofts! Our young adventurers were learning about the world beyond their school's doorstep.

Ludwig Bemelman's beloved picture book about Madeline begins, "In an old house in Paris that was covered with vines lived twelve little girls in two straight lines." Pictured on the first page are the twelve lasses walking two by two, their hats askew, along the Champs-Élysées. In towns and cities, one passes schoolchildren walking two by two with a teacher in front and another behind like sentinels guarding a flock of magpies. In the annual parade of Princeton University, classes of alumni walk in sequence, starting with the earliest graduates—a small contingent of proud, fragile old men—and ending with a large crowd of boisterous seniors. In watching this spectacle, one sees life pass by before one's eyes. Processions most powerfully convey the present; neither wanderers nor ramblers, people on walks are *in the process* of traveling from here to there. It is no wonder that traditional processions created by kings, priests, generals, academics, protesters, and activists convey the most poignant journey of all: from birth to death.

When we would finally move to a permanent schoolhouse on Fackler Road, there would be six acres of open land to explore. Our walks would become very different in terms of their focus and findings. Our findings would be birds, turtles, rabbits, deer, woodchucks, and frogs. Our places would be meadow, marsh, and woodland. Our new habitat, the schoolhouse, would be surrounded by a natural world teeming with life, a world waiting to be discovered.

Within the new schoolhouse would be many journeys. From the moment children lined up in the morning to go to class until they disbanded at the end of the school day, they were "in process." The littlest ones would be asked to tiptoe silently through the halls, their eyes wide with curiosity as they peered into the classrooms of other children. Then there would be journeys made by children who wanted to share with others what they had made. Miniature chefs would show off cookies that they had baked in the school's kitchen. The children's daily journeys would mark their place in time and space.

—⁓—

Our years at Walnut Lane were full of epiphanies. Perhaps being packed into a space too small for comfort led to our readiness for wisdom's spark to kindle our imaginations. Unexpected enlightenment came one year in the form of a thin volume entitled *The Wit and Wisdom of Woodrow Wilson*. Reversing current methods of research, several children memorized excerpts from Wilson's speeches about education in America. For accomplishing such a feat, they had none other to thank than the playful octogenarian who compiled the book, William McCleery. Mr. McCleery's credo was drawn straight from the Wilson material.

> Education is not, after all, an affair of filling and furnishing the mind, but . . . of informing the spirit; and nothing affects spirit but spirit.
>
> —Woodrow Wilson, October 2, 1907

In addition to several well-known plays, Bill McCleery had written a book for children called *Wolf Story*. He had created this wonderful tale with his own son years earlier, and he now sought to recreate it with our schoolchildren. Hence, one day, he came to Walnut Lane, sat down in an easy chair with the children gathered around him, and began to read *Wolf Story* aloud. While doing so, he growled and howled, grumbled and chuckled—much to the delight of his young audience. A year later, Bill transformed *Wolf Story* into a play for the children to perform.

Little did we know how powerfully the children inspired this eighty-eight year old playwright. In the glow of their satisfaction, Bill conceived a project that neither he, nor anyone else had ever imagined. When the wild applause for *Wolf Story* died down, he asked, "How many of you would like to listen to wise words about education spoken by one of our former presidents, Woodrow Wilson?" All hands went up. "Okay, I'll bring them around next week and we'll have a go at them."

So began one of the most unique educational processes I have ever witnessed. Bill returned to the school a week later with his book of excerpts from Wilson's speeches in his pocket. It was just after lunch. The children clambered for a place close to his easy chair and held their breath. Perhaps this would be a sequel to *Wolf Story*! After giving them a short account of Woodrow Wilson as an educator, Bill pulled the book from his pocket and began to read.

"You are not as beautiful as some animals or as cunning as others, but you have the one great power of mind and the power to draw from the reservoir of the minds of all the men and women in the world. The cultivation of the mind is the best and most profitable thing you can do." Bill paused and peered over his glasses at his audience. They held on.

He turned a page and selected another excerpt. "Education is the process of limbering up the mental powers. No amount of information alone makes an educated person. Libraries are places where our information can be laid up where we can get at it easily. The educated person knows where and how to get his information; the ignorant person does not." Silence.

Bill went on, his voice intoning every word. "Luckily we are not the first human beings. We have come into a great heritage of interesting things, collected and piled all about us by the curiosity of past generations. Our education consists in learning intelligent choice."

Some listeners were gazing through the window to the world beyond. I doubted that their daydreams included Woodrow Wilson. Bill didn't seem to notice, and droned on: "It is a great deal better to see one thing than merely to look at a thousand." What a sly old fox!

Even so, Bill wasn't making much progress during this week's reading. The beloved wolf of the previous week's story had retreated to his den and the children couldn't find him anywhere in this maze of wise words. At one point, a little boy's nodding head hit Bill's left knee accidentally. Scrutinizing the young man with twinkling eyes, Bill concluded the session with, "The pathos of this situation is that I cannot impart to you from my experience anything that will keep you from being just as great a fool as I was at your age." The lad was too sleepy to notice.

The Broadway playwright put his book down, sprang rather unsteadily to his feet, thrust his hands into his pockets and puckered his brow. "I can see that you all have somewhat less energy this week. What's wrong? Have you not had enough sleep?"

"I thought you were going to tell us what happened next in the wolf story," replied a brave voice from the floor.

"Wolf story? Oh, yes, the wolf. Well, he's asleep today . . . and just like some of you, he is unable to grasp the wonderful words of Woodrow Wilson."

"I got some of them . . ." ventured a child. "I liked the part about not being as cunning as some animals. That made me think about the wolf."

"Oh, yes, of course. Well, you might enjoy the rest of the words if you took the time to learn them by heart. But then, that's too much to ask. Unfortunately, children nowadays don't learn great things by heart." Bill reached for his overcoat.

There was a stir in the pack. "Yes, we do! We memorize lots of things, Mr. McCleery!"

"Like what?"

"'Six times eight equals forty-eight,' or 'I pledge allegiance to the flag,' or—"

"So you do! That's all very well and good. But learning by heart is different from memorizing. When you learn something by heart, you plant it so deep that it grows inside you and leads you to all sorts of new places. When I was your age, I had to learn poems by heart and they still open new doors for me to walk through." Bill cleared his throat, took in a deep breath, closed his eyes and began to recite: "Something there is that doesn't love a wall, That sends the frozen-ground-swell under it . . ."

"I know that one! It's about frost," piped up one of the girls.

"Good for you! It is about *Robert* Frost." Bill headed for the door. "Well, I've got to go now. I'd leave these words of Woodrow Wilson behind if I thought any of you could learn them by heart, but that would be too much to ask of children these days."

"Wait, wait, wait!" they protested. "We *do* know how to learn things by heart! You just think we don't."

Bill turned around with disbelieving eyes. "So you say! But what would Mrs. McIntyre say if I asked you to do something that you are incapable of doing? I'd rather not. She'd tar and feather me and throw me out." With that, he donned his Irish cap.

Such a retort brought on a flood of protest. Bill paused and stared at the floor, deep in thought. Then reluctantly, *very* reluctantly, he removed the book from his pocket and laid it ever so gently on the table. "Well, we will see. I'll leave these wise words of Woodrow Wilson with you for the remainder of the year—six months. If during that time any of you can learn so much as a sentence by heart, I shall be very surprised. In my opinion, it's a lost cause." He shook his head, shrugged and trudged ever so slowly out the door. It was hard for me to stifle a chuckle as I looked through the window to see Bill doff his cap as he drove away.

No sooner had Bill departed than the children scrambled to make copies of the essays in his book. Each selected and pocketed one excerpt. Throughout the week that followed, the hallways, bathrooms, and sanctuary resonated with the chanting of eighteen declaimers. "Learn by heart," became their mantra. By week's end, the children declared that it was time to summon Mr. McCleery back.

"Bill, whatever you did, it worked."

"Good. I thought it might. I'll be there. The sooner, the better."

Bill returned the following Monday. The children were ready for him. This time when he sat down in the easy chair, they stood before him shoulder to shoulder like a fire brigade. One by one they recited the words of Woodrow Wilson, their eyes fixed on him throughout. He beamed and applauded loudly at the end of each child's performance— and in particular for a six-year-old whose lisp could barely express the syllables she had selected:

"We hear arguments now in favor of a shorter college term. It is said that the lessons of the first two years of college are learned in the high school now. Two years is enough for a college course, these persons say, so graduate the men when they have finished their sophomore year. Well, no man who ever knew a sophomore can use that argument. The sap is rising in the sophomore, but it has not got to his head yet."

The recitation came to an end and the victorious troupe bowed to their thespian. Bill roared with approval, "Well done, my friends! You've proven me wrong! I shall have to revise my opinion of today's youth altogether."

This was no charade. Bill was thrilled to the bone. However, he was not done with them yet. "Now, let me ask you a question: How many of you can tell me—in your own words—what the excerpt that you recited actually means?" His question hung in midair while the children looked uncertainly at one another. Bill continued, "Unless you try to understand Woodrow Wilson's thoughts, you cannot fully communicate his meaning to others, least of all to yourselves. The wisdom lies in how well you know what you're talking about."

"But the ideas are too old for us!" protested one of the boys. "How can we know about sophomores if we've never even been one?"

"True, you'll have to wait quite a while to be a sophomore. But do you know anything about sap?"

"Sap is the juice that goes up inside a tree when the weather warms up."

"Right you are. Now, think about sap rising inside you when your learning warms up. I don't expect you to understand all of the great man's words, but I will suggest that each of you talk to your parents about the lines you've chosen. Together you might all come up with something wonderful."

The children agreed to discuss Woodrow Wilson's excerpts with their parents. That process took some time. Bill returned a couple of weeks later to see what they had come up with.

"Anybody have any ideas?"

"I do! We talked about it at home. Education is like making a building with blocks. The people who lived a long time ago started by making the base and then people who came later built it up higher."

"Where do you fit into the building process?"

"I put my blocks where there are empty spaces."

"So that other people can build where you leave off?"

"Yeah."

"That's wise. You got it. And what about you?" Bill pointed to another child.

"I think I want to see a thousand things more than just look at one thing."

"Ah, well . . ." Bill sighed. All in all, he was pleased with their progress, for they had interesting, if not always relevant, interpretations of their texts.

"So now that you have learned these sayings by heart, how would you like to go on the road with me?" Bill rocked back and forth on his heels and waited.

"You mean, say them in front of an audience?"

"Why not? Nothing would please Woodrow Wilson more than to have his thoughts about education declaimed by the children of Princeton Junior School. It would do his heart good."

I was as startled by this suggestion as were the children. Was Bill promoting a play based on words that would etch the wisdom of his hero on their minds forever? The children clapped enthusiastically and the "Woodrow Wilson Declaimers" was launched.

During the winter, we coached the children in projecting their voices with the use of a microphone. When the weather warmed up, they began their journey, delivering Woodrow Wilson's wit and wisdom to thinkers of every kind, including residents of retirement communities (many of whom remembered Woodrow Wilson), trustees at the annual meeting of the Woodrow Wilson National Fellowship Foundation, and judges attending the annual Medina Seminar. Accolades were generous: "Astonishing . . . Inspiring!" The judges were unanimous in their praise. The best comment of all came from the Chairman of the Woodrow Wilson Foundation:

> Please pass along my deepest thanks, on behalf of our Board of Trustees, to Bill McCleery and the wonderful students from Princeton Junior School who graced our meeting with such a well-performed recital last Thursday. All of us were impressed by the spirit and dedication of your students, and it was thought-provoking to hear Woodrow Wilson speak through them.
>
> Haskell Rhett

True, the children's recital celebrated Woodrow Wilson as educator. Moreover, it celebrated children who allowed wisdom of their own to mingle with the wisdom of an educator who had preceded them by fifty years. Perhaps their greatest wisdom was demonstrated in the way they leaned forward and softly prompted Mr. McCleery who, during his own concluding recitation, was so carried away that he occasionally forgot his parts of the excerpts:

"Sometimes, when I go through the Princeton campus at night, and see the brilliant display of lighted windows, I know perfectly well what is going on in those rooms . . ." Never very steady on his feet, Mr. McCleery would pause in front of the line of declaimers, rocking back and forth with his head down.

"There is some studying . . ." whispered a voice from behind him. Mr. McCleery's face lit up and he continued.

"There is some studying . . . a lot of good fellowship . . . a lot of fun; but . . . they have not found out what fun it is to use their minds; that the . . . the . . . the . . ." A long pause. The audience held their breath.

"That the best fun in the world . . ." whispered another voice from behind the beloved old man.

"Oh, yes. That the best fun in the world is to do something hard with the mind, and do it successfully.'" With a triumphant flourish, Mr. McCleery spun around and bowed to his protégés. They bowed back. Wisdom was at play.

I am sure that this letter from one of our students cheered up Mr. McCleery when he was very ill.

Dear Mr. McCleery,

I was the wolf in your play. I liked being the wolf. It was a funny part. I remember you telling me to project, and now I am the loudest kid in my class, at least when I want to be. Remember, all of us are pulling for you! I hope you get well soon.

Sincerely,
[Student]

Bill died shortly after receiving this letter. He had received from this boy and the other children as well, a gift that only the young can give to the old as they travel off: the gift of thanks for imparted wisdom.

—⚡—

Often, I refer to the children's folktale, *The Little Engine that Could*, when describing children's sheer determination to overcome various obstacles in their way. As in the case of the little blue engine, the seemingly powerless child can pull a heavy load over a high mountain, all the while repeating, "I think I can, I think I can, I think I can." Upon reading children's academic progress reports, I have often perceived their fortitude in overcoming insurmountable odds. They believe in themselves and climb their hills, academic or otherwise, bravely. Their wisdom wins the day.

> One day Willy the lizard went out for a walk. He wanted to go to the seashore, but he was very far away from the ocean. Willy had to go across two roads with cars on them. He was a very tiny lizard but he was very brave. Willy looked both ways and when there were no cars coming he ran as fast as he could. He huffed and he puffed and when he didn't think he could go any more he looked down and his foot was in the sand! Willy felt wonderful! The water was so cold and refreshing. Willy couldn't be happier.
>
> The End
>
> Student

I have watched Annie, a four-year-old paraplegic, lurching on her sticks to imitate the ferocious troll in a play of *Three Billy Goats Gruff*. I have seen a child who, although flattened by her parents' divorce, was able to adjust to the change and migrate from one parent to another like a small bird who instinctively adopts the sound patterns of the birds in her new neighborhood. I have witnessed immigrant children assimilating a new language within three months and then teaching it to their parents. I have flinched with the diabetic child who regularly tests his sugar with a prick of the finger. I have marveled at the way in which a class of children will gladly jump the hurdles of new academic material thrown their way.

Our school crawled over a mountain of disappointments. In our eight-year search for a permanent home, we examined vacated churches, barns, firehouses, even a former schoolhouse. We explored vacant mansions, storefronts, office complexes, and a science lab that reeked of formaldehyde. In every case, our bids and proposals were rejected— by planning boards, neighbors, even our own trustees. Throughout our years of wandering, we continued to promise our school families that the day would come when their children would occupy a single schoolhouse in a permanent location. Needless to say, a number of parents gave up and took their children elsewhere. If it were not for those who believed in us, who looked beyond the obstacles to the little engine's vision for its load of exuberant learners, we never would have made it. We all learned from the children how to trust the train and enjoy the ride.

A world for children had been our vision from the beginning. No matter where we found ourselves during those early years, we created a common place for everyone, young and old, to gather. Whether we were meeting in a church basement or sanctuary, a sandbox or park, we shared a common task: to learn from one another how to become wise. Even with the addition in 1996 of yet another habitat, a large room in the basement of Princeton Theological School's Tennent Hall to house our brand-new class of two-and-a-half-year-olds, we were united.

> Who really knows what has driven the staff of this school and made them so committed to their work? It has certainly not been the pay, nor the working conditions, which in those early days were cramped and far from optimal for the teaching of young children. Still, we have continued through all the growing pains of a new school: the hard work, the excitement, the frustrations, and the disappointments. The inevitable tragedies when death took those we loved and cared for.

The reason has a lot to do with loving what we do, knowing that there is nothing more vital or seminal than helping a child (and his parents) to learn. It has a lot to do with a respect for those we do our work with . . . in a spirit of caring and professionalism. [Mrs. McIntyre's] work exemplifies how in life, as in history, conservatism and radicalism work hand in hand. We must, on the one hand, conserve all those practices that bring out the best in our children and in each other. We must on the other hand be bold and radical, moving forward with new and different visions of how things could be.

Every staff member has shaped the vision and made it happen. I am honored to have contributed in my small way to making PJS a reality.

Teacher

—◁◅◆▷▻—

The raising of some children is pretty much left up to them. Such was the case of two brothers, Paul and Mike, whom I met during one of my long walks with the dog in Vermont many years ago. My own children had summer jobs and I was often alone on my daily ventures into the farmland around the village. I was crossing a sun drenched hayfield one day when two boys emerged out of nowhere—disheveled and flushed with summer heat. "Hi! What's your dog's name?"

"Angus. What are your names?" And so began a friendship with two of the most unusual children I have ever met. They walked with me for about a mile that day before disappearing into the woods as swiftly as they had come. I was left with the distinct feeling that my daily walk would never be the same. During our time together that afternoon, I had learned that the brothers loved dogs but couldn't understand why Angus didn't have a job. I had learned from them that when foxes sleep out in the open, they curl up into a ball and wrap their bushy tails around their noses and feet to protect them from the cold or wet. I had learned how to recognize bear prints. I had learned where the best streams for fishing were and—by the way—how old the boys were (seven and nine) and where they lived—right across the street from me! Why had I never noticed them? Perhaps because they preferred the life of the woods to the life of the village.

The boys' father had been a metallurgist—robust, fiery and inventive. Their mother—a member of the Abenaki tribe—had blessed her sons with an affinity for wildlife that only a native-American mother could engender. The family had lived from season to season hunting, fishing, going to tribal gatherings—until the day when their father crashed his motorcycle and broke his neck. The accident left him paralyzed from the waist down. When I met Paul and Mike, their mother had moved away. They were living with their father in a small apartment complex framed within a converted barn.

Paul and Mike possessed very little by comparison with other children. Crowded into three rooms with a father whose physical handicap and emotional intensity took up a lot of space, they were obliged to "make do." It is no wonder that they spent as much time as possible out of doors. For a while we became acquainted by way of our walks. I would no sooner start out across the hayfield with Angus than with a "Whoop!" the boys would sprout up before me. During most of the walk they frolicked with Angus who looked upon them more as siblings than human playmates. Over time, Paul and Mike showed me their hideouts, habitats and favorite climbing trees. While other children were hiking and picnicking, Paul and Mike were trapping rabbits in the woods. While other children were playing tennis, Paul and Mike were fishing in the brooks.

After the field was hayed, the brothers chased one another along the tops of the huge rolled bails that were lined up along the edge of the field. Angus leapt up and chased after them, eyes rolling and tongue flapping. This wonderful sport came to a sudden halt one day when Mike fell through a crack—into a nest of bees. The poor boy exploded into the air slapping and screaming. We dragged him to the nearest wet spot and plastered him with mud. He returned home so swollen that I felt I had to meet his father and explain what had happened.

We found the boys' father lying on a couch in what I can only describe as his lair. Bedding, dishes, food containers, papers, guns, traps, fishing rods, beer cans—all were crammed into a space no larger than a single car garage. My initial shock was soon allayed by his greeting. "Well, well, who have we here? So you're the one who my boys take off with all the time? The place isn't much to look at but make y'self at home. Paul, clear off that chair and go see what we can give her." Paul swiped an army blanket off the chair and rummaged through the pile of dishes in the sink.

"Dad?" Until now, their father hadn't noticed the mud covered, disconsolate lad poised like a statue in the doorway. Mike's eyes were so swollen that if he had tears, they were not able to flow. Their father heaved around to look at him and uttered a loud snort. "Dad, the bees got me."

"Come here, you poor kid!" Mike stumbled over to the couch. His father wrapped his arms around him and tousled his wet hair. "I bet you won't run on those bails again, eh? Go wash up. You'll be fine once you get some food in you." Mike disappeared through a clothesline full of fishing waders.

Food? I looked around. There were potatoes, tomatoes, cucumbers, radishes and lettuce stacked up on the windowsills. "Yep, they come from the boys' garden out back. We bring them in before the pests get 'em—if you know what I mean," he chuckled. I did not know what he meant.

Shortly, Paul produced some lemonade, bread and cheese that he laid out a bench near the couch. Angus was contenting himself with a bowl of water and some Cheerios. When Mike emerged puffy and shiny from the bathroom, his father nodded his approval and we all settled into the delicious snack. I got up to leave an hour later. The boys' father—with great physical effort—hoisted himself onto his feet, grabbed two crutches and reeled toward the door. With a wide grin, he drawled, "Great to have you here. Thanks for everything. Come again!" I nodded. My brand as a flatlander had been effaced.

Ever since they arrived a few years before, Paul and Mike were well known to people in the village. After all, with their father so hung up, who was going to watch the boys and see that they didn't get into trouble? The boys were warned against crawling through the culvert under the road where the mill stream roared. As they grew older, they earned pocket money by mowing lawns, climbing and trimming trees and painting porches. They were taught to make correct change when serving as cashiers at yard sales. The butcher at the general store showed them how to cut meat off the rabbit carcass that they had skinned and gutted at home. The boys cooked, cleaned (sort of) and did the laundry. They occasionally came across the road to my house for lessons in baking. I still have a photograph of Mike, aged seven, holding the large chocolate pot upside down over his head to catch the drips on his tongue. They learned how to trap and shoot from their father, who built a rig by which to prop himself up in the back of the pickup truck. He taught Paul to drive along the logging roads. If they were lucky, they would bring home a rabbit or turkey to feast upon. When Paul finally reached the age of twelve, he and others his age were allowed on one appointed day to hunt under the supervision of an adult. He was the first to fell a stag. I was back in Princeton when their father sent me the newspaper story with its photograph of Mike—gun over shoulder, foot resting on the dead animal's girth. I looked hard at the boy's beaming face in the picture. Was this merely an expression of triumph? Or were his eyes revealing another spirit—that of the beloved woodland companion whom he had just killed? He was, after all, a member of the Abernaki tribe. His ancestral hunters were deeply connected in spirit to the creatures they killed for food and clothing.

The boys attended the village elementary school up the road, trudging back and forth in all kinds of weather, even when the temperatures were well below freezing. Teachers admired their spunk. Children envied them their freedom, little knowing how much responsibility rested upon their young shoulders. After fifth grade they took the school bus down the mountain to another school. I heard only two things from their father about their experience there: 1) Mike gave a friend the Heimlich maneuver and kept him from choking to death. When someone from the local newspaper asked how he knew about the Heimlich maneuver, he replied, "Dad showed us how. He said it might come in handy." Mike must have learned a lot about safety from his father. During one night-time sledding excursion, he saved me from being run over by a snow mobile by whipping out a flashlight. 2) Their mother kidnapped them from school and held them for six months before their father got them back.

In addition to their wisdom regarding the necessities for survival, the boys were kind hearted. When their father fell down, they helped him get up; when my baby grandchild cried for attention, they played with her; when an elderly neighbor struggled with a bag of groceries, they carried it inside. I often wondered how they would "turn out," as adults, given their extraordinary childhood.

When the boys were teenagers, they left the village and moved to Stannard Mountain. In an effort to stay in touch, I called them by telephone and set out one day to find them. After several miles of driving, I discovered their house, tucked into the edge of a woods. Their father greeted me with his usual broad smile and showed me a number of carvings he was hoping to sell at the next pow—wow. He and the boys had constructed a "lift" to lower him into his basement workshop. The house was compact, clean and organized to give him as much freedom of movement as possible. But where were Paul and Mike? "Oh, them? They're living out back in the woods."

"Out back," I found them busy at work hanging two hammocks. They had made a tent as large as the house by connecting and stringing waterproof canvases from tree to tree. Within its pliable walls were collected everything that two boys could possibly need for a summer residence: couch and chairs, table, carpet, lanterns, cots, pillows and sleeping bags—even a clothing rack. Outside the tent in a nearby grove were a shower and sink—connected to the house by a long hose. As I approached, they hailed me and invited me to inspect their habitat. I learned that they had lived in the tent long before and after the previous summer. As I explored its nooks and crannies, I wondered: was necessity the mother of this invention? Was this not a wise way to separate from—yet not abandon—the father who so loved and needed them?

What was it that so moved me about these two? I think that I was seeing firsthand how—when put to the test—two children could handle their circumstances responsibly, given the freedom they had to run amok. Wisdom had its way with them.

—✺—

There is hope for us all, even when the connection with our common humanity seems virtually broken. Ten-year-old Jose came to us from the inner city of Trenton by public bus and borrowed bike. Having already spent four years in an overcrowded, understaffed school, he was wiser to the ways of the world than most children his age. What's more, he let everyone know it. His mother, a strong single parent of three children, wanted him to take advantage of the individual attention that a small school such as ours could offer him. He very quickly took advantage—but mostly of other children by exploiting their weaknesses in order to show how clever he was. The rules of the classroom were lost to him. He showed little respect for his teachers and applied himself to his schoolwork with no more than a lick and a promise. When asked to concentrate, he claimed that he was too tired, having spent half the night on a couch in the reception area of the office complex that his mother cleaned every night. Besides, enthusiasm for school was simply not cool.

At first, assuming that he would take a few weeks to adjust to our different approach, we waited. Usually, other children from massive school systems came around once they got over their fear of success. Why not Jose?

I finally lost my patience. It was after lunch, and the children were playing outside. Suddenly, there was an awful commotion over by the sandbox. The teacher reported that Jose had whipped out a sharp pocket nail clipper and held it to the neck of another child. "He was annoying me," was the only explanation he had given for this deplorable act. I was furious. As I glared into Jose's face, it was all I could do not to forcibly erase the cocky expression I found there. How dare he do such a thing? His act had seriously threatened another child's safety. Furthermore, he was eroding the very trust that held our young school together. I could think of only one thing to do short of expelling him on the spot. I made a couple of telephone calls.

"We're going to take a little tour, Jose. Get into my car, *now*." He complied in slow motion.

Our first stop was the emergency room of Princeton Hospital. Dr. Hancock awaited us. He held out his hand to Jose in vain. "Well, Jose, I wonder whether you have ever thought about the effects of a stab in the neck? No? Well, here's what can happen." The doctor proceeded to give Jose a graphic anatomy lesson, leaving no doubt in our minds about the dire effect of neck-stabbing. During this exercise, we were in the ER's hot spot where a stretcher bearing a blood-soaked patient rolled by in time to confirm the wise doctor's every word.

At the end of his cautionary tale, Dr. Hancock looked at me with raised eyebrows. I thanked him and took a somber Jose back to the car. "Now, we're going to visit another kind of school, Jose." He didn't speak during the twenty minute drive to the Training School for Boys in Skillman. As we drove up, we saw some older boys working outdoors in a bare yard surrounded by a high fence. They were raking and bundling leaves under the surveillance of a uniformed guard. They paused, stared briefly through the wires at the boy in the car, and then resumed their work.

"This is a school?" asked Jose.

"Sort of. It's a correctional center for boys who have violated the law and need to spend some time away from their communities."

"Is it a jail?"

"No, not a jail. You'll see that later. But first, do you want to get out and look around?"

"No. I get the picture."

We turned our backs on the boys behind the fence and made our way through the Hopewell Valley toward Princeton. There we dropped in at Borough Hall, where we were welcomed by Officer Stanley. He appraised Jose with a quick glide of the eye. "So, buddy, you want to see what a jail looks like?"

"Not really."

"Oh?" His voice took on a muted tone. "Well, now that you're here, you might as well take a look. No one's in here right now. It's perfectly respectable." The policeman led us to a cell, unlocked it with a flourish of his key chain, and held the door wide open. "Go on in, if you want. See what it feels like."

Jose stared past the man into the empty cage. "No thank you." This was the first "thank you" that I had ever heard from him.

"Suit yourself," Officer Stanley intoned as he closed the cell door with a bang.

We left soon after and headed back to the school. On the way, Jose leaned back against the seat and shut his eyes. "I got the message, Mrs. McIntyre."

I had to believe that he got the message. At home that evening, I tried to make sense of it all. I was still mad. Figuratively speaking, he had jabbed at the jugular of the school. Whether or not the tour that afternoon had made any difference to Jose, it made a big difference to me. I had drawn the line of demarcation for him to see. He stood at the fork in the road and would have to make a choice regarding which way he wanted to go.

Parents were calling for his departure. Certain questions gnawed at me: why should the school community tolerate such behavior? Did he not see a difference between right and wrong? Should he be reproved or reprieved? Reproof weighed in heavily. As for reprieve, I wondered whether Jose's lack of consideration for others was in fact born out of fear. Had he been so humbled by the hierarchy of the street that he had to disguise his true self? His mother was a proud and loving woman working day and night to give her children a good education. His behavior distressed her and she punished him. Her pleas for him to have another chance brought me to my knees. How could we do less? He had to decide whether to rely upon his acquired street smarts or to discover his inherent wisdom and proceed accordingly. To choose the latter would take courage and commitment. It would be our job to foster him every step of the way. With most of the teachers behind me, I decided to let him stay.

Jose's teacher was a superb golfer who watched her students with the same eagle-eye that she applied on the fairway. The class covered great distances from point to point. Jose was no exception, and was soundly praised for his efforts. As he gained self-confidence, he cooperated with the people around him and began to achieve good academic results.

Five years later, that same teacher was outside her house, working on the chimney. Two boys on bicycles approached, parked, and came across the lawn to greet her. "Hi! Do you remember me? I'm Jose. This is my friend Jimmy. We've just biked all the way from Trenton." They shook hands vigorously, and then he continued, "You always told me, 'Results, not excuses!' Well, you don't have to worry any more. I'm going to Trenton High School, tenth grade. I don't do drugs, and I made the honor roll. And I'm in the youth group in church." After reminiscences and glasses of water, Jose and his friend took off toward town. His teacher kept on building her chimney stone by stone—a remarkable undertaking by a remarkable woman.

—⁓—

When my son, Jamie, was fifteen years old, my dying father asked to see him alone. They were deeply connected, despite the seventy years between them. Jamie tiptoed softly into the Barracks' little parlor where my father lay in a hospital bed, his face illuminated by the glow of the hearth. His breathing was labored but he wanted to talk.

"Well, Jamie boy, here we are, once again. Only this time is the last."

"I know."

"I love you, Jamie. We've had many good times together, haven't we? You're a wonderful boy with lots ahead of you. Now, I want you to remember something very important. Remember that you have to find in life the thing that you do best."

"I'll try, I promise."

"If you can find your own special way, then you will be able to reach out to people. You'll be able to live with them and love them better."

"I'm getting there, I hope."

"Good. As for me, I found out that people liked my stories. Telling a story about something was the best way I could connect with people. It made a difference."

"You've told me a lot of stories."

"I hope you'll remember them as my way of loving you, Jamie."

"I will."

"Now it's time for us to say good-bye."

"Thank you, Bu, for loving me so much. I'll always remember you."

"Goodbye, Jamie boy. God bless you."

"Goodbye, Bu. I love you."

Jamie wrote Bu's last words down on a yellow pad. I prayed that he would find his own special well way as well.

A child at the school posed the question to me, "When I am your age, will my father be an old man?"

"Perhaps a very old man," I replied.

"When my father dies, I'll cry. I love him."

Still smarting from my own father's death, I asked, "Do you tell him you love him?"

"Yes," the child nodded. "Fathers don't get told as much as mothers." How did he know?

There were several other deaths in my family around that time. Numbed by the shock of so many losses, I absorbed myself in my work. That forced me to reach beyond my own needs into the needs of others. Before long, the hollow hoed by grief was filled in by children who intuitively helped me to see beyond its rim. If it were not for them, I would have buried myself in sadness. In a letter to parents in the spring of 1988, I wrote, "I wish to thank the many of you who supported me throughout the season of my father's dying. You and your wonderful children strengthened me daily to go through the home-hospice experience." Fifteen years later, in the spring of 2003, Maboo died. I wrote the following note to my wonderful faculty and staff.

> Thank you for the wonderful ways in which you have let me know that you care for me and my family. Food, flowers, notes, telephone messages, hugs—all of these things have helped me to adjust to this vast change in my life. You are "my sail to windward and the breath of God is a-blowin'."

Some children seem unaware of the finality of death, even when it has robbed them of a parent. A boy in our school lost his mother to cancer after a year of struggle. I wonder whether his poem revealed his sense of an oncoming storm.

> Strikes fast blinding light,
> Sky darkens quickly again;
> Thunder coming soon.
>
> Student

Before she died, his mother wrote letters to him and his brother, to be opened and read on each birthday of their childhood – and perhaps beyond.

Other children often ask when the deceased grandparent will return, or whether the deceased parent is going to be away on their birthday. One child I know strayed from the viewing of his grandfather and visited other chapels in the funeral home, only to return and tell his mother that Chapel 6 "has the best." Are these children denying death because they live so much in the present? Or, are they putting death "on hold" until they can safely tolerate the pain of loss? Surely Alice, no more than twelve years old, must have known that her mother needed her to be close by during the final weeks of a long illness. Alice slept in her mother's room every night and comforted her in every way she could. I believe that when her mother died, a part of Alice died too. I wondered at the time whether such a wound as Alice felt could ever be healed. When recently I saw her—now the mother of two children—I concluded that she had weathered the storm and her wisdom had healed her.

In some cases at school, the disruption and apprehension caused by a child's grief was so great that we could do little other than watch and wait out the sadness. While it was not always evident in the child's achievements, we could see it in his or her play and writing.

> Black Holes are so scary to me. Will I ever see inside? The sun might become one. What makes them? Do scientists know? I wish I knew all the answers. When I get older I will figure them out.
>
> Student

This child spent weeks at his grandfather's bedside, helping his mother take care of him.

There have been times when a child led me so close to the door of my own departure that I could almost reach out and turn the handle. One summer vacation, while reading aloud to my four-year-old granddaughter, I tried to clarify what a chapter was. I explained that chapters are stages of a story—beginning, middle, and end—just like stages in life. I remarked that she was living the first chapter of her life. The following morning, she crawled into my bed at 5:30 a.m., declaring, "I'm awake."

"I know. It's early. Can we go back to sleep?"

"Nana?"

"What?"

"When you get to be a hundred, will you be dead?" Her clear blue eyes searched mine from only six inches away. Was she looking up my chapter—she, aged four, and I, seventy, swaddled by bed sheets?

Her question roused me. I was tempted to retort, "Given questions like that, I may be dead by noon." But I thought better of it. After all, she was ingenuously doing what children do: searching for clues to a mystery that cannot be solved. Instead, I said, "I hope not, lovey. A few more winks of sleep will help me to live longer." I shut my eyes and wriggled under the covers. Waiting is difficult for most children. She left me alone to ponder.

A child such as this one is a beginner who hasn't lived long enough to stack the cards. There is nothing to lose. Big questions pop up, hungry questions that want answers, now. We have all been hit at one time or other, sometimes in the most inconvenient moments. We adults have lived long enough to know that some of the answers are impossible to find. Maybe later, if I ever get to be a hundred, I will know the answer to her question. My memory flowed back a few years to the bed in which my late husband was dying, his fading eyes exploring the doctor's face as he asked him how many hours he had left. He learned that he might have six.

Further sleep was out of the question. I got up and went downstairs. There was my granddaughter, sitting alone on the sofa, waiting. I held out my hand. "Let's go walk on the beach and watch for the sparkle to come." We grabbed some bread for the gulls and left the house.

Do children live so much in the present that they cannot allow absence to be permanent? Is the unspoiled wisdom of their souls daring the world to look beyond life? I recall a day in my eighth year when I became conscious to both the inevitability of death and the possibility of life beyond. That morning, I discovered my mother weeping. She was sitting in her bedroom with her face in her hands, rocking back and forth.

"Maboo, what's wrong?"

"Don't worry, little Nan. I'm just having a good cry. Henrietta is no longer with us and I didn't have a chance to say good-bye. I'm going to miss her terribly. She was my best friend."

I remembered Henrietta as an old lady who taught my mother all about a poet called Dante. I knew that my mother had really loved her. She had often taken me with her to Henrietta's big house for tea. While they spoke Italian to each other, I was allowed to play with the china animals in the glass case.

"Is she dead?"

"Yes, she's gone for good, darling."

Henrietta wouldn't come back to us. Her life was over. I caught my breath as I thought of all the people I loved who were old, especially my Granny. She was going to die soon. Maboo and Bu would die later. Then, much later, it would happen to me. Death was no longer an idea, but real.

Maboo stopped her rocking and leaned forward to give me a hug. "Henrietta has gone to God, little Nan. That's where she belongs. He has loved her ever since He created her. There is nothing to fear."

As we hugged, I caught my eye in the mirror on my mother's dresser. The freckled face reflected there, flanked by lanky braids, smiled back at me. In this moment I awoke again to what I must have known always: that death is the end of now life and the beginning of new life. I thanked my mother then and I have thanked her ever since for throwing a log onto my inner fire. She attested to the wisdom of my soul that enables me to relate to those who have died and whose presences continue to imbue my life with love.

———

In my opinion, nothing is more heartbreaking than the death of a child. On Labor Day weekend a year before the school moved to Fackler Road, I was again in the Vermont kitchen, this time washing and gently blotting the lush raspberries that I had fetched from the garden. Julie was at the lakeside snatching a final swim before supper. As I culled the last berry from the mash at the bottom of the pail, I listened to new messages that had been left on the answering machine while I was outside. The last recording from one of the school parents pierced the kitchen's peace.

"Juliana, it's Charles! Our Amelia is gone! There's been an awful accident! She's been killed!" His sobs washed the rest of his words away and I waited, stunned. For a while I heard nothing but huge intakes of breath. Then the horrible story flooded through: "She died this afternoon. A heavy stone bench fell on her and crushed her. We were playing tennis with friends. Their kids and ours were playing hide and seek. It was getting late so we stopped and called them." His voice faltered. "Amelia had been hiding under this bench. As she was coming out from under it, it toppled over and she was pinned underneath it. We all tried to lift it off but we couldn't do it fast enough. By the time we got it off she was gone." After a fumbled telephone number, the message went dead.

I replayed Charles's message again and again, swept by the tides of tears that flowed through the telephone line. Julie, having paused at the doorstep to listen, came over to share my disbelief. Was Amelia really gone? Amelia, the little girl whose paintings of flowers and rainbows brightened every wall? Amelia, the little girl whose eyes watched my every move when I mixed colors or wrapped clay? Amelia, the little girl who taught me how to see things as if for the first time? My tiny guide had died. I cried for Amelia, for her mother and father and brother, for her teachers and friends. The whole school cried. To know her was to love her, and to love her was to learn the secret of beauty she so gently and generously shared in her wonderful paintings.

Lora, an artist who had been Amelia's former teacher, was in England on the day of Amelia's death. Lora and her husband were walking the coastal path at Land's End when the call came through. Later, they described how, at that very moment, the huge sky broke to reveal a rainbow as wide as the ocean below—Amelia's best rainbow ever.

The following Tuesday was Princeton Junior School's opening day. "Opening" is hardly an adequate word to describe the outpouring of that day and the days that followed. From every corner of the school, gifts of love flowed into grief's deepest crevices. Dinners were cooked, errands run, babysitting provided, comfort and prayers offered despite general confusion regarding God's will. I am sure several of us wondered whether God had not, in fact, made a terrible mistake. Buoyed by such a swell of love, Amelia's family navigated through the rapids to create an unforgettable funeral service. The art room in the new school was enlarged by a loft and dedicated to Amelia. Her portrait and two of her paintings hang there. In Princeton Cemetery, her burial site is situated near the street, where every passerby can see the statue of a sculpted angel child encircled by flowers, her arms outstretched to the heavens. Now, years later, I sometimes notice ribbons in the angel's hair, or flowers in her hands, or toys in the grass at her feet.

Amelia's death broke the heart of the school family. Our love could never make up for her loss but it helped. Years later, I received a letter from Amelia's family.

> It is hard to find the words to thank you for the many ways you have touched our lives. It is such a gift to have four children who have all loved going to Princeton Junior School and have all had their innate thirst for learning nurtured and given wings to fly. The many ways that you, the teachers, and the school community supported us and helped us heal after the loss of [Amelia] are immeasurable. She will always be a part of our family and a part of the Princeton Junior School family.

The memory of Amelia lives on. To this day, children see her portrait in the art room and ask, "Who is she?"

"She is Amelia, your art angel."

—◆—

Often, when traveling around the school, I have observed teachers on their knees. The explicit reason: eye-to-eye contact with their students. The implicit reason: wonder. Wonderful as well are the words of one alumnus.

> Looking back on PJS, it seems almost too good to be true. In second grade we designed our own country with our own currency and government—it was all based around *The Rats of Nimh* because that's what we were all into

at the time. Joe Stiglitz came in to give us a lecture on economics! All the teachers I had were totally nurturing and made me feel creative and excited. It was really the perfect environment for me to grow up in . . . Teachers at PJS tailored the curriculum to the needs and interests of the students. I felt very special and stimulated. I really felt free to be myself and explore different interests. It was amazing.

Alumnus

Joe Stiglitz, a parent, had knelt down on the floor with the children and—while stacking coins from all over the world into little piles—explained the International Monetary Fund. No clearer lesson could have been taught than this—by a Nobel Prize winner down on the floor amid his son's friends. He challenged the children to design their own currency:

> So we drew money which had rats on the bills, or mice, which the boys chose, and we brought in things and bartered with it and made up the whole system, which I remember as being very complex for second grade . . . Just the ability to present topics in really creative ways and have the students get so much out of it—all of it was fun!

Alumna

—ᗧᐯᐯᐸ—

In the preschool we began with the little ones—three, four and five year olds—to introduce germinal programs that would eventually grow into academic forms later on. For instance, their hours of play with Froebel blocks prepared the grounds for mathematical construction later on. In the elementary grades, our school's educational program synchronized with New Jersey's core curriculum and national achievement tests. Reading, writing, math, science, social studies and geography—Spanish, music, art, drama and sports—all provided grist for our students' mill. In the words of a trustee and long-term friend of the school:

This School leads children to be open to their intrinsic aesthetic selves. It is through the arts that children can develop and draw forth all their capacities for learning. The result of this creative approach is that the School's foundations for learning are formed by the whole child— mind, body, and spirit.

It all boils down to the trilogy of love, work and play in their various manifestations.

At every point in the School's nine year span, we paid attention to our children's various stages of development. Many great educators lent us a hand: Whitehead, Dewey, Piaget, Montessori, Steiner, Elkind, Thompson, Evans, Levine, Bruner—to name a few. I embraced Italy's Reggio Emilia approach to early education, for many of its principles were akin to our philosophy and practice: e.g., acknowledging the "100 languages of children," learning through experience of the senses, exploring materials with others, expressing individual points of view, interacting with the environment and sharing learning with the entire school family. One child's sensory perceptions:

> We walk around the school observing what is all around us. As the wet grass seeps through our shoes, the cold breeze sinks through our coats. The big bright moon hangs in the blue sky as the squirrels feast on nuts getting ready for winter. We sit on the bench waiting for sounds to come to us. The smell of pine sap lingers in the air tickling my nose. I feel the rough bark run along my fingers. The red, yellow, green and brown leaves fall to the ground as my fingers rub against the moss . . .

Increasingly, provocative questioning characterized our approach to children in the elementary grades as we taught them academic subjects. We wanted them to explore and discover some answers on their own rather than rely on prepackaged solutions. We encouraged them to voice their questions, to live in their questions and to search everywhere for answers without fearing the unknown. If they were to adapt to the world outside of our school, they would have to learn to think for themselves and solve problems creatively. In every subject area we encouraged them to collaborate with one another and to learn by experience.

> "I think it's useful to work in teams because then both of you can work together and have two brains instead of one (or sometimes many more than two brains). Your special job is to help the other people and when they do something wrong you say 'Keep practicing' and 'Don't give up' or, 'the sun was probably in your eyes' or something nice, not something mean."
>
> Student

Teachers learned by experience as well:

> Thank you for trusting a novice teacher and having faith in me even when I made gigantic mistakes. I have learned so much at PJS. It will always be the foundation of my teaching.
>
> Teacher

Teachers drew upon their own interests. Projects were woven into academic subjects. It was at this early time in our development that a writer for a local newspaper interviewed me.

> Mrs. McIntyre says that having to discipline themselves to use only what is "absolutely essential" has made for a greater use of imagination on the part of the teachers. She likens it to improvisational theater.
>
> "I don't think we would have predicted this strength coming out of these teachers, who are calling on their own resources," she remarks. "I hope that we remember this discipline if we ever get our own building."

Praising her teachers as being "very, very committed" and "a loving, flexible bunch of women," she adds, "They can teach anywhere."

Barbara Johnson, Town Topics, September 25, 1985.

In a letter I wrote to teachers and staff one summer:

> I think of you all at this mid-vacation moment and hope that you have had time to rest and rethread that fundamental fiber that you weave into others so well: the thread of your own learning . . . My goal for us all is to live as fully as possible, to love as fully as possible, and to give as fully as possible. Then, to take time to rest and nurture ourselves. When we gather again, our school family will provide the loom.
>
> J.

Admiration for our teachers is reflected in this letter from a parent.

> It's hard to put into words how these teachers' different personalities and approaches have brought out the best in Johnny and his classmates, but suffice it to say, their warmth, caring, creativity, intelligence, thoughtfulness, and dedication have worked wonders.
>
> Parent

———

The winter trimester, the darkest and coldest time of the year, was for us a time of extraordinary creativity. It was an exciting time for children. They *lived* their education. Their energy, undaunted by cold and darkness, turned inward to break new ground. They were pioneers. It seemed that there was never enough time to do all the things that we wanted to do.

Our enjoyment of winter deepened when, later, we occupied our own schoolhouse in the country. Natural light flowed through the windows. A fire glowed in the fireplace and children were bathed in its warmth. We worked hard every day. We also made time for nature walks, identifying the tracks in the snow, and feeding wild birds.

Winter

Darting, running, leaping,
Fluttering here, then there,
Dotting the snow with boot prints.
Oh, why do humans have
The desire to leap and dance
Like snowflakes on the horizon,
Filling the serenity of the
Snow with joyous sounds?

Student

Wherever we were, as we entered the winter holiday season we reminded ourselves to attend to what was truly important, to see the light, and to allow unimportant things to slide into darkness. Making time for important things leads to enlightenment. Do we discern what is truly important? Is it a sink cleared of dishes or a child on your lap listening to a story? Is it the third trip to the mall or an afternoon on a sled with a child? Is it watching your favorite show on TV or helping your child prepare for a test?

One winter, I wrote the following letter to the school community.

One Reason for a Holy Season

It is not surprising that religions have their holy days during this season. The great stories about the Creator that are told at this time are stories of light breaking through darkness. Darkness falls early. Long shadows lick our heels as we rush home in the late afternoon. We welcome the light that nature gives us: the sun, the moon, and the stars. We illuminate gathering places and sacred spaces with candlelight. Let us all light our inner hearths during this holy season and invite children to warm themselves thereby. Let us regard every child as a gift bringing us new and unique experiences. During the very short day of their childhood, children enlighten our days and help us to grow in wisdom and imagination. Without a doubt, there are heavy moments, but they are redeemable because we are sharing life with a child: the essence of creativity and hope. During this midwinter season, let us shed a light on all children near and far, remembering that they are our gift to enjoy and to cherish with thanksgiving.

J.

Sometime later, I received a poem from a fourth grade child that perfectly exemplified what I meant by "the essence of creativity and hope."

What is hope?

Hope is getting a new relative.
Hope is believing in yourself.
Hope is the name of an angel that God sent down from heaven to be my mother.
Hope is a blessing from heaven.
Hope is something to believe in.
Hope is anywhere you don't feel confident.
Hope is a caterpillar turning into a butterfly.
Hope is the best guide we have.
Hope is a great thing.
That's what hope is.

Student

On another occasion, we hosted our first candlelit winter party. The children filed into the room following the tempo of beautiful music. They formed a circle three-deep around a central table on which stood a large candle surrounded by twelve smaller candles. I talked about light as it related to the seasons, various holidays, the inner light of learning, and gifts from the heart. I lit the central candle as a symbol of our community and our caring for one another. Then a child from each class came forward, one by one, to light one of the smaller candles. At the lighting of each smaller candle, the child's class quoted a phrase or sentence that represented their experience of light. The ceremony ended with a moment of silence. Children understand from experience what light is all about, and these phrases told us a lot about their wisdom. Somehow, this simple ceremony took care of all the differences of religion, nationality, age, and stage of development. Like plants, children lean toward the light:

> Light represents joy, happiness, and very special love. It represents the friendships in people, no matter what the color of their skin may be. Light represents the progression of peace with other nations.

> Grade V

It is true: an extraordinary output was typical of our winter months over the years. With less light, less space, less distraction from the outside world, we centered ourselves. This is not to say that there were no low moments when we became exhausted and our spirits dampened—as my letters to teachers attested:

> 1) . . . Parenting today is very difficult, as many of you know. Parents are anxious about parenting, and need a lot of support, even when their anxieties drive us crazy. We must remind ourselves of the many opportunities we have to educate, to nurture, and to help them make appropriate decisions for their children. They are our 'customers' and companions. Without them, there would be no Princeton Junior School.

> I write this letter in hopes that our School environment will again become conducive to the kind of learning that we all espouse. Please take advantage of our conferences with our parents to reaffirm our faith in them . . .

> 2) . . . During the past few weeks, twenty-three parents have come to me to express their anxieties re a number of subjects: curriculum, discipline, diversity, homework, and placement, to name a few. At least a dozen children came

to me to express anxieties as well. Part of the unrest seems to be the February blues, a condition that usually springs up with a spring vacation. Several of you are also feeling unusual pressure at this time. You have met the challenges of unrelenting cold weather, parent-teacher conferences, admissions screening, and core curriculum. I know how hard you all have worked during the winter trimester, as the children's growth and progress attest. You deserve some time off and a good rest. As that won't happen for another two weeks, I encourage you all to hang in together, and with your willowy wands, transform the blues into yellows and greens. As we support one another in our efforts, we will undoubtedly feel stronger, and the children will sense that there is something in the air, and breathe deeply . . .

J.

The winter blues did not last. Winter was followed by spring!

Spring is a season where things come alive again.
Spring is as beautiful as the prettiest flower you ever saw.
Spring is like a fairy, beautiful and light.
Spring is when birds and other animals give birth to their young.
Spring is flowers blooming like stars twinkling.
Spring is bees buzzing like fairies flying.
Spring is as long as a snake.
Spring is very beautiful.
I love spring.

Student

I had only to listen to the words of this young poet to "come alive again." I learned from my conversations with parents how ready they were to share and engage in the transforming work of the school. I have them to thank for starting a newsletter, funding enrichment programs, volunteering their time and talent to countless school events: field days, auctions, rummage sales, book fairs—to name a few. I have parents to thank for welcoming newcomers, for providing transportation, for donating toys, educational equipment, books and food. Most of all, I have parents to thank for trusting us with their children, for their willingness to learn along with us how to educate and love them. We grew in wisdom together, be the weather fair or foul.

—◆—

PART II: BUILDING

Our attempts to find a suitable building in which to house our whole school proved to be fruitless, given the inevitable cost of remodeling to meet code requirements and the incredible arguments posed by prospective neighbors at zoning and planning board meetings. So, at the suggestion of a wise colleague, we began to look for a piece of raw land upon which to build a new schoolhouse. Our new scheme led us to a beautiful ten-acre farm site on Fackler Road, not far from Princeton. At first, the elderly owner was reluctant to sell her family farmland to a school. In addition, the homestead was a historic landmark that could not be altered for school use. Thanks to another interested buyer and the diplomatic skill of our lawyer, we were able to work out a plan that the owner finally accepted: we would purchase the field and the other buyer would purchase the house. We figured out how much acreage we would need, crawled through the subdivision process, raised the funds and purchased our patch of land.

I took frequent walks on the prospective school site with my dog. These walks were dream-time for me. My greatest regret was that, after fifteen years of devoted service to the school, Margaret was no longer around to see the fruits of her labor. Shortly after the school site was purchased, she withdrew from Princeton to a Quaker retirement community in North Carolina where she lived until her death in 2005. Before she left, she illumined her huge "goodbye party" with a radiance reminiscent of the Han Dynasty. For her love, her humor, her wisdom and her grace I am deeply grateful.

—⁂—

This I Know

This farm is a sight for my wondering eyes,
A site once hand-mowed by the farmer's scythe.
I dream that together we'll seed such a place,
Wherein wisdom and children will grow face to face,
Where families will learn how to work and to play,
To listen, to laugh, and to love every day.

J.

What I envisaged then materialized after eight years of labor. Buying land was one thing. Gaining approval from the Planning Board of Lawrence Township for the construction of a school was another. The creation of a "world for children" that we could call our own took several turns with neighbors, municipal principals, traffic engineers, architects, contractors, inspectors, banks—a-*maze*-ing!

Our efforts to obtain a loan with which to build the school were thwarted by eleven commercial banks during the first two and a half years of the five-year period allowed for construction. They considered the school too high a risk. As the months slipped by, several trustees became apprehensive and decided not to wait any longer for funds to build a school. Instead, they focused their efforts on finding and converting a commercial space to be leased by the school for ten years. As much as I welcomed a chance to gather the whole school beneath one roof, this plan cast a shadow on my dream to build a school from scratch.

Although the Planning Board of West Windsor approved of the school's leasing space in a large warehouse on Alexander Road, I was not enthusiastic. However, the plan fell through when the owner of the building declared bankruptcy and informed us he was going to sell the warehouse. We would have to negotiate with his successor if we wanted to continue our project. When I was asked by a couple of the trustees to go with them to Trenton to negotiate with the new owner, a substantial developer of commercial real estate in the region, I went with a heavy heart.

It was late afternoon, cold and dark. During an hour of hard discussion, Mr. Simmons—the developer—assured us that we would be *very* unhappy as tenants in his newly acquired warehouse. He claimed that he would be a tough landlord, that the surrounding parking lots were perches for predators, and that furthermore, he intended to install a large dialysis unit in the proposed school space. Such a source of blood-stained waste materials would be hazardous to any other tenant in the same building. After a few murmurs of protest, we rose to leave. "I would like you to remain, Mrs. McIntyre. I have something I want to say to you. Sit down." The trustees left me there alone with Mr. Simmons in his office. "You never wanted your school to occupy that warehouse in the first place. I could see it in your eyes."

"I suppose so." His deft observation left me dangling. I looked around at the clerical clutter in the receding light and wondered why I was there. The place was silent save for the hum of sleepless monitors.

"Well, I've got news for you. I always wanted that piece you bought on Fackler. The old lady never gave me a chance. You got yourself a gem."

"Thank you. It wasn't easy." What was he getting at?

"Now I know I can help you." He settled back in his chair. I felt my blood quicken. Was he about to make an offer for the field? My silence must have goaded him.

"Don't you want to know? You think I'm the bad guy, but I can help you to make that property into a wonderful little school—far better than anything you could do in my tacky building."

"Are you an angel?" Silly question.

"No, I'm not giving you any money, if that's what you mean. I reserve being an angel for my grandson's school. For you, I can do something better. Have you ever heard of the N.J. E.D.A. here in Trenton?" Yes, I had heard about the Economic Development Authority. We had applied for a loan once, only to be rejected. When I told Mr. Simmons, he urged me to try again. "I know the new Director. She and I have worked together on a lot of projects. I'll call her tomorrow and you can bet she'll give you a hearing. She has kids of her own and is interested in early childhood education." I was startled by his comment and tried to respond, but he hoisted himself out of his huge chair and with a flick of the light switch ushered me out. I suspect that my favorite black hat remains with all the other stuff in his office to this very day.

As I drove home, I chuckled. Perhaps Mr. Simmons was not a bad guy after all. By definition, E.D.A. supports non-profit organizations in their efforts to create an environment for growth and opportunity. E.D.A. is required to use a percentage of the state lottery funds to provide collateral for loans to non-profit organizations. I had been buying lottery tickets unsuccessfully for years in hopes of winning some money for the school. Wouldn't it be a hoot if, after all my trashed lottery tickets, we ended up building the schoolhouse on the strength of an E.D.A.- backed loan?

Sure enough, we did. Within a few days of that memorable conversation in Trenton, representatives from E.D.A. unexpectedly dropped in at the church on Walnut Lane to see "what was going on." Unfortunately, what was going on was the dissection of countless dead fish in the sanctuary-cum-science lab. Entrails everywhere—the whole place reeked. Even so, the children's enthusiasm hooked the E.D.A. folk and after many further visits, E.D.A. guaranteed a loan to build our school on Fackler Road. (At one point, the Authority recommended that the School plan to install fans in its science room.)

I wrote a letter of thanks to Saint Simmons, the so-called villain who blindfolded me, turned me around and pushed me in the right direction.

———⁓———

The Barracks had fireplaces everywhere. On the third floor there were wood-burning stoves to warm the two bedrooms beneath the roof. Bu hung a hefty, knotted rope from one of the windows so that we could shinny down to escape an attic fire. (I failed one practice by falling into the bayberry bushes below.) On the second floor, there was a hearth in my parents' bedroom. Often at night, I heard them, wrapped in its warmth, reading Trollope novels aloud to one another. The fireplace in Davie's room was cold; he generated heat without it. On the ground floor were three hearths: one in the dining room, one in the big parlor, and one in the little parlor which was a former kitchen that had served as a hospital for the wounded during the American Revolution. I viewed the little parlor's hearth as the heart of the house.

Legend has it that the ghost of a Hessian soldier hovered around this little parlor hearth. We children spent hours waiting for him to show up. When he finally did, I mistook him for a house guest, so simply and quietly did he appear to me. I liked him and spotted him often. I shall never forget the presence of this mysterious companion of my childhood.

When, as a child, I gazed into a flame-filled hearth, I wondered why fire, so bright, so beautiful, so playful, was so mysterious. Its flickering dance invited my imagination. Did I have a fire burning inside of me as well? Could it burn me up? Could it be that when the fire went out, I would die?

Maboo loved a good fire. As strict as she was about bedtime, she could not resist the impulse to chase the fire truck if she heard its siren during our bedtime prayers. I remember once being pried off my knees during the Lord's Prayer ("Lead us not into temptation . . .") and dragged by Maboo down Edgehill and Mercer Streets to watch the old Maxwell house burn to the ground. So frequently did we chase fires that the fire chief finally prohibited Maboo from doing so—on the grounds that she and her children were a hazard. She complied, reluctantly. I have often wondered whether Maboo's gentle demeanor could suppress her emotions for only so long, until a fire siren released the blaze within her.

The children at Princeton Junior School "caught fire" one dark, rainy day when the pastor of our second church home suggested that we gather and sing in the church's little common room. We had long noticed the hearth there, filled with dusty logs, scrunched paper, and a few brittle evergreen boughs. Never did we expect the pastor to startle us into song. That day was one to remember: the pastor's rich tenor accompanied by a chorus of trebles singing to their hearts' content before the dancing flames.

Several years later, during the schematic design phase of our new schoolhouse, we called upon natural elements—air, earth, water, and fire—to help us imagine a world for children on the beautiful site. The plan called for a hearth at the center of the school to give warmth and light to a commons wherein the school community would meet every day. We imagined that the hearth's welcoming glow, the streams of sunlight, and the mellow patina of old barn beams would warm the school family. We initiated a tradition at the site before construction to keep our hopes and dreams alive: bonfires at harvest time.

Prior to the first bonfire, a few of us went to the field and staked out the footprint of the proposed schoolhouse, delineating all the interior spaces: the commons, the hearth, surrounding classrooms, etc. The wood for a bonfire was gathered and piled by children and adults on the exact spot where the school's hearth would eventually be. They hauled branches and brush from the nearby woods, broken furniture from basements and attics, scraps and palettes from Grover's lumberyard. The fire chief from Lawrence Township had to approve of the heap and assign a team of firefighters and a glorious, melodious fire engine to the bonfire site before we could strike a match.

Although the school's layout was strung only by stakes and tape, its space felt real to us as we crossed the field and entered the virtual school through the main door and filled The Commons. Someone placed a high stepladder for me to climb upon. Once aloft, I asked for a moment of silence so everyone could enjoy the vast canopy of stars and the sounds of nature in the enveloping darkness. Inwardly, I prayed that the silence would draw us all to look beyond ourselves, beyond the pile of dry timber, the field, the colorful trees, and upward into the heavens, where the autumn sky awaited our gaze, its galaxy twinkling back at us.

Then, to the stirring melodies of Vivaldi's "Four Seasons," six torchbearers encircled the wooden construction with flaming rag-wrapped tapers. A quick poke into the dry wood and the bonfire spiraled into life, drawing from the surrounding crowd a resounding "Ohh . . ." From that moment forward, the annual bonfire's wild brilliance, reflected in the eyes of all around, became the symbol for the school's spirit.

> It is warming me
> Sparks are coming out to me,
> The flames are dancing.

> Student

Once the school was built, the bonfires took place in the nearby meadow, drawing into its radiance a great variety of activities and events: hayrides, square dancing, storytelling, native-American dances, clown shows. Warm cider and donuts, pizza and pretzels were abundant. Even when the flames died down, the bonfire offered one final blessing: smoldering coals for the children's marshmallow-tipped sticks.

When the bonfire was reduced to ashes, families faded into the surrounding darkness to wend their way home. A few of us stayed to clean up the cauldrons and gather trash into bags. The school kitchen soon transformed into a bistro in which we enjoyed our friendships over a glass of wine and what was left of the pizza.

Over the years, the bonfire became a complex event. The fire department sent more firefighters as well as more equipment. The fire chief—in passionate adherence to safety requirements—insisted that the bonfire be constructed by adults according to his specifications— and furthermore, that children not be allowed to set the blaze or to dance close to the flames. His routine inspections of the schoolhouse grew more rigorous. Only when we surprised him with a massive birthday cake during one of these inspections did he loosen his grip and allow us to stable our wooden rocking horses in The Commons. I grieved upon hearing that he died recently without my being able to give him a final hug.

Our schoolhouse finally grew up in the field. At the very spot where the bonfire had blazed, The Commons' hearth now glowed. On cold winter mornings, children with frost still clinging to their eyelashes would fling their jackets and backpacks aside and cling together in its warmth. How enthralled they were! Had some of them never approached a hearth before—never been charmed by its lively flame?

—∼∼—

For years, I had been dreaming about the ideal physical layout for a children's school. Now was time to watch my dream come true. During my travels through the greater world with Jim, I had noted the creation of central assembly spaces by communities both modern and ancient: town greens, courtyards, marketplaces, atria, cloisters, stone circles. These commons were often shaped like squares or circles and surrounded by walkways, streets, or structures dedicated to the life of the community. This shared world could be interior or exterior, or both, if the central space contained pathways leading outward to the surrounding area. I recall a school in Africa where the children sat cross-legged in a circle on the cool, newly swept earth, their bodies dappled by sunlight that filtered through the foliage above their heads. This was their common ground for learning by heart the lessons intoned by their elders. At a school in England, upon the clanging of the bell, the academic quad's central courtyard overflowed with students rushing from one class to the next, hailing or slapping one another's palms as they zoomed along the crosswalks. Somehow, these moments in the grassy courtyard of their lives provided an intersection between the immediate and the infinite: the immediate—getting to the next class—and the infinite—connecting with a fellow soul.

Never commonplace was this common space! In graduate school, I had rendered a plan for an early childhood center that resembled a village, commons and all. If children all over the world liked to meet and greet one another in common, should not the children of Princeton Junior School do likewise? As always, children led me to the heart of the matter: connection. We sought every way possible to create a commons in which such connections could be easily and naturally made.

When we interviewed professional architects, we found several who offered schemes couched in magnificent designs that separated rather than united people. At last an architect came along who showed us an existing school that he had designed wherein a central commons surrounded by classrooms provided a spiritual home for the school community. We welcomed this architect with open arms. During the years that we collaborated, I felt that my dream was indeed coming true. We created a school environment where children could discover the wisdom in themselves, in nature, in others, and in God only knows what else.

The architect found a barn for sale. Dismantled and trucked in from Canada, the barn trusses arrived at 5:30 a.m. one chilly March morning. The red taillights of the huge flatbed truck blinked at me through the heavy fog as if to say, "Here we are, at last." Over the ensuing days, we watched the giant crane hoisting first one, then another truss into place. What had been used to support a farm building now became the armature for our schoolhouse.

—∿—

Occasionally during the year of construction, schoolchildren visited the site with our project manager. Everyone had to wear hard hats and listen carefully to the contractor, who explained in detail whatever stage of work lay before his team. Once the lesson was over, the children broke ranks with shouts of glee and scrambled up the huge mounds of soil that the bulldozers had set aside. Like momentary kings and queens, they surveyed the land from the peaks of their mini-mountains. I always felt a twinge of regret in calling them down to return to the subterranean space that their school inhabited.

—∿—

During construction, it was all too easy for me to make a *faux pas*. It was late spring and the children were bursting with energy. One day, word came to me from the construction site that the exterior concrete pads—doorsteps leading into the classrooms—would be placed very soon, weather permitting. My thoughts immediately flew to the possibility of taking the children to the site to learn about concrete as a construction material, how it cures quickly and eventually creates a permanent, stone-like material. They could watch it harden to a broom finish only an hour after being poured. They could walk on it four to five hours later. Also, the children could learn about how the ancient Romans used concrete for the construction of aqueducts and bridges that survive to the present day. The Romans even knew that adding horsehair made concrete less liable to crack while it hardened, and adding blood made it more resistant to cold . . . details sure to delight children.

The possibilities were endless. Why not turn this into a multilevel lesson? The teachers agreed. Sand, gravel, water, concrete; tubs, buckets, shovels, trowels; ancient civilizations; how multidimensional! Grown-ups in a sandbox—what could be better? Inevitably, something better did pop into my mind: why not invite each child to impress his or her handprint into the warm concrete of the doorsteps before they hardened? Their prints would proclaim to all who entered through those classroom doors, "Welcome to our world!" Giddy with hope, I called the contractor who called the superintendent, who called the subcontractor who called the township engineer to see whether such folly was permissible. General approval was granted on condition that the handprints be shallow and made at exactly the right time, i.e., when the concrete had partially cured. Triumph! At pick-up time that day, I rounded up some parents who were willing to transport the children at a moment's notice. When I told the children, they were thrilled. After all, they were being given a chance to do what is normally forbidden. We all waited for a couple of days, poised for flight. Then suddenly, the call came. We sprang into action and dashed to the site. It was very hot and we knew the concrete would harden quickly. The doorsteps awaited, their soft, smooth concrete looking like peanut butter in the afternoon sun. With workmen, teachers, and parents hanging on to them for dear life, each child leaned over, pushed one hand into the warm concrete, and held it there for a moment before carefully lifting it out. By the end of the hour, sixteen doorsteps were studded with handprints of every size and shape (a few being those of adults, I noticed). The children were elated. Artists of today, they were no less eager to make a lasting mark than were the Paleolithic artists 32,000 years ago whose handprints dot the walls of the Chauvet Caves in southern France.

A disgruntled building inspector came by a week later to examine our children's handiwork. Summarily, he rejected our doorsteps on the grounds that several handprints were too deep for safe crossing. The workmen were ordered to break them up and pour new ones. I was appalled. We had to tell the children what had happened. They were not impressed by our assurances that it was better to break doorsteps than legs.

A literal *faux pas* could be far more intractable than a social one, that sad event during the final stage of construction demonstrated. I have thought a lot about what I learned from the children who saw their project come to such an unhappy ending. No amount of explanation could assuage their disappointment. The hand printing had been fun, to be sure, but more important to them, I think, was the loss of a permanent mark in the school that they were helping to build every day. An instinctive human longing to leave a legacy had been rebuffed.

Should a great millstone have been fastened around the neck of the inspector? He had officially and arbitrarily put an end to the doorsteps. Reason: they were stumbling blocks. Recently, when I recalled the event with the contractor, he sympathized. "I am sorry it happened that way. In the real world of construction, there are far greater risks than hand prints in concrete."

———ᨆ———

A month later, a miracle made up for the doomed doorsteps. The new schoolhouse was nearly complete. Eleven classrooms, a library, art room, music room, kitchen, and offices spiraled from the central barn structure that formed The Commons. How were we to garnish this gathering place with the kind of furniture that would both harmonize with the oak barn timbers and provide for children a safe, hospitable environment? From Miss Morrison's colorful stash we could furnish the classrooms, but what about the halls, the library, art room, music room, and offices? What about swings and climbers, sandboxes and shovels for outdoor play? We had run out of funds for custom-made bookcases and cabinets. Our old standby, rummage, couldn't cut the mustard this time. We wanted furniture with *character*.

The new schoolhouse was going to open for business in September, assuming we got our Certificate of Occupancy. Although furniture deprivation had seldom been an issue, it now took on alarming proportions. For years I had claimed that a child who has nothing to do will dream up something to do, but now, apprehensive and devoid of imagination, I could find such a child nowhere within me . . . not even the child who would use pillows for furniture and the floor for his or her atelier.

Then, one Saturday, I was awakened at 6:00 a.m. by the telephone. Who could be calling at this ungodly hour?

"Hello?"

"Hi, Mrs. McIntyre." The soft, singsong voice could only belong to Greta Reiner, one of our school parents. Deaf as she was, she mouthed her message through the wires on that sweltering June morning. "I'm sorry to call you so early, but do I understand that you need nice furniture for the school?"

"Well, yes . . . in a big way." She picked up the vibration of my voice.

"I can help you get the furniture you need."

Was I dreaming? "You can? How so?"

"It's too much to explain over the phone. Can you get a truck and meet me at 7:00 a.m. at the Gulf station on Route 1?"

What could Greta possibly mean? I peeked at Jim lying next to me sound asleep. He had been awake on and off for the past several nights with a sore back. He needed the rest. Perhaps I could sneak out and return before he woke up. "Okay, Greta." I tiptoed from the bedroom, made a pot of coffee with a note for Jim and drove straight to the Gulf station.

The window of Greta's car framed her broad, playful smile as she inquired, "And where's your truck, Mrs. McIntyre?"

Thus began an adventure that I am convinced only God and Greta could have created. Softly droning, Greta informed me that two state mental institutions had closed and were being dismantled. Furthermore, all NJ employees, including Greta, were authorized to go to the sites and purchase whatever contents appealed to them at minimal cost.

We rented a large U-Haul truck as quickly as possible and sped to one of the institution sites—only to find hundreds of state employees waiting in line to enter one of the huge brick buildings. Once a dormitory for the mentally ill, this building was now under the control of the state police, who stood guard while prisoners from the Garden State Penitentiary stripped the interior of furniture and equipment. The upper windows and doors had been flung open to the dazzling morning sunshine. Beds, chests, tables, chairs, commodes, walkers, not to mention such personal effects as helmets and straitjackets, were flying headlong into dumpsters below. Customers had to scamper among the green-clad prisoners to retrieve the furniture before it smashed. Since the police allowed no one to speak to the penal colony, the whole scene transformed into an elaborate dumb show, a pantomime expressing far better than words the miracle that was taking place.

For two hours, Greta and I dodged and darted in the crowd and came away with eight small oak chests, all for $10. The party was on! During the next two weeks, Bill Sorrel, a friend who had just returned from the war in Iraq, helped us to haul truckloads of heavy pieces from both institutions. Bill played a very important role in getting our school equipped for opening day, not only by retrieving oak furniture that we had purchased from two mental institutions, but also by helping me scour the storage warehouse of Princeton University. He deftly removed the slate chalkboards from another school's demolition site and even transported play yard equipment from a neighbor's backyard (always with permission, of course). Soon after that summer of 1998, he returned to the heat of Baghdad where he fought in a special unit of firefighters. We heard from his wife that he sorely missed his friends at Princeton Junior School. Upon hearing this, the children created dozens of valentines the following February, which he received while fighting the fires in Iraq.

Oak furniture that the state would have confiscated was now rescued by the school to furnish its new world for children. I wondered whether any of the furniture had been occupied by my brother, Davie, for he had lived in one of the institutions briefly. Now deceased, could he be the angel who performed this miracle?

Throughout the summer of 1998, men, women, and children gathered in the parched field adjacent to the new schoolhouse to scrub, sand, and polish dozens of items—refectory tables, sofas and chairs, benches, bookcases and cabinets—converting them from grimy institutional props into works of art. Children painted the cubbies and coat trees with bright enamels. The summer drought enabled us to work outdoors and finish the furniture in time for the opening of school. Cost? Approximately $800 to furnish 18,000 square feet of space. The library tables and chairs were trucked down to the Garden State Penitentiary Workshop to be stripped of years of varnish, thanks to the whispered advice offered by one of the convicts. When the restored library set came back a month later, we found a note taped beneath one of the chair seats.

I know by the number stamped below

125

This chair was made here years ago
By me.

Harry, #20175

I think of Harry's chair as a prayer that supports the wisdom of anyone who sits in it. Little does he know how many people he has helped to educate!

During this same summer, Jim and I learned that liver cancer would take his life within a very short time. It was hard to believe that this energetic, healthy man would be so swiftly and unexpectedly attacked, but cancer had the upper hand. As he and I watched the final phase of the school construction, we realized that this beautiful project would be our last one together. It would never have come into being were it not for his strategic planning and determination to see the project through. During the parched summer weeks, Jim insisted that I go on the furniture "adventure" despite his weakening condition, for in his opinion, everything we had worked for hung in the balance. The school had to open on the scheduled date with all its furnishings in place. So we arranged for me to work for the school while he slept—5:30 a.m. until noon—and then to spend the rest of the day with him. One of our school parents, a compassionate Guatemalan woman, came to the house regularly to help both Jim and me. She was an invaluable assistant, helping him to clear his files, his closets, and bookcases—to get ready for departure. As they sorted through his papers, she consoled him by reminding him of how much he had accomplished and how much of the world he had seen. When the new schoolhouse opened its doors in September, Jim was there—barely—greeting everyone with a triumphant gleam in his eyes. The Japanese Scholar Tree that stands in the center of the circle before the entrance is a living tribute to him. The fountain that Julie and I created in the main entrance with river stones from the field was dedicated to him. At his funeral, I found a letter on the table from one of the boys at the school:

Dear Jim,

I will miss you. I hope Mrs. McIntyre will be able to get along without you. Thank you for helping the school and the new building. I hope the school will get along on its own. Have a nice time in heaven.

Love,
[Student]

—∿—

Once in the new schoolhouse, we no longer walked around the town of Princeton. We were surrounded by acres of freshly graded dirt. The groundhog population having scattered, we looked for fresh deer tracks, rabbit warrens, and birds' nests. The children came to Fackler Road with a new sense of adventure.

> The way a chickadee landed beside me
> With its feathery body covered in snow
> Made me think of all I can see,
> Of all the places I can
> And all I can do.
>
>   Student

—∿—

In one of our teacher's descriptions of the school's final habitat on Fackler Road, Mother Nature and human nature work in unison.

> After all, how many schools can boast such a beautiful environment where birds twitter and trill, where seedlings dodge children's footsteps and thrive, where trees are named after people, where a Well [kitchen] welcomes its faculty with sweet smells and produce often grown on the premises, where a dog psychologist is in residence—the list is endless! You'd have to see it to believe it. I loved my time at PJS. I wouldn't trade it for a million bucks! We got down

to basics: basic values, basic skills, basic emotions. Such a strong foundation for all ages and for all times.

Teacher

—⟋⟍—

As I had hoped, The Commons became the school's sanctuary—a place where those who gathered beneath its lofty trusses were acknowledged, protected and cherished. The Commons made room for the power of wisdom to come into play. A beautiful fossilized ammonite, ancestor of the chambered nautilus, was attached to the chimney. It reminded us to grow from our center outward toward the world beyond, from being to becoming. Only when we regard education as a matter of the spirit can we live out the wisdom so generously bestowed upon us at birth by a loving God.

Early every school day, children of all ages and stages met in The Commons. On dark winter mornings, a fire burned in the hearth. On sunny mornings, light streamed through the stained glass of the east windows, causing colorful sunbeams to ricochet off the timbers. The place buzzed with everyone's news until the bronze school bell clanged for silence. Colorful wooden hobby horses, unit blocks, chess games, and jump ropes were quickly stored. Children ran indoors from playing kick ball. The various classes formed lines to hear special announcements, to stretch and breathe deeply, and to walk to their classrooms down hallways that receded from The Commons toward the north, east, south, and west.

Friday assemblies in The Commons quickened the pulse of every child. Spanish fiestas, choir recitals, black history festivals, talent shows, book fairs, inventions, demonstrations, and countless other class presentations brought us all together at the end of the school week.

The Commons' book fair, a colossal show masterminded by the school's librarian, always fascinated me. Among the colorful books for children and parents moved a spirit that I can only ascribe to wisdom. While adults stood chatting at the display tables, the children became lost in the world of literature, oblivious to everyone and everything around them. Seated at one of the tables with my author-sister Margery,

I could easily see young readers pulled as if by a magnet into the picture books laid out before them.

> What is a book? It is your key to knowledge. It is an adventure on paper. It inhales you into a new world as you turn the pages. The only way to survive is to master the characters and the surroundings. As you read, you make new best friends. Books are the secret keys to the universe's secrets, from front to back.
>
> Student

At noon, The Commons held dozens of children who ate their brown bag lunches at folding tables that they had set up. Their conversation filled the air. At mid-afternoon there was another gathering, this time to say good-bye or to enter yet another phase of the day, the after-school time when free play became a matter of primary importance. During this period, The Commons again became transformed according to how its occupants wanted to use it—as a castle, a forest, a dungeon, or a stage. I once strung a large parachute from the trusses above. Its voluminous canopy provided children with yards of billowing khaki fabric with which to shape a new world of caves and crevices. In a drama class:

> At first I did not know what we could be using [the parachute] for. However, the class was instructed to be creative. As a class, we proceeded to use this large prop in acting the story from the Bible of Jonah and the whale.
>
> Alumnus

Chess and checker games covered the tabletops in The Commons during the late afternoon time. Many children become wizards at both games.

Throughout the day, The Commons accommodated travelers of all kinds. Classes passed through on their way to the library. Individuals crossed to the front desk to get a scraped knee bandaged or a bloody nose plugged. Visitors touring the school paused in The Commons to gaze upward. Parents met there for a cup of coffee and conversation. Rainy day exercise, celebrations, and displays all enlivened The Commons, week after week.

From its onset, this generous central space was an arena for visiting performers as well. Many a Monday night, if you drove by the school, you could practically see it levitate to the strains of a rehearsal by the Blawenburg Band. The Princeton Symphony's "Bravo!" program brought classical music to the school through live instructional performances. Upon the percussionists' arrival, our children rocked with delight to hear drums, rattles, wooden blocks, and cymbals resounding from every corner of The Commons in response to the call of the marimba. These percussion sessions always included a lesson on how to compose music with pots and pans. "Bravo!" inspired children to incorporate music into their lives and express themselves artistically, either by learning to play an instrument or by heightening their appreciation and enjoyment of classical music.

On other occasions directed by Dickens the Clown—my cousin— the children staged mock concerts using bicycle bells, whistles, and kazoos. Once, McCarter Theatre's teachers invited our older students to participate in Homer's *Odyssey* and Shakespeare's *Tempest*, plays that transformed The Commons into ancient Greece or an island on the Mediterranean Sea. Still other programs included musicology, folk singing, papermaking, and poetry.

Dance communicates the movement of the human soul and spirit in ways that no other art form can. Such was the case in 2005 when a world-renowned Indian dancer gave our students a glimpse of the glistening dances of India in The Commons. She was accompanied by three other dancers, the youngest being her daughter who was one of our students.

Birds of prey found their way to The Commons' highest trusses during visits by the Raptor Man. I sometimes wondered whether the birds, once they reached such an inaccessible perch from which to view their young audience, would ever agree to return to the falconer's glove. Fortunately, his chunks of ground beef appealed to them more than the juicy little people below.

There were times when The Commons became a little too generous! Creating a learning environment while at the same time offering hospitality to our visitors and parents was a challenge. On one hand, we tried to ensure a quiet, distraction-free place for the students. On the other, we encouraged parents to park, come in, meet, have coffee and read the walls for documentation of their children's latest accomplishments. It was always difficult to hush the very people whose enthusiasm for our school was so high that they volunteered their time, talent, and money to enhance it. Somehow, we achieved a balance. While visitors congregated in "The Well" (kitchen) or The Commons, the hallways during class time were quiet enough to hear a pin drop.

—⁓—

Manifestations of wisdom cannot be measured or mastered. However, they are apparent in the creative activities of children. They emerge naturally when children connect with others and feel respected, understood, and loved, and when their imaginations leap into play. In young children, these images of wisdom may take the form of words, pictures, plays, songs, or dances. In older children, they may take on more abstract forms, concepts, strategies, and inventions. Whatever the child's age or stage, wisdom longs to be revealed. Children are surprised and delighted by wisdom, for it helps them to become who they truly are.

> Then I [wisdom] was beside Him, like a master worker;
> and I was daily His delight, rejoicing before Him always,
> rejoicing in His inhabited world, and delighting in the
> human race.

> Proverbs 8:30-31, The New Oxford Annotated Bible,
> Third Edition, New Revised Standard Version,
> pp. 914-915.

"Master worker" can be alternatively be translated as "little child." I'm not surprised.

One day in early April, the beds of our back garden were filled with twigs and debris from a recent storm. Birds were flitting from feeder to feeder in search of seed. Competition among the winged rivals was too sharp and shimmering to be chivalrous. Their songs of love would have to wait.

My grandson Georgie entered the scene. The surprising arrival of a seven-year-old master worker stunned the garden community. Birds scattered to the surrounding brush amid cries of alarm. Squirrels dashed for cover.

I had purchased a few flats of annuals to line the borders of the perennial beds once the soil was tilled. Pansies lay in the shade of the fragrant wisteria vine like harbingers of hope awaiting their time in the sun. Large containers filled with fresh potting soil stood on the dry wall overlooking the lower terrace. A shovel, cultivator, and trowel leaned against the lattice fence in readiness for the rituals of spring. The whole garden hung in abeyance.

Georgie went straight to work. Grabbing the shovel, he cut into the packed soil, his enthusiasm driving deeper by the minute. Unwittingly, we became his lackeys.

"Nana, come over here and see the worms. They're spitting dirt!" He made no attempt to remove them.

For several hours, Georgie waged war with weeds. At last, standing up and mopping his brow with muddy fingers, he hailed my husband. "Dick, we've got to move that bench over here where people can sit and watch the pansies I planted." We? The bench weighed at least fifty pounds. Reluctantly, we—his grandparents—staggered the length of the garden bearing the heavy wrought-iron Victorian curio to the designated spot. It turned out to be a great idea, for we now can sit in the shade of the arborvitae and watch the birds and pansies grow.

"Nana, we need to build a fountain over here so you can hear the water when you eat outside." (What water? "Over here" was nowhere near a water source. Had this bossy boy botanist considered the cost of such a project? On Mother's Day he called me up to remind me that I needed a fountain over by the lily bed.)

"Dick, we should put birdseed and worms into the birdhouse there so the birds will want to build a nest in it." (Later, after he climbed down from the tree, we discovered the roof of the new birdhouse was adorned with a large pink petunia.)

"Nana, you better get two humungous pots to put on each side of these steps and I'll plant roses in them."

At first I met his incessant requests with misgiving, for I had my own ideas about how I wanted everything to be planted. For me, sequence, scale, color, and texture were all of great consequence. But as I watched his small figure laboring day after day with the shovel to break the clay-sealed soil, it dawned on me that he was truly inspired. The garden awakened to his touch. Seedlings responded happily to his arrangements. I found his diligence not dutiful so much as devoted. His imagination flooded our tired old garden, transforming its rather conservative design into a palette of colorful inconsistency. Border plants crowded together in cheerful clumps. Geraniums, scraggly from months indoors, were consoled in their pots by clusters of snowbells and mountain pinks. The sundial, longtime solar indicator of the upper terrace, now occupied a pivotal place below the wall, where birds at the feeders could determine the hour for courtship. Delicate impatiens, planted alongside some stepping stones by Georgie's tireless fingers, would soon live up to their name and garnish the ground around the hosta and fern.

I bowed my head to the creativity of this young master gardener, for he was indulging his Creator. Creativity must be the point of connection between mortals and their Maker, the intersection between the temporal and the eternal. This must be where transformation takes place, where joy is born. What do Georgie and other children know that I have to relearn? However impulsive he may have seemed, I suspect the breath of God blew Georgie into our garden. There, he was a virtuoso at play in God's presence.

It has often been said that play is considered a child's work. Likewise, that gardening is considered an adult's work. Farming is considered hard work, no matter who does it. The six-acre site of Princeton Junior School now needed some hard work of a different kind. The Planning Board stipulated that the property must be screened by bordering trees. (Was this to protect the neighbors from the sight and sound of children at play?) The newly planted trees resembled a legion of soldiers marching around the grounds—hardly a welcoming sight. When it rained, the fresh dirt around the schoolhouse dissolved into a sea of mud. Landscaping was out of the question for the time being, as we had very little funding left for anything besides grass. It would have to become a "lawnscape."

Unexpectedly, the mess was transformed into a masterpiece. Two architects, a husband and wife team whose children attended the school, put the question to me: "Why not consider the development of the school grounds as an opportunity for the education of the children?"

"Opportunity for the children?" was my bleak reply. At that moment, all I could think of was a youthful bucket brigade out in the field, scooping up and throwing mud in every direction. No sooner had I opened my mouth than they deflected my doubt by introducing me to a landscape architect whose sole focus was to develop landscapes for, by, and with children. This visionary woman led me to a whole new way of thinking about the school's grounds. She encouraged me to visit the Coombes School in England that had spawned a national program. I visited the school during one of my frequent trips there. The Coombes School was nestled in an old estate situated in the heart of the Surrey countryside.

"So you want to learn about our landscape program?" the headmistress's words clipped. "I suggest you take a tour with two of our children. They can tell you much more than I, who sit behind a desk." She hailed two children passing by on their way to class. "Tommy, Sarah! Please forego your mathematics and guide our visitor around the grounds. Mrs. McIntyre has come all the way from the States to find out what we do here." Needless to say, the children threw down their book bags and complied with her request. During the following hour, they opened my eyes to a world beyond the walls of their classrooms, a world full of surprises.

"This is our fish pond. We found a spring under the cattails and dug it out. It took many weeks. Tommy's father helped us line it with plastic and we dumped goldfish in. They like it because it is in the sun and that makes them look 'specially pretty."

"When we discovered that the rabbits mostly lived here we decided to let them keep their habitat. Their babies are really cute. We leave lettuce and carrots at the doors of their holes."

"Our teacher knows all the creatures in the woods. She tells us to write notes to them. We put the notes under the ferns before we leave for home in the afternoon. When we come back the next morning, she lets us go to where we left the notes. And there are notes back to us! We bring them to our classroom and pin them on the wall."

"This upside-down boat has been here a long time. We use it to make plays about shipwrecks."

"'Here is our math play yard. The white lines are math sentences and games. We come out here when the blackboard is too full to put anything more on."

"This mound is where we play King Arthur and his round table. The road crew brought in loads of broken concrete. We piled it up and packed soil all over it and planted grass seed."

"This black spot is where we burned London. We built London out of cardboard boxes and when we were finished studying about the great fire of London, we came back to school at night with our teachers and burned it."

And on and on. I learned about shrubs that attract butterflies, a pen for sheep, a medieval herb garden near the kitchen door, a poetry place, and much, much more at the hands of my young tour guides. Their landscape was for them a living, breathing classroom that reached beyond any book they could read or lecture they could attend. My problem was solved.

With very little gardening experience, I launched the British program—"Learning through Landscapes"—at Princeton Junior School. One of the school parents, a professional horticulturist, happily took over, as my knowledge of gardening began and ended with the planting of bulbs, as the following instructions imply:

> Should any of your students wish to plant during these last relatively warm days, please allow them to help themselves to some bulbs and to heed the following procedure: 1) Dig a hole six inches below the soil line. If by chance you encounter another old bulb, gently cover it up, pack it down, and try another place. 2) Put a tablespoon of bulb food in the hole. 3) Place the bulb in the hole right-side-up. 4) Fill in the hole with dirt. 5) Press the dirt down with your foot. 6) Cover the area with mulch.

J.

The Learning through Landscapes program connected children with their school grounds in such a way that nature became their teacher and mentor.

During the following years, the school's six acres were developed by faculty, students, and parents into a series of outdoor learning sites. One parent in particular became our inspiration. The students discovered ecosystems: the habitats of animals, birds, and insects, the life cycles of plants, the behavior of weather, and the energy of the elements. Spaces were created as outdoor classrooms for other subject areas as well: literature, math, history, art, music.

Parent

The tireless efforts of the school's founders, supports, administration, and teachers are not lost on the children here. Their enthusiasm for protecting the environment is as much a part of the learning experience as ABCs and 123s.

"There was a bird's nest in our play set," a fifth grade girl reports, "and we respected the mother and her babies. We went to see them two at a time so we wouldn't disturb their home."

Each fall, every class plants seeds in the Hilltop School Garden. As the plants grow, the children care for them. They harvest vegetables, as well as wheat and rye, which they winnow and grind into flour. The resulting pumpkin, zucchini, and multigrain breads are shared by the entire school community. A giant compost bin built by the students themselves overflows with fertilizer for the garden.

Another lesson involves collecting pokeberries, onion skins, and walnut hulls, boiling them to create natural brews, and then using the resulting dyes to stain pieces of cloth which are then used to make quilts and create art for school plays.

Parent

One of the program's requirements was that each of the fifth-graders adopt a tree for a year. Often, when I looked out the window of my corner office, I saw these students scrutinizing their trees with notebooks and pencils in hand.

Finding out that my tree
Is a maple tree
That will grow to sixty feet,
Finding out that Iona's
And Zoe's trees
Will grow little berries
That robins love to eat,
Finding out that Ebony's tree
Is infested with ladybugs
That ants fight,
Finding out that Steven's tree
Has little red helicopters
That will spin like my green ones,
Finding out is fun!

Student

Learning through Landscapes provided a synthesis of traditional teaching and modern experimentation. The architects who had awakened me to the opportunity funded the initial plan, the materials, and an inspired parent and teacher whose expertise drew the landscape into every aspect of the school's academic life.

Every spring the children plant a hilltop garden that grows grains and vegetables for homemade bread and soup. Their allée of river birches leads to a labyrinth that they made with smooth river stones. Trees, forsythia hedges, flower and berry gardens that attract butterflies and birds, gourd birdhouses, patches of wild grass, swamp gardens, a library reading garden—all have been planted and cared for by the children. There is no doubt about it: Children love dirt. They love to see things grow. Even the "soldiers" marching along the borders have surrendered to their tender care. The landscape that our children have developed cultivates the school. Years later, I received the following note from the landscape architect who introduced me to the concept of Learning through Landscapes:

> It has been such a pleasure to be involved with and see the transformation from a treeless landscape to a learning garden! It has also been a pleasure to come to call you a friend whom I love!"

Landscape Architect

I overheard one girl say to another while they were planting shrubs beneath my office window, "This is just like making a baby. You just dig a hole and put in the seed and watch it grow."

How did their attention to the natural surroundings affect the way the children learned in general? They came to our school to build a basic foundation that would support their education for years to come. The landscape offered them a rich resource for scientific investigation, observation and calculation. Its animal habitats, vegetation and water invited them to explore and discover. It compelled them to describe its beauty in words, colors and shapes that they had never used before. Its history told them about Revolutionary battles, Lenape tribes and the farmers of Maidenhead. Its woodlands were a sanctuary for birds. Its garden called for laborers and harvesters. Yes, the children learned a lot from their landscape—but most important of all was that through engaging with it, they came to love and understand the world around them more deeply. They cared enough to become responsible. Their powers of perception penetrated other parts of their lives. The building of a strong academic foundation depends on one's engagement, one's caring enough to understand more deeply, and one's sense of responsibility. In the light of wisdom, one thing leads to another.

———⁓———

In the spring before I retired, our school's neighbor, Edward, invited me over to his house. I went with some reluctance as he seldom called me without a complaint about our students kicking balls over his fence—or our night lights disturbing his sleep. To my surprise he offered me a glass of wine and asked me to sit down. "I hear you are about to retire. Is there anything at the school that you have wanted to do but haven't had the money to do?" I hesitated, reviewing the many things the school couldn't afford, such as new computers, or a school van. "Those are commendable, but I meant something YOU have wanted that maybe nobody else would think of—something special . . ."

I began to see what he was getting at. "Well, Edward, this may seem crazy to you, but I have always wanted to see a labyrinth laid out in the school's woods."

"A labyrinth? What for?" I knew he'd be skeptical.

"To be a place where people can retreat from the busy life of the school and have some time alone, to think." I remembered Andrea's Alone Place.

Edward frowned. "How would you go about making it?"

"I'd give the project to one of the classes. They could study the ancient world and work up a design such as a Cretan labyrinth. Then they would map it out mathematically.

"What material would you need?"

"River stones."

Edward took a sip of his wine and thought a while.

"Are you sure you want to do this? How much would it cost? Where would you find the stone?"

"River stone is expensive because it's rare. There's a quarry along the Delaware River that sells it. Probably about $4,000.00."

Edward grunted, fished a check from his jacket pocket and wrote in an amount to cover the cost of a labyrinth. "Don't forget to clear the dead wood and poison ivy first."

The labyrinth took a few weeks to design and build. The fourth grade students were studying ancient Greece at the time, so I challenged them to create a Cretan labyrinth in the northeast corner of the school grounds. They spent days measuring and staking. They lined the path with smooth river stones that were chosen individually from the Delaware Quarry. Every stone bears the fingerprint of the child who placed it. When the project was finished, I invited Edward to come and walk it and see for himself what a powerful experience it was.

My grumpy angel winced. "No, thank you very much."

Unlike the simple spiral set in the grass years before, the path of this labyrinth wound around trees, reversing and advancing until it finally reached a center encircled by small boulders. The path to the center is now carpeted by emerald-green moss. In the fall, the surrounding maple trees gild its curves with golden leaves.

> While I sit under his roof of green leaves
> He guards me.
> While I stare up at his great branches
> He guards me.
> While I play in his shade
> He guards me.
> He is my guardian, the Norway Maple,
> And I will stay here for now and cherish him.
>
> Student

The labyrinth is a place of peace and beauty, a place apart, where dappled light, wild roses, and alternating birdcalls provide a sanctuary for the occasional visitor. For many, the journey to the center of the labyrinth rekindles the spirit that underlies all learning. Wisdom leads one to linger there.

One of the children in Grade IV came up with the following words, which are now affixed to a boulder at the entrance to the labyrinth.

> A labyrinth is an ancient symbol that represents wholeness.
> It is said to help you find your inner self, to give you courage,
> wisdom, power, dignity, and love. This labyrinth is made
> with six tons of river stone. We all helped shift and move
> the stone. We were taught about the energy the labyrinth
> supplies to people who walk its powerful, spiraling path. It
> will always be here and will represent our efforts and our
> gift for many years to come. We invite you to find your
> inner self. Who knows what you will find there?
>
> Student

The statement is followed by the request: "Please remain SILENT as you walk the Labyrinth. Thank you." I have often seen children skip or trot along the mossy path to the center, but rarely do I hear a word.

Whereas the journey suggested by the nautilus is outward from the center, the journey suggested by the labyrinth is inward to the center. This is an important distinction for a child. In the labyrinth, as one moves ever nearer to the center, things that have been widely separated become more closely connected. At our center lies wisdom that envelops every aspect of life, both here and now, and beyond our knowing.

I believe the labyrinth located the spiritual center of the Learning through Landscapes program. In all the turning and returning, tracking and backtracking of our life as a school family, we were and still are following a path toward our own center and mission.

—⁓—

While walking the halls one September morning, I paused outside a classroom door, captivated by the sight of children listening intently to their teacher. They were all leaning forward on their desks while her words wound around them like a hug. "We're here to explore. You'll discover new ways to find out information, learn it, and share it with others. But most important of all, I want to know what each one of you is most curious about. What do *you* want to learn? What is your question? Whatever it is, write it down on a piece of paper." They did so. For the remainder of the year, those scraps of paper were woven into the basic curriculum so skillfully that the overall fabric was seamless. No child's curiosity was cut off; they learned more as a group than they would have learned individually.

One teacher had a passion for birdlife. So did her class—although at first, they didn't know how or why. She led them into a study of birds early in the year. She knew a great deal about the subject and gave them countless experiences of bird watching, identifying, feeding, and tracking. Throughout the year, each child carried out research into the life cycle of his or her favorite bird. In the spring, each wrote and presented a research paper accompanied by photographs, drawings, poems, and stories, as well as a replica of the bird formed by the child's own hand.

> Do you remember building the cage for the papier-mâché hawk and how, after applying three layers, we put it in the shower to dry and my little brother turned the shower on?
>
> Student

> The bird in flight then became a bird perching on a branch. It was a family event we all participated in, for better or for worse.
>
> Parent

The handmade birds were beautifully and lovingly executed. The children gave their reports to other classes and their bird sculptures were exhibited for all to see. To top it all off, the students took a trip to the Raptor Trust, where they could observe the birds they had studied.

> Glowing eyes beside an oak tree,
> They seem to be watching me.
> As the snow falls from the sky above
> An owl watches over me,
> Over me as I watch over him.
> As the snow falls from the sky above
> Everything seems to be still.
> All of this time the owl has been watching over me,
> Watching me,
> And always will be.
>
> Student

I believe that the children's yearlong curiosity about birds was due in large part to their teacher's passion. Essential to experiential learning is the fusion of passion and curiosity. In a child, this synthesis releases extraordinary energy, along with the will to learn whatever skills are necessary to satisfy his or her hunger for knowledge. Through the bird projects, children acquired skills in observing, recording, researching, rendering, and communicating, to name a few. They were hardly aware how many skills they had mastered. Perhaps they were even less aware that they had opened the door to a greater understanding of their own wisdom.

> We researched our birds in class. Soon spring break started and we began our projects and rough drafts. We made life-sized replicas of our birds. When we got back to school we read fantastic books about our birds. We saw cool movies with some of our birds flying. We finished our rough drafts and started our final copies. We later finished our beautiful and colorful projects. We then put our birds on display. We finished our final copies and put them with our birds. We enjoyed the birds of prey unit. I hope you have enjoyed my article.
>
> Student

Other comments about the project:

"I was excited to present my memorized facts to the kindergarten class and give an oral presentation."

"I liked that everyone in the class had a different approach to making the bird sculptures."

"It was great to see my bird at the Raptor Trust."

"I liked spending time with my family working on the project."

"It was fun dissecting the owl pellets. We found bones and vertebrae."

"I liked time writing poems because we got time to sit and think about our birds."

"On Grandparents Day it was the third time making my presentation. I felt better about myself because I improved every time."

Not only did the children gain confidence while learning through experience; this way of teaching also gave our teachers confidence. The school was transforming them by enabling them to try methods they might not try elsewhere. They took chances, and I trusted that their endeavors would bear fruit. They did. Children acquired knowledge far beyond the circumference of their curriculum. Not only did they learn to read, write, and compute; not only did they develop self-discipline, tolerance, and compassion; their spirits also soared and they had *fun*. Often, they were reluctant to leave at the end of the day.

Lest you think that this description of the educational process is mere fantasy, it is not. Lest you wonder whether the children in our school ever "sobered up," given the heady draught of play that imbued their earliest academics, they did. They took cognitive learning seriously and acquired knowledge by use of reasoning, perception, and critical thinking. However, we never allowed them to forget their natural endowment: wisdom. For wisdom was the source of their creativity. Creativity was their key to developing new and original ideas, relationships, or plans. They played with words, concepts, and strategies, looking for chances to match what they were learning with what they already knew. We heard the cry, "I got it!" when their wisdom was released and they moved from being into becoming. There was a spiritual dynamic at work here. Not to acknowledge spiritual awakening in education is to be asleep at the wheel.

> The amazing thing is how all these projects became family events . . . We all saw the project constructed from start to finish and listened to many practice sessions of the oral report. [Our son] was reliving his many years at Princeton Junior School through the projects that served as milestones in his educational life. As we visited schools, his hand was often raised, asking if this particular school asked students to do research projects and what form they took. He wanted to make sure that this exciting and satisfying form of learning was also practiced in his next school . . .

> I realized how much we had each learned about a particular subject and how much we learned about each other . . . Each project has been a wonderful milestone representing time spent together watching him make decisions, creating visuals with a variety of materials, putting facts and pieces together, and presenting them in a cohesive and intelligent form. Most of all, it has been wonderful to see how he felt about himself at the end of each accomplishment, each project getting better and more put-together as the years went on. It is seeing the nautilus shell with its progressive

chambers growing and deepening with complexity . . . It
is a great way to measure a journey of learning.

—⟋⟍—

Learning through Landscapes enables a child to perceive what is
unfamiliar or even dangerous about nature and make it safe, accessible
and familiar. However, there have been times when I have feared nature's
fury, despite knowing that storms exhaust themselves. I have feared
people's fury, despite knowing that tantrums burn themselves out. I
have feared anxiety's fury, despite knowing that worries implode. Over
time, I have learned that fury has limited power and often fizzles out
like a firecracker. I have seen rage dissolve into giggles. Despite fury's
fleeting moments, I have found that fear is not so easily dismissed.
When other things have been put aside, fear can remain in the soul for
quite a while, waiting patiently for opportunities to destroy faith.

There have been times when Mother Nature has dealt such a heavy
blow that my trust in her has faltered, and I have learned more from
the landscape than I ever wanted to know.

Crashing blue thunder, loud booms on the clear water, wet
rushing ocean.

Student

Today, I am looking through the window at the colossal waves that
heave against a beach along the New Jersey shoreline. The setting sun
that peers through the clouds after hours of rain is gilding the sea foam
with an unearthly light. This gorgeous natural phenomenon before
my eyes is the "low" of a hurricane gone astray. Rather than whip the
beach to a pulp, the storm has wandered out to sea, leaving its beautiful
breakers to merely slap the sand. How different this spectacle is from
the one long ago, when the same stretch of shoreline was attacked by a
hurricane so fierce that people fled for their lives. My family was living
at the shore at the time, during my father's stint with the US Army Air

Corp. It was late afternoon when the winds flew in, whipping us as we ran home from school. With great relief, my mother greeted us at the door and ordered us to stay away from the windows. We huddled in the hallway until military trucks arrived to evacuate families who lived along the beach. Crammed like sardines into the truck bed, we forged through streets flooded by sea water to a distant hotel. My heart leapt when I spotted my father waiting for us with arms outstretched to receive his wide-eyed, terrified Davie.

People were running in every direction, shouting at the tops of their lungs in order to be heard over the screaming wind. We were herded into a huge ballroom on the eleventh floor of the hotel. It was all horribly confusing. Chandeliers swayed overhead. Everyone rushed to the windows to watch the Steel Pier float out to sea, the cage doors of its zoo banging back and forth, freeing frantic creatures to leap into the waves. We watched, spellbound, as human figures dove off the pier, the ferris wheel reeling above them. Then the glass windows began to blow in and we scrambled for cover under a mammoth oriental rug. My father never let go of Davie, who was trembling from limb to limb. Retrieved again by the military, we and hundreds of others were taken from the drenched ballroom to a huge underground convention center. Through this pitch-black maze, we groped hand in hand, following Davie's cries as he clung to my father's shoulders. Bravery was beyond my reach. I felt that the world had dumped me upside down. The prospect of becoming separated from my family in such a teeming, airless underground tunnel filled me with terror. At last, after several twists and turns, we reached a large room that contained two sofas and some easy chairs. My panic somewhat assuaged, I fell into a fitful sleep for the rest of that night on one of the sofas, head to foot with my older brother. The roar of wind and water far above intensified my vivid dreams of people plunging into the waves beneath the tottering ferris wheel. Would they ever be seen again?

> Devastating waves,
> Dangerous to many things;
> Lives changed forever.

> Student

The following day, the storm subsided, and we emerged from the soggy hole to return to our neighborhood. The streets were jammed with cars lying upside down in the sand. One school bus had found its way onto someone's front porch. The boardwalk lay strewn all over the beach as far as the eye could see. Amid the twisted rubble, a zebra munched coarse dune grass. Our neighbor's house was tilted. Another house was split in two—half on one side of the street and half on the other. We found our house to be in comparatively good shape, with furniture piled up in the corners and sand everywhere. The fright of the night lessened when I discovered Goldie, my pet fish, swimming serenely in her bowl inside the piano.

The hurricane was classified by insurance companies as a natural disaster, an act of God. The disorientation such chaos caused was undeniable. Yet we, the young survivors of that hurricane, discovered a whole new world to explore. Every day brought new adventure. The scavanging was lovely. The momentous storm had wreaked havoc up and down the beach. Tumultuous waves had washed ashore an extraordinary array of flotsam and jetsam: boat wreckage, auto parts, beds, bicycles, baby carriages, kitchen appliances, lamps, swing sets, not to mention the shards of shells and ceramics that formed little mountains in the gutters. The boardwalk sprawled, half-buried in the sand, its planking smashed beyond repair, its twisted steel railings providing tangles of treasures for such scavengers as ourselves. One day, while swinging upside down from one of these railings, we spotted two small monkeys watching us with great curiosity from a safe spot. Freed from their cages, they had miles of beach to roam in search of interesting sights.

Terror doesn't fade easily, even though we found ways to make the most of the mess the storm had created. For years, I cringed at the sound of thunder. During one summer, a merciless camp director, knowing full well of my terror, decided to teach me a lesson by assigning me to spend the night in the horse barn whenever an electric storm threatened. Her theory was that I would conquer my fear by throwing burlap bags over the heads of panicking ponies and leading them out of the burning barn to safety. I spent those barn nights in anxious anticipation, wondering which pony I should pick to bear me out of the barn with my head in a bag.

The way the owl winked at me,
The fierce eyes staring,
Peering out through the dark elm—
It's given me a fright,
Yet somehow has made me
Braver, has given me hope,
Strength to overcome all
My fears.

Student

The question I put to all who teach is: how can we help children find a way to alleviate their fears? Their inner wisdom is there, waiting to be known and shown. Our school enables children to explore the world of the community and the world of nature, as well as the world within themselves. But when, as in the case of a hurricane or an abusive camp director, a child's confidence is shattered, fear takes control. I look back on Jose's situation and think that he and I had to meet one-on-one in order to build mutual trust before it was too late.

In the education of children, opportunities for fear are recurrent. As Franklin D. Roosevelt so eloquently stated in his inaugural address, ". . . the only thing we have to fear is fear itself—nameless, unreasoning, unjustified terror which paralyzes needed efforts to convert retreat into advance." Roosevelt was referring to the suffering caused by the Great Depression. I am referring to the depression of children when their wisdom is threatened. Fortunately, children are resilient by nature and able to spring back quickly.

Fear had no place in our school—neither then nor now. I pray unendingly for the children I know, that throughout their lives they may reflect God's image deep within their souls. When their hunger for growth is satisfied, they are transfigured. When they find themselves in a situation that neglects or frustrates them, the image fades. Neglect disfigures, sometimes indelibly. Depriving a child of the miracle of his or her own being is the closest thing to evil that I know.

When faced with or defaced by an abusive person, in particular a beloved person, children sometimes shrink behind whatever armor fits— e.g. lying, cheating, stealing, or bullying. They sometimes internalize their pain in order to please or placate the abuser. They sometimes try to restore adult rifts. I once heard a child beg his divorcing parents to give him another chance. Whatever children do to assuage their fear, the resultant depression is gravely injurious. In situations of injustice, neglect, rejection, or abuse, their spirits may be scorched—or even worse, may flicker and die.

> I got stitches at the hospital where she hit me but it was by accident. I wasn't listening and so my mom got mad and the accident happened.
>
> Student

—⚘—

Adults involved in childrearing need to do everything possible to honor the wisdom of children while teaching them the tools of life's trade. As children tend to learn from the inside out, we must listen to their cues as we reach for them from the outside in. Only then can they naturally and confidently protect their vulnerable selves from blows dealt later in life by breaches of their trust or innocence. For children who long for the deep satisfactions of love, responsibility, and freedom, our society leaves much to be desired.

> Stay where you are or else—
> They bite you if you don't watch it.
> Eat your greens or else they will eat it for you.
> Get out of the way, Ah!
> Ouch, that hurt!
> Slow-moving animals coming through,
> All day long they eat like a horse
> Under some trees.
> Run for your life!
> Use your hands and say good-bye,
> Say, Goodbye Dino! Goodbye!
>
> Student

I believe that calamities wrought by humans are more devastating than natural disasters. We children of the Second World War years were apprehensive about a possible enemy attack. My father was the head of the Personnel Division of the Air Force. Memories of our two years in Arlington, Virginia, form a frightening collage of whispers behind closed doors, blaring air raid drills in the middle of the night, bloody stories in the comic books, propaganda leaflets that seemed to have dropped from the sky with images of Nazis torturing American children—all convinced us that the enemy hated children, probably the children near Washington most, and that our lives could be snuffed out in a moment.

How did we cope with our anxiety? As usual, we children retreated to our imaginations. War games provided a perfect way for us to handle our souls' disorder. On the battlefield of our school playground we learned to shoot with our fingers, taunt with our tongues, and twist truth without consequences. Our teacher was tense a good bit of the time; she sent the rowdiest classmates to the janitor to be spanked. Although I was never suffered his yardstick, I was in the target zone a good deal of the time. My tormentors regarded me as the new kid on the block, a "creepy yankee" whose northern accent and orthopedic boots provided subjects for their scorn. I was neither a Catholic nor a Jew, just a wasp. I remember one day being stoned while on my way home from school because I had told my enemies when they demanded to know what religion I belonged to that I was a Protestant. Never a courageous fighter in the field, I spoiled my homecoming by pulling the wings off of butterflies, grabbing the food dish from our hungry dog, needling my brother and stealing from a guest's purse. I earned myself a break from school by proclaiming exposure to scarlet fever. My exploits were those of a young casualty of war games.

Recently, I watched a news clip about children who live in one of the war-torn regions of the Middle East. After slowly delivering shocking images of a bombed-out neighborhood, the video finally zeroed in on a group of children of all ages—playing hopscotch amid the rubble. War must have become so real to them that they resorted to peace games.

———

All in all, the school family was at peace, holding within its hug a hodgepodge of multicolored and multicultural folk. Yet, as in all families, there were times when crises—both personal and public— brought everything to a standstill. Rebounding from shocks was never easy, but thanks to the extraordinary efforts of many, the school recovered and discovered an even greater unity.

On the morning of September 11, 2001, our custodian frantically dragged the school's television into my office. There, several of us watched in disbelief as first one, and then the other World Trade Center tower collapsed to the ground. Was this spectacle an earth quake—or was it man-made? With mounting alarm, we viewed the same images over and over, now seeing the planes that perforated the buildings' sides. We could only watch, wait, and wonder while listening to TV commentators' babble. My vision clouded with memories from my childhood: Could this be the end of the world? Will whatever it is come this way? Then came the plea of all mothers: "Oh, God, where are my children? Please save them from harm!"

My fears were abruptly jarred by the telephone. The voice on the other end pleaded, "Will you take care of my child? I've got to find my husband. He works in New York."

"We'll take good care of Sasha, don't worry."

The terror of the other mother's voice yanked me out of my panic and I looked around at the people in my office. They were frozen. All past and future seemed bound together in this moment. "God, help us to remain calm and act wisely." We turned off the TV for the time being, held one another's hands, formed a circle, and prayed for strength to quell our fears and do what we believed God wanted us to do now: take care of the Princeton Junior School family. Perhaps the courage that I mustered at that moment came from a boy angel clinging to my shoulders and crying out how to go.

While five of us were gathered in my office, the rest of the staff and faculty were busy with the children and had no idea what was going on. An FBI agent whom we had scheduled to come that morning appeared out of nowhere to begin the fingerprinting that the New Jersey Association of Independent Schools required for accreditation. Somehow, his presence and purpose added to the unreality of the morning.

I shall never forget the courage of my colleagues. Telephones began to ring off their hooks. One of us answered them to assure callers that school would remain in session for as long as there were children to be cared for—even overnight, if necessary. The mother who had called us initially called again and again. Her questions were shared by dozens of others: Had their spouses made it to work that morning? Were they alive? Were they in the blizzard of ashes that fell over the fleeing crowds in lower Manhattan? I tried to calm people's fears, but it was hard to do when I, too, teetered. In a weak moment, I darted out of the schoolhouse, jumped into my car and raced down the road, propelled by an apparent need to mollify one of our parents. About a half mile into the dash, I realized that I was running away from the very place where I should be, where I *must* be. I mustered what little courage I had and turned around.

Two of us made the rounds of the classrooms to give the teachers a moment to come to my office to learn about the cataclysm that had just occurred fifty miles from our doorstep. They were visibly shaken. Time hung in the balance as we talked over what to do. Should we inform the children? No, I told each of them to go back and conduct their classes as usual. They should have as normal a day as possible. It would be better for their parents to communicate (or not) what had happened in the outer world today.

The teachers were as anxious as I was—about their spouses, their children, and their responsibilities to a school full of other people's children. How could we keep fear at bay? I felt that telling the children about the explosion in the big world would thrust them into an anxiety that they could not understand or control. I remembered all too well how it felt to be gripped by storms beyond my control, some of which were man-made. I was determined to do everything in my power to preserve the peace at 90 Fackler Road.

Some children were picked up early. Other children waited indefinitely as one or both of their commuting parents searched for a way home. We dreaded to think that some parents might never come home. To our enormous relief, a call came through that afternoon from the "lost" husband. He was safe, alive, but unable to get through to his wife. He had missed his train that morning, had avoided being mashed in the mayhem of downtown Manhattan, and was now trying to find a train to bring him home. For a while, we were the conduit through which a number of other parents communicated with one another. News broke that two other planes had headed for Washington, one hitting its mark at the Pentagon and the other hitting the ground in Pennsylvania. Could we be in the next line of fire? Everyone was scared. It took several hours before we knew whether our commuters were dead or alive. Fortunately, none of them was killed.

Somehow we got through the day. Parents were found, families were united, and the doors of the school closed in the early evening. We had done everything we could to give the children what they had dashed into school for that morning for: a day of fearless learning.

As I suspected, parents differed widely in their opinions regarding how much to tell their children. Some preferred to keep the news from them altogether. Others told them everything, with TV images included. One father even took his four year old son to the smoking abyss to "learn history." Needless to say, September 12 was ablaze with children's interpretations, most of which showed up in their play. As I wandered around the school to see how everyone was doing, I noticed a group of children in the play ground's sand area. They were flailing their fists and shouting terrorist threats as they demolished the elaborate sandcastle they had just built. Later that day, I came across a different group of children engaged in block-building in The Commons. There stood two very tall towers amid countless other, lower block buildings. I overheard one boy remark, "We just need to build them up again." I left them to continue their play. Children had reminded me once again: if you let fear overwhelm faith, you will miss a new beginning, new trust, new life and a new testament of God's love.

Having read and listened to a number of opinions, I came to the conclusion that children need not revisit the events of 9/11 while at Princeton Junior School. Their families had a wide range of strategies to handle such overwhelming information. Rather, we should focus on activities which emphasized the good, the creative and hopeful aspects of human nature, and we should address children's individual concerns as positively and simply as possible.

In the October following 9/11, I reported to the Trustees.

The world has changed irrevocably. It is more important than ever for children to learn basic skills—not only in academics, but also in human relations, assuming the latter is required for survival. Working with children as we have during the past fortnight, we are reminded that in the beginning, they want to create, in order to help and to heal. It is our hope and prayer that, as they grow into maturity, they are motivated not by fear, but by faith in their God-given strength.

J.

In November, I reported again to the Trustees.

It is apparent that children are weathering the after-effects of September 11, although the general tone of the school is more shrill than in previous years. Teachers have experienced occasional episodes of jittery behavior on the part of both parents and children. Efforts are being made through the Gather Round program and Coffee with Juliana to calm people down. For all of us, a sense of family at school is of paramount importance. Despite these ripples, the year is off to a good start.

J.

—⁓—

Children are apt to dive into the wake of bad news and wonder how they can rescue people. They do so not because they know how, but rather because they are so passionate about life that they will do all they can to bring it back again when it gets lost. For instance, the question, "Can we do something for the people who had the tsunami?" hung in the air until we sent off some clothing. Soon after 9/11, a child asked, "Can we do something for the people who got hurt?" There was no doubt in my mind that "doing something" was important to children who wanted to express their compassion and find their own solutions through hands-on projects that they created themselves.

The child was waiting for an answer. "We will find a way to help. In the meantime, we can do something every day here at school to help those people. Close your eyes for a minute. Imagine that you have a bow and arrow. Now find a piece of love in your heart. Shoot it with your bow and arrow—all the way to those people who have been hurt. Somehow, they will feel the love you have shot to them and that will make them better. You will feel better too, my love."

—◆—

Fear appears in many forms, some enlarged by our imagination. Often, when our vision is dimmed in the shadow of our fears, we need to remind ourselves that for every shadow, there is a corresponding source of light. A case in point is documented in my Headmistress's Report in October, 2003:

> I was beginning to worry about the School's breathless beginning when I remembered that new life often gasps before it stirs, and stirs before it stands. This fall the opening of School was marked by unpredictable circumstances: the deaths of two parents and a teacher's husband, the absence of classroom space for Spanish, music, drama, and special services, the no-show of a teacher on the first day of School, the falling of plaster from The Commons' ceiling and the shortage of lunch help. However, we are fortunate to have been spared by the Lawrenceville Tornado, to have been featured in The Princeton Packet, Lawrence Ledger, and TV's WBZN News, to receive an unexpected gift of prime property in Atlantic Highlands, and—most important of all—to have 131 students eager to enter the school every day. Let us count our blessings.
>
> J.

I cannot continue without mentioning with deep gratitude the unexpected gift of a property in Atlantic Highlands. The giver was Tom

Simpson, a great friend of Jim and me who had discerned a parallel between the educational philosophy of his late mother's school and our own. A creative individual, Tom had spent his life transforming properties from "almost lost" to "remarkably found." Having given away two other properties to institutions of higher learning, he chose Princeton Junior School to be his third beneficiary and left America with a knapsack on his back to spend the rest of his life in Italy. We were stunned by his generosity. Although it was tempting to keep the house on the New Jersey shore, we sold it and launched a capital campaign with the proceeds. Tom's memory lives on in the shell forms that he crafted for his garden in Atlantic Highlands and that we have placed here and there in our school garden beds. The concrete scallop shells beneath the berry bushes of the Library Garden were handmade by this loving, modest angel.

—◦◦◦—

Children are vulnerable. Paradoxically, the "childish" qualities of openness and trust that can be easily exploited are, in fact, the very qualities that lead to creative transformation. Like the biblical character David, children may seem to have relatively little to sling when faced with the Goliaths of life. However, the stone they have in their pockets is wisdom. They have already used it to overcome many a mammoth in their path. If we educate them to trust in themselves and use the wisdom that God has given them, they will work miracles. How can we assure them that the stone in their slings is their most powerful weapon? We must look them in the eye, listen for what lies behind their words, laugh with, not at them, love them, and learn from them. We must not undervalue their daily transformations. Our world hungers for wisdom of the kind these children sling.

—◦◦◦—

When I was a child, I had a friend named Billy who taught me how to smoke, shoplift, and sneak into cinemas by way of the fire door. Our smoking was discovered by my mother who cured us of the habit by insisting that we smoke corn silk instead. Our shoplifting came to a halt when a saleswoman in the Five-and-Ten Cent Store caught us red-handed and sent us to the manager. Considering our ages, he kindly but firmly told us that there would be severe consequences "next time." Our furtive film-viewing ended when we tiptoed through the Garden Theatre's fire exit right into the arms of a policeman. Despite Billy's cunning, he had no common sense. One day, while in the middle of proposing marriage to me, he asked for a loan of two dollars. He knew that I had two dollars in change, thanks to that morning's clean sweep of the news stand on Nassau Street. I didn't want to give up my bounty—either now or in a future marriage.

Although that proposal diminished Billy's allure, I was not finished with stealing. Money, chocolate chip cookies, honors that belonged to others were all my pickings during the time of my life when I most wanted to be noticed and praised. I suspect that my misdemeanors were not uncommon among children my age.

However, a few years later when a student in the eighth grade, I was brought up short. During a test, the teacher left the room for a few minutes. People started to ask one another for answers to questions on the test. I allowed a neighboring student to copy answers off my paper. At the end of class, we all handed in our tests and proceeded to the lunchroom. The following hour was replete with accusations—the non-cheaters accusing the cheaters of cheating. No one pointed a guilty finger at me or my accomplice, much to our relief. After lunch, six of the cheaters marched themselves to the Headmistress' office, confessed their crimes and were suspended for three days. I glided into school the next day unabashed—until our teacher announced that the Headmistress required the whole school to attend a "special assembly" that morning. As I entered the auditorium, my stomach was churning.

The headmistress began to speak in measured terms: "Thank you all for coming. I won't take much of your time. However, I need to inform you that six of your fellow students have just been suspended. By cheating on a test, they have violated one of our school's cardinal rules of conduct: integrity. Therefore, they must take the consequences." The Headmistress paused while a general murmur swept through the audience. "Nevertheless, I want you to know that rarely in my time as your Headmistress have I been so proud of six young women. They adhered to the highest moral principles by coming to me and admitting their mistakes. They knew full well that they had done the wrong thing and they had the courage to face the consequences. For such a turnabout I have the highest respect. I do hope you will feel the same and welcome them back in three days' time."

I was stunned. It took me five years to confess to the eighth grade teacher that I, too, had cheated on that day. She looked at me thoughtfully, shook her head and smiled. "You've lived with your guilt for five years? You've paid the price. Let it go."

—*m*—

Once we were on the school bus, returning home from a field trip to Baltimore's Inner Harbor. We had visited the National Aquarium, taken a water taxi to Fort William, and dined at the Cheesecake Factory. The children had spent some time buzzing around the Inner Harbor in search of souvenirs. Each had brought five dollars to spend, so everyone on the bus had something to show off—unless it had already been eaten. I sank back into the unforgiving bus seat and listened with half an ear to the excited chatter of the twelve travelers, until one comment caught my attention.

"Hey, take a look at what Brucey got! Where'd you find that? Cost a lot more than five dollars, I'll bet." I peered down the aisle at the boy in question, but he slid further toward the window, out of my sight. It was too dark to see what had caught people's attention, and I was too tired to check out the inquiry. I slept most of the way back.

The following day, the fifth-graders' trip to Baltimore made headlines with the younger children who looked forward to the day when they, too, would make the trip. The Commons during lunch hour hummed with stories, not the least of which was the story of Bruce's souvenir. I approached Bruce's table. Like a king, he lolled amid a cluster of pawns, rotating his wrist slowly so as to display the watch that he had procured in Baltimore.

"Bruce, when you are finished your lunch, please come to my office." His eyes clouded as he dismissed his admirers and jammed a half-eaten banana into his lunchbox. A few minutes later, he appeared at my office door. "Come in and shut the door behind you. I have a question." By this time, Bruce had regained his composure and was able to settle easily into a chair across from mine. I searched his face for a clue to his thoughts, but found there a carefully emptied stare. Beyond repair? Could this handsome lad, groomed to perfection by affluence, be wanting? I leaned forward and took his left hand in mine.

"Let me see this watch, Bruce. You bought it yesterday? Where?"

"At one of the booths near the water. Everybody found stuff there."

"What did it cost?"

"You told us to bring only five dollars. That's what I did."

"It looks like a very fine watch for only five dollars. Did you bring extra money with you?"

"No. I just said what I brought."

"May I have it for a moment, please?" Bruce reluctantly loosened the wristband and gave me the watch. I turned it over. It was a Tissot. "Bruce, I believe this watch is worth a lot more than five dollars—more like three hundred and fifty. Now, look at me straight and answer my question. How did you buy it? Did you use a credit card?"

"My card's at home. My parents don't allow me to take it on school trips."

I judged from Bruce's polished veneer that credit cards were no mystery. "Bruce, if you really wanted or needed a watch, I expect you would have only to ask for one. Am I right?"

"Maybe."

"So why did you settle for one you found in a vendor's booth? Why not Brooks Brothers?"

"It was more fun this way."

"What was more fun? Did you bargain?"

"I just watched other people bargaining and trying them on."

"And you tried one on as well?"

"Sort of. Someone else took it off and left it on the counter." Bruce stopped abruptly. The story had gone too far to retrieve.

"Bruce, I think I know what happened. I did the same thing once."

Bruce's eyes, fully loaded, met mine. I continued: "Look, Bruce, I'm inviting you to tell me the whole story. Don't hide from me; I'm not here to punish you. Don't hide from your true self. You may get lost. If you continue to do things like this, you will be severely punished."

The truth crawled out: Bruce had simply donned the watch and left the scene.

"Thank you for telling me. You have taken off with someone else's property. You realize that you don't really own it, don't you? It still belongs to the vendor in Baltimore. It's his, unless you pay for it."

"Yeah."

"Did the attention you got from others make your shoplifting worthwhile?"

"It did up 'til now."

"So it wasn't simply that you needed the watch to tell the time. Bruce, listen for a minute: the admiration and respect that you most long for comes from somewhere else. It comes from inside you when you stop pretending and do the best you can every day. You'll just feel better. Also, it comes from your friends and others around you as they get to know the real you. No frills are needed. Just be yourself." (I wondered whether his parents had ever told him this.) "Right now, I really admire you because you had the courage to tell me the truth."

"What do you want me to do with the watch?" Bruce asked bluntly.

"I suggest that you write a letter to the vendor in Baltimore and tell him that you have his watch."

"I can't do that! He'll turn me over—"

"I doubt it. The truth sometimes leads people to forgive. It happened to me that way."

Bruce looked incredulous. Eventually, with some prodding, he accepted the letter paper I offered and wrote: "Dear Sir, I took a watch off your counter yesterday and now I am sorry. Sincerely, Bruce."

"How do you plan to return it?"

"Are you going to tell my parents?"

"That's up to you. What more can you say to the vendor?"

Bruce thought long and hard. "I could tell him that I'll pay for it."

"No way! You were only allowed to spend five dollars. Is that fair to the others?"

"I guess not."

"Why don't you tell him that you have only worn it for a few hours and you would like him to inform you how you should return it. Maybe he has a post office box. For now, we have to send your letter by way of the manager of Inner Harbor."

Bruce added another line to the letter asking what would be the best way to return the watch. We sealed and stamped it and I mailed it on my way home. The watch remained in my desk drawer. We never heard back from the vendor. After a month, I called Bruce into the office. "Bruce, we've had no answer from the vendor. What do you think we should do with his watch?"

"I'll take it back next weekend. I'm going down with my parents to see cousins who live in Baltimore."

"Did you tell your parents what you did?"

"Yes."

"What did they say?"

"They said I did the wrong thing but they were proud of me for admitting it. My dad even said I had a lot more courage than he did when he was a kid and stole something."

Following this incident, Bruce's swagger changed to a walk. He downsized his wardrobe. As for me, I was finally able to bury some of my old fears along with his new ones.

———

It was after lunch at Princeton Junior School. I was in my office with the door shut, trying to fight off a snooze while composing a long-overdue report to the New Jersey Association of Independent School's accreditation committee.

Suddenly, shouts of distress came from the play yard outside the window. Two third-graders were brawling. A teacher intervened and the skirmish seemed to die down. I could not hear the discussion that ensued, but eventually the two combatants, one large and the other small, stomped out of the play yard behind the teacher. I wondered how long it might be before they arrived at my office door. I turned again to the required report for the NJAIS accreditation committee. The computer screen stared back at me with the air of an interrogator.

What could I tell the committee about the school's social service program?

There it was: a knock on the door.

"Come in." The two boys shuffled in and stood before me, their chests heaving. "Hello, what's up?"

"Ms. Benson told us to come and see you," the large one mumbled.

"Why? Did she send you to help me write my report?" Not funny. I motioned to them to sit down. "So why *are* you here?"

The small one shrilled, "We were out on the playground and I wasn't doing anything and Burt came up behind me and twisted my arm around and it hurts a lot!"

"He's lying—he always follows me around and whines at me. He never leaves me alone! I'm *not* his babysitter."

"Well, I'm sorry to see you two here. It seems that you have broken the very rules that your whole class agreed upon at the beginning of the year." They hastened to justify themselves.

"No need to prove each other wrong—blame is not what interests me. My ears hear more than your words." Silence.

Feeling the heat of their anger, I could see that this was going nowhere. I asked them to take a deep breath and have a piece of chocolate and think about how each would tell me his side of the story. Meanwhile, I turned off the computer, praying for words beyond the screen. The chocolate helped. The boys sat and stared for a while, waiting for me to begin.

"Listen to your hearts. I wonder whether you haven't broken them as well. Have you forgotten who you are?" Silence. "Let's begin with you, Henry. Tell us your side of the story."

The shrill had gone out of Henry's voice, but within its timbre were the tears that I had heard so often from the victims of the large boy in the other chair. "I wanted to play on the climber but he pushed me off the ladder and told everyone that I was a wimp. He ordered me to go over to the baby swing. I wouldn't. Then he called me a mother———— so I threw sand in his face." Henry's story confirmed my hunch that the brawl had involved more than the heckling of a small boy.

"I never called you that! I said 'thumb-sucker' and you know it. You're just making it up to get me in trouble."

I took a deep breath. "Either way, name-calling will get you nowhere. So, Henry, you threw sand in his face? That could have really messed up his eyes!"

"It served him right. He's always hurting me, even when I'm not near him."

"Nevertheless, we only have one pair of eyes. Henry, do you believe that Burt was telling everybody the truth about you? Think for a minute. Do you agree with him that you are a wimp? Or a baby? Or whatever else he called you?"

We waited while Henry stared hard at what was left of his grimy fingernails. Does truth need to cause such a delay? Finally, with a fleeting look at his adversary, he murmured, "No." A snort from the other chair filled the air.

"Henry, deep inside yourself you know that you're none of the things Burt said about you, so why do you worry? Other people know it as well. Try to remember who you really are and use your willpower. Dig deep. Don't think wimp; think *will*."

"Will?"

"Yes, will. You *will* try to remember how good you are. When you do, you'll become stronger. Don't you see that your fear makes you easy to tease? Now, go over to Burt and take a close look at his eyes. He's not going to bite you." Henry veered around Burt's glare and peered at his eyes. "Do you see any sand in them?"

"Not *in* them, but there's sand around them."

How did it get there?"

"Me."

"Then you're the one to remove it, please." I handed him a tissue that I had moistened with water from the bottle on my desk. Slowly, tentatively, Henry blotted the sand from around the eyes of the boy he feared the most.

I looked on in suspense. "What do you say, Burt?"

"You want me to say thank-you but it still won't take away his whining. You just wait—he'll start all over again as soon as we get out of here."

"He may surprise you. Now, Burt, tell us your side of the story before we all have another chocolate."

"He always whines for attention—"

"Tell your story, not his."

"My story is I can't put up with whining anytime. It hurts my ears so I can't concentrate on getting a thing done."

"What do you want to get done?"

"School stuff. You know what I mean."

"No, I don't know what you mean. What school stuff?"

"Like in class and homework."

"Is homework a problem as well?"

"In my house it is."

"Why is that?"

"At night my baby sister whines all the time so my Dad hollers at her and then my Mom yells at my Dad and he yells back and that hurts my ears."

"Have you ever asked them to stop?"

"Are you kidding? I'd be killed."

Henry was gazing at Burt. "Do you think they'd really kill you—dead?"

"Better me than each other," was the grim reply.

My mind raced through all the conflict resolution solutions I had been taught, but none seemed to fit this impasse. Bully, bullier, bulliest . . . where did it begin? I couldn't erase the memory of Burt coming to school most mornings with his backpack unzipped, with dark rings under his eyes, with his head down. During the course of the year, he had shredded the confidence of several other children and triggered the censure of parents by broadcasting filthy words on the playground. In light of imagined consequences, I had let the matter alone, despite the urgings of some colleagues who supported the view that Burt would be better off in a different home as well as a different school.

"Burt, have you ever known a bully?" Silence. "Well, right here in this room, there's a bully who needs to make things right. Do you have any ideas?"

"Who, me? I'm O.K. I don't mind being the way I am. I like it. This kid's a whiner".

"Do you think you'll become any stronger or safer by making Henry look weak? Why did he have to resort to throwing sand in your eyes to get back at you for the way you treated him? What are you afraid of, Burt?"

"Nothing scares me. He could have blinded me!"

"Yes, that's true. Throwing sand is extremely dangerous, as Henry knows. But to get back to bullying: there must be a better way than twisting someone's arm for you to show everybody how strong you are."

"I could lift weights."

"Don't be funny. Weights may make muscle but they don't guarantee strength."

"What do you mean?"

"I'm talking about *root* strength, not brute strength. You know about trees. What feeds a tree?"

Burt sighed as if doing me a favor. "Roots."

"Right. When a tree has a strong root system, it's healthy. It'll put out branches for birds or even boys to build houses in. It'll provide shade during the hot summer. You're like a tree, Burt; when you become deeply rooted, you'll grow and help others to become strong as well. You'll have nothing to fear."

"I told you I'm not afraid of nothing, Mrs. McIntyre."

For a while, Burt stared at a tree outside the window. It was a tree that he had helped to plant two years before. Was he listening? What was he thinking? Were we going to stand by and watch this bully burn out the other children at the school? His future and the future of the school were both at stake. I had to douse the flame now. I had appealed to his wisdom so that he could become a source of strength for others.

"You may not be afraid of anything, Burt, but bullying won't make you any stronger. When you clobber somebody smaller than you, you break the taproot that feeds you. It isn't worth it! What you did was wrong. You're twisting your own arm behind your back."

"Yeah, and it hurts a lot," crooned the small voice from the other chair.

I suspected that Burt's helplessness at home was recycling in the form of bully brawls that were tearing the fabric of the school apart.

I pushed on: "Furthermore, Burt, you're hurting the school that loves you. If you don't believe me, ask your teachers. You'd be surprised. They love you and know you are truly a good person who wants to learn and make friends. It will take willpower, but you can do it. You will become a tall, proud leader who is a source of strength to all around you."

Burt's eyes returned to squint at the chocolates. "You giving me the same spiel you gave him?"

"In some ways, yes. You two have a lot in common. Deep down in the soil of this school, you are the same size."

My words dangled in the air. Could either of these boys possibly know how much I loved them? They needed to believe how good they were, both of them. The whole point of this school was to provide them with a place where they could help one another to learn and grow.

Burt retorted, "What you say isn't going to make my sister shut up. She's the one who starts trouble in my family."

"Perhaps, but she's so little that she can't tell people what hurts her. I take it you haven't twisted her arm?"

"Not yet. She's just a baby."

About to be yanked from her birthright? I felt the pressure rising in my veins. "Listen, we're in this school family together to build each other up, not to tear each other down. It has to be this way if we are ever going to get anywhere in life. In this family, you are brothers who need to help each other to succeed. Whining and bullying are not in the ballpark. If you feel stuff like that coming on, please remember who you truly are and use your will to overcome it. That's what courage is all about." I passed the chocolates. "Whenever you see someone's heart breaking, don't ignore it—try to mend it. You have the power within you to do so when you believe in yourselves and in each other! I need your help to make this school a place where everyone feels safe and free, and where it is fun to learn. *Please*. Do you both understand?"

"Yeah." Their voices finally harmonized.

We all stood up. Should I have asked them to shake hands and apologize to one another? Probably. But instead, I asked them whether they had ever wanted to be friends. Yeah—once, long ago, before the fights. Then the hit-or-miss question: would they like to be friends again? The boys slowly nodded. I asked them to place their hands between mine. For a precious moment I felt their palms pulsating between my own. Then, suddenly, they were gone.

Relieved that the "hearing" was over, I returned to my report about social services at Princeton Junior School. Once again, I sensed that it was I who was on trial. We had discussed the problem of bullying often in faculty and staff meetings. Should I call the Division of Youth and Family Services, as some teachers had insisted that I do, to suggest there was domestic violence in Burt's household? There were no signs of physical abuse on Burt's large frame. Would DYFS shape Burt's future? If I put off calling DYFS, would I and/or the school be accused of neglect? What would the Board of Trustees say? Or the accreditation committee? That this is a school where bullies are fed chocolate and advised to follow the devices of their own hearts? This situation was 'make or break' for both the school and me. I put my head down on my desk and prayed for wisdom.

As it turned out, I stood my ground on behalf of the bully, hoping that we could solve the problem within the school rather than have him labeled by social services as a problem kid who would become 'a case.' In the following weeks, Burt's parents filed for divorce, cursed me for devaluing their son, and withdrew him from our school. We never saw him again. A year later, I heard that he was doing very well in another school. A model of citizenship, he was on the honor roll and had lots of friends. An unexpected and welcome solution!

Needless to say, Henry became ebullient.

In the carousel of childhood, children reach for the gold ring of courage whenever they get a chance. Although they know that to attain courage they sometimes have to lean way out, to grab and hold on, they believe that they will recover balance somehow. To them, the prized ring is worth the risk.

One very dark night, while a young mother was traveling along the New Jersey Turnpike in the fast lane, something went wrong and the engine failed. There was a lot of traffic on the road and she had neither the time nor the power to change lanes and stop on the shoulder at the right of the highway. Her only alternative was to coast to a stop alongside the guardrail in the center of the turnpike. Cars in those days were generally much longer than those today, and hers was no exception. As close as she got to the guardrail, the tail of her car stuck out into the fast lane. In a panic, she turned the flashers on and tried to rouse her sleeping boy in the back seat. To stay in the car would be dangerous. To leave it also would be dangerous, as they were situated between two exits. Cell phones had yet to be invented.

Within a few moments, the mother and child were swiftly walking south as close to the center guardrail as possible, buffeted by the currents of cold air caused by speeding cars. The boy marched ahead, resolutely singing "Onward Christian Soldiers" over and over again. His shrill treble dispelled the roar of his mother's fear. Finally, they made it to the next exit. This book could not have been written otherwise.

Fear spoils. Fear is the opposite of faith. Fear smothers the soul and stifles the spirit. Fear of judgment can curtail a child's capacity to enter a new chamber. Fear of failure can diminish a child's courage. Children who are too frightened to take a risk are *at* risk of losing the very faith that has led them so far.

Some childhood fears are rooted in family soil. Consider the child who longs for a parent's presence rather than presents, or who hides under the rug when declared guilty, or who gulps now but vomits later, or who startles in the dark. What would be the anxiety of a child whose gender was unwelcome to either or both parents? I have known a father who was so disappointed in his daughter's gender that he hardly gave her a moment of appreciation for the extraordinary advances she made in school. No matter how she excelled, she failed in one respect: she was not a boy. It was not until years later when the girl admitted to being a lesbian that he took notice and tried to convince her of her femininity.

Other fears are rooted in school soil. Consider the children who lie, cheat, or run away, who are afraid of showing an interest in learning, who forfeit imagination to procure perfection, who stall and say nothing at all. We who care for them must be lovingly present. When we see them doubting or abandoning their wisdom, we must assure them that they need not be afraid, for we support them. We must pray that children who have been spoiled by fear will respond to love. Such times when we can be present and help drive out their fear by our love are 'make or break' moments for both the soul of the school family and the soul of the child. The words of Harry Fosdick ring in my ears during these moments:

> "Grant us wisdom, grant us courage,
> For the living of these days,
> For the living of these days . . ."

Once, a man with a gun scaled the wall of a playground in Trenton, landing amid dozens of small children. They were hastily herded into their daycare center, leaving him to shoot it out with the police who followed. One of the children was the baby brother of two of our students. Upon hearing the story, I wondered how their mother had managed to raise three children to be so open, trusting, and imaginative while living in an inner city neighborhood such as theirs. Her daughters never failed to greet others with a smile and to throw themselves wholeheartedly into all school activities. When I asked their mother to tell me her secret, she replied, "They never go out without me or another person I trust. I always tell them that I love them and they are with me in my heart, always. They must treat everyone with respect, but if they sense danger, ask for help. I have given each one a cell phone with numbers they can call." Such a statement would make little difference if the gunman were wielding an assault weapon.

Sometimes, a terror is healed by a single act of love, as in the case of my experience with Larry. It was Christmas Eve and I was eleven years old. My cousin Larry was visiting from the work farm in Doylestown where he lived year-round, except for holidays. Larry was thirty-five, broad-shouldered, energetic, and friendly. That some people called him a "retard" did not bother us children. We regarded him as another child, albeit an overgrown one. His sudden outbursts of laughter, affectionate hugs, and loud interruptions were part of the orchestration of The Barracks at holiday time. Furthermore, we were fascinated by his extraordinary ability to make music with everything, from the water glasses on the dining room table to the bells in the tower of Trinity Church. These he played beautifully.

Every Christmas Eve, Larry was invited to play carols on the church bells prior to the midnight service. No other honor could delight him more. For years, he mounted the steep spiral stairs of the bell tower, straddled the bench in front of the keyboard, and struck its batons with joyful fists. With his booted feet flying back and forth along the pedal keyboard, Larry inspired the gigantic bronze cup-shaped bells to hail the throng of worshipers as they entered the candlelit sanctuary below. For years, I loved listening to Larry's bells pealing the story of Jesus' birth in the middle of the night.

However, on this particular Christmas Eve, Larry forced a series of changes in me. It was late afternoon when he invited me and my brother to join him in the bell tower that night. Never having watched him play the bells before, we begged our parents to consent—and they did. We could hardly wait until the bells sounded the last quarter before midnight and we scampered up the spiral staircase to the bell chamber above. There we found Larry in a state of utter jubilation. We squatted on the floor below the bell ringer's platform, mesmerized by the staccato of Larry's fists as he struck the batons. This set in motion several levers and wires that were attached to the metal clappers that struck the bells. It was all wonderfully deafening! We clapped our hands over our ears.

Suddenly Larry stopped mid-carol and stared down at the two of us with a frozen expression. Amid the echo of the bells, he rasped, "I think I'm going to be sick. Don't move. I'll be all right in a few minutes." With that, he swung down from his perch and shuffled toward the small door through which we had entered the bell chamber. Yanking a key from his pocket, he locked us all in. Then he pivoted and headed back in our direction, eyes glazed, lips spitting foam. I watched with horror as the unleashed fury of a grand mal seizure bashed his body against the wall, the platform, and then one bell that let out a loud bong. Rebounding, Larry staggered toward me, his face as grotesque as a gargoyle's. I can still feel the revulsion that gripped me at that moment. Grabbing the key that lay on the floor, I escaped from the bell chamber and fled down the spiral staircase, away from my brother's voice calling, "Come back, please come back! Larry's fainting!" It was only when I heard Larry's voice that I froze in my tracks. "Please come back! I'm okay now! Please don't tell anyone!" Despite great qualms, I dragged myself back up the stairs to the tower. There, Larry, fully recovered, swore us to secrecy. "The rector will think I'm crazy. He won't let me play the bells anymore. And besides, he doesn't like me hanging around his congregation." We gave him our word, reluctantly. Satisfied, he climbed back onto the bell ringer's bench and shepherded the oblivious worshipers home with an endless "Gloria in Excelsis Deo."

I kept my promise to Larry and told no one about his seizure in the tower until after his death eight years later. The secret was very costly. Whenever he came to visit during the next few years, my memory of that night in the tower confined me to my bedroom with a stomachache. My parents questioned me, to no avail. Not even Christmas dinner could lure me into Larry's presence.

Larry himself healed me. It was Easter Day and I was fourteen years old. I was bicycling around town, taking in the sights and sounds of the beautiful April afternoon. My dog, Sally, ran behind me as I wove my way through several neighborhoods. At one point, I was separated from Sally by the thick hedge that surrounded the parking lot behind St. Paul's Church. Without looking back, I called loudly, knowing that Sally would spring into view and race down Moore Street to catch up. And so she did, bursting through the hedge right into the path of an oncoming car. The screech of brakes, the awful thump, the piercing cry whirled me around in time to see Sally collapse in the middle of the road, blood running from her mouth. In a minute, I was beside her, beside myself with anguish and remorse, imploring her to come back. She fixed her eyes on me, tapped her tail a couple of times, and with a deep sigh, died. Neighbors surrounded us, stopped oncoming traffic, and asked me for my family's telephone number. One of them called home but got no answer. I lay down on the street next to Sally and wailed.

"Hey, you can't just lie there in the middle of the road!" someone commanded. "You'll be killed as well. Let's pull the dog over to make way for the cars." Before I could protest, a man sprang forward, grabbed Sally by the tail, and began to drag her over to the gutter, leaving a bright trail of blood. Everyone had a different idea of what to do next. Call the vet? "No, she's dead as a doornail." Cover her up? "With what? "Put her in a box? "The blood will soak through the cardboard." "The dog should have been on a leash." The talk went over my head as I stood staring at Sally, certain that I had killed her myself by calling her without looking to see whether a car was coming down the road.

Suddenly, from out of nowhere came a great shout. "Leave them alone! I'll take care of them!" People jumped aside to make way for my cousin Larry, who, having spotted us from afar, skidded his heavy old bike to a halt in the bloody gutter where I crouched next to Sally. I was too confused to run. With a gentle, "You poor little girl," Larry pulled off his huge jacket, wrapped Sally in it, then lifted and folded her limp body around his broad shoulders. With his new Easter necktie, he tied her feet together. Then, directing a stunned me to get on my bike, he made his way on his own bike through the crowd and pumped up the hill. I followed him as he peddled slowly along Nassau Street ahead of me, all hunched over with the dead dog around his neck. When we reached The Barracks, he ever so carefully lifted Sally's body off his shoulders and carried her into the garage. "Now let's clean her up so when everybody comes home, she'll look beautiful." Together, we washed Sally in warm water, wrapped her in a soft old blanket, laid her outside under a tree, and waited for our family to come home.

I was cured of my fear of Larry that Easter Day. A few years later, he died of a seizure while swimming. His gravestone in Trinity's churchyard bears the inscription, "Make a joyful noise unto the Lord!"

Larry was a child whose wisdom was manifested through his music. I was a child whose wisdom was manifested through my curiosity about the bells he played. Somehow in that tower, both of us lost our wisdom. Without it, we had no anchor. We lived in fear: I, of a repetition of his violence, and he, of my betraying his secret.

Only when a second event as traumatic as the first came along did Larry and I break the grip of fear and make friends again. In that moment, my image of Larry changed and he was no longer a monster, but a rescuer, a healer. A transformation from looking to seeing the real person took place.

There are countless "languages" that children find to connect and communicate. It is through acts of creation that children find their wisdom. During my childhood, I stumbled into the light frequently as people perceived my eagerness to draw and paint. When I was in fifth grade, one of the stores on Nassau Street was transformed into a studio. As I bicycled past the window on my way to and from school, I caught sight of easels, brushes, pots of paint. My late grandfather, an impressionist painter, must have clapped his wings when I enrolled in a class that met there once a week after school. What bliss! Leaving my bike collapsed against a tree, I entered a world so saturated by color that I could not help but reflect its radiance. Only last month did I finally throw away a picture that I had painted in that studio sixty-eight years ago. It had been rolled up for years, so the paints that defined three small unicorns on three small clouds had chipped and slipped off the surface. Nothing remained but a trace of the underlying drawing, along with a few scabs of color. What a shame not to have framed it back then and hung it on the wall! It manifested my wisdom at that time of my life.

As a sculptor today, I often marvel at the emergence of form out of raw material. Whether one sculpts by adding or taking away, by modeling or chiseling, one works to discover the essence of a thing by playing with substance. When I make a portrait, I have to remind myself that the likeness of a person is not a precise replica of the person's features, but rather, a glimpse of that person's spirit glowing through the material. I play with bits of clay, adding and subtracting, always attentive to the moods and movements of the person whose character I desire to portray. The portrait emerges as a presence. This usually happens unexpectedly. It is wiser to leave a portrait alone than to overwork it and lose the very thing that I have captured. What really matters most—more than pedagogy—is the process of discovering a child's essential character. Academic learning will follow.

Wisdom played this game during an initial admissions interview as well:

During his admissions interview, you played with him, and somehow in the time you had with him you saw the creative spark—his unique character, his Jacob-ness—and more importantly, you valued it.

Parent

I once made a portrait of Sarah, who was seven years old. During every session, she painted pictures on large sheets of white paper that I had laid out for her on the tilted worktable. As she became totally absorbed in her work, I rolled my tripod clay stand from one place to another in order to study her features from different perspectives. During the hours that we spent together, she rarely looked up from her painting, tilting her head this way and that as she applied her brush loaded with brilliant color. Was that tilt of the head—so familiar to me now—a gesture of Sarah's wisdom? While painting in the studio, she seemed to be swept from the here and now into another sphere where her soul rejoiced in color and form. I doubt whether she even noticed my maneuvering. The final result was a portrait of a child whose intense downward gaze reflected the power of her concentration. Our sessions always culminated in the kitchen, where we talked over a cup of tea and thick cinnamon toast.

After Sarah left each time, I would clean our work spaces and put the paint pots, brushes, and clay tools away, all the while scrutinizing the clay portrait on the tripod. I felt closer to her, more aware of who she really was. "You are beginning to be you. Don't be lonely; I'll come back tomorrow."

One day, Sarah was sitting with me in the kitchen when Dick came in. They greeted each other warmly.

"Your portrait has become very real to us," he told her. "Last evening when we walked through the studio before going upstairs, I patted you on the head and bade you goodnight."

Sarah tilted her head and looked up at him with a slight smile. "I know . . . I heard you."

Did Dick's playful remark about talking to her portrait open the window to her imagination once more? Were they daydreaming together? I believe so.

It all has to do with the connection between the grounded self, who listens and watches, and the soaring self, who rises to the sound of beautiful music or flares at the sight of beautiful art. When a connection is made between the two spheres of the same self, an epiphany occurs. For example, when an audience securely seated in the concert hall is swept away by Tchaikovsky's "Pathetique," you will see their faces transformed by the huge sound that sweeps the self into the realm of the soul. Music and art are only two examples of epiphanies. There are as many others as human experience allows. Paul Muldoon, winner of a Pulitzer Prize for Poetry, provided many such moments for us—not only in occasional evening readings of his poetry, but also in conducting a poetry workshop for his daughter's third grade class. Paul considered eight-year-olds to be natural poets and wonderful writers because they have a vision of the world that is still "untrammeled by preconceptions of what poetry is." He saw their wisdom.

—⁓—

As I grew older, I knew that art would be an important language for me to master. I devoured whatever assignments were thrown to me in art classes at school, even when they were no more demanding than making Valentines in February or snowmen in November. I welcomed every opportunity to produce a thing of beauty, either by imitation or original design. Slowly, my skills with material and construction developed. So when I came into contact with Miss Stevens, I was ready to make a new leap.

"Miss Cuyler, it is time for you to join me here at the table, please." I had been daubing blobs of paint onto my picture with increasing annoyance. In no way did my composition convey the subtle beauty of the still life set up on a table nearby. Although I had turned my easel slightly to avoid Miss Steven's scrutiny, I could feel her eagle eye boring a hole in my back. I put down my brush, readjusted the easel, and approached the large wooden table where Miss Stevens always presided. The hush in the art room was broken only by the swishing of brushes in water jars. I knew the others would listen closely so as not to miss the wisdom that inevitably emerged during these table visits. None of us could deny the aura that Miss Stevens cast as she sat so quietly, so colorlessly, so endlessly at her table. Before her lay several large books opened to show reproductions of great works of art dated as long ago as the Paleolithic Age.

I sat down next to Miss Stevens, trying not to bump her thin, veined hand as it turned the pages of one of the big books. I held my breath as one painting after another flipped by in succession, their bright images flying off the pages like birds from a cage. "Don't go so fast!" my inner voice protested.

Miss Stevens gave scarcely a glance toward me or my painting. After bypassing several images, she finally came to a stop in front of a still life by the French painter Paul Cezanne. "I want you to look at this painting carefully. It will tell you everything you need to know." I stared at the painting before me. It depicted a rustic table partially covered by a rough white cloth. Among the heavy folds lay several ripe pears, a lemon, a peach, and an apple. A white china pitcher and sugar bowl, both enhanced by flowery patterns, were tucked in among the succulent fruits. Placed behind this assemblage was an earthen pot and a sturdy straw garden basket full to the brim with still more fresh fruit cushioned by a white napkin. My mouth watered as my eyes took in their brilliance. Each fruit sparkled against the subtle blues and grays of the kitchen scene.

"Well, what do you see?" Miss Steven's question broke my trance.

"I see fruit on a table."

"Of course you do—but what about the fruit on the table? How does it affect you?"

"It makes me want to eat it."

"Good. I'm sure that's what Cezanne intended. How do you think he produced such an impression?"

I stared more intently at the still life on the page before me. "He didn't do it like a photograph, but the fruit looks so real. You can almost reach out and touch it."

Miss Stevens droned on. "Cezanne studied things in nature very closely, over and over, until he knew them by heart. When he painted fruit, for instance, he didn't just show what it looked like. He showed its essential being."

"How?" I wanted to beg this crone to tell me how I, too, might make things in my paintings look so true. But telling wasn't her way of doing things.

"Well, look again. Are the background colors warm or cool?"

"Cool."

"And what about the fruits?"

"They're bright—in front." I shot a look at Miss Stevens. She was obviously waiting for more. "I like the way the pears look so juicy."

"Now you're getting warmer. Cezanne cared a lot about fruits on a table in a kitchen. He painted them all the time." Her voice trailed off. It was my turn.

"I tried to paint my fruit so that it looks good enough to eat, but it doesn't."

Miss Stevens peered over her glasses at my painting on the easel and raised a wispy eyebrow. "Go get an apple from the still life and bring it here, please."

I selected the biggest apple and brought it back to the table. Miss Stevens watched while I examined the apple from every angle. "What colors do you see?"

"Red."

"Is that all? What else?"

"I see orange near the stem and gold in the hole where the stem comes out. There are parts where the red is darker—"

"More intense?"

"More intense. And look, here's a place that's almost yellow."

"If you keep the apple in one position so that part of it is in shadow, what happens to its color?"

"The shadow part gets darker."

"Turn the apple again."

"Then another part gets darker."

"Miss Cuyler, how much better you see now that you've taken your blinders off. First impressions never tell the whole story. Let's take another look at "Still life with Fruit Basket." How did Cezanne reveal his vision of fresh fruit to a girl who lives seventy years later?"

I gazed at the painting again. I could see that each fruit was embellished with flat planes of color that had been laid on with a square tipped brush. The most intense colors were in the places where the fruit was fattest. The darkest colors were in the shadows. Cezanne's apple had sections of red, orange, gold, yellow, and green. Not confined by a line, the apple fairly rocked. "He did it with colors!"

"Exactly. And with a few other things too—but they can wait until later. For now, you have learned enough from a great artist to keep you busy for quite a while. Put the apple back in the still life and get to work." Miss Stevens turned away. "Miss Brown, it is time for you to join me at the table, please."

People of long ago communicate with us by means infinitely more powerful than internet chat or twitter. Music, art, dance, drama—all symbolic forms—help us to sense a world beyond. By showing me the still life by Cezanne, Miss Stevens had given me a bridge across which I, the young artist with an urge to paint, could travel beyond the span of my lifetime to empathize with a great artist of yesteryear. She had helped me to cultivate an aesthetic point of view from which I would contemplate and instinctively comprehend a thing of beauty created by another. At her request, I had reflected upon images left behind by an artist whose painting helped me to access the wisdom with which I came into the world. I returned to my easel knowing that I had found a new friend—the artist Cezanne—who would teach me how to convey the spirit as well as the form of an apple. Cezanne lived in a place and time far away, yet his painting spoke to me as if I were in that very kitchen today. He and I loved the same things! I wanted to thank Miss Stevens for introducing us, but when I looked back at her, she and Molly Brown had already entered the cave of Lascaux at Montignac, France, to view paintings made by people who lived 17,000 years ago.

I have visited ancient Neolithic sites and been awestruck by the power of their mammoth stone circles. Their mysterious markers give no more than a few carved hints of their origins. Yet they are deeply compelling. How could Stone Age people have cast a spell so far as to mesmerize visitors of modern times? Their stage of human endeavor has often been regarded as primitive. Why not say passionate? They engineered tons of stone over miles of rough terrain and erected them in patterns that drew attention to the revolution of both the sun and moon, the celebration of both life and death, and the recognition of both temporal and eternal time. The Neolithic people could hardly be called neophytes. They placed colossal quartz crystals at the entrances of their stone circles. These portal stones, lying on the surfaces of magnetic fields, oscillate frequencies of rosy light long after the setting of the sun. One evening, as I watched the full moon rise and temper the glow of the great quartz lanterns, I felt transfixed. For a moment, I was living there and then. In terms of shared humankind, it all made sense.

I have had the same sort of experience when coming upon places that I call "children's traces." These traces are signs that remain and show the former presence of a child (or children) no longer there. They can be made of anything—objects found in nature, Legos, blocks, pillows. Whatever the objects, they are chosen to create forms of great importance to the maker. These traces remain to be discovered by others who come along the way. When I am the one who does so, I stop and stare, for these traces communicate now, as did the traces of ancient people, the ingenuity of the human spirit.

For children in whom creativity is preserved, life is full of moments of tension between reality and imagery, known and unknown, time and eternity. Building with blocks, playing with numbers, expressing with stories, illustrating with pictures, debating with arguments—all of these actions demonstrate a child's capacity to organize and synthesize. This is their way of making sense of the world around them. However, we must help them to also learn from the wisdom of others before them who have tilled the fields of art, math, science, and humanities. Those farmers who cultivated and enriched the soil leave much behind for future generations.

It was not surprising, then, that we took our fifth-graders on pilgrimages to such places as The White House, Fort William in Baltimore, or Independence Hall in Philadelphia. They had much to learn from those venues so permeated by past lives. Once, when a class was on a tour in the White House, a US Secret Service tour officer paused in his description of the Red Room to answer a student's fervent questions about the room's history. So impressed was he by her curiosity that he unhooked the red velvet rope that separated the visitors from the room's principal space. "I can recognize a future docent when I see one," he remarked, as he allowed her to enter the room and share her enthusiasm with the people who had gathered behind the rope. To see her standing proudly in this historic space, braids aflame with red beads, hands fluttering to her lips, was a sight to remember. What better example of wisdom could we find than this child declaring, "I want to know the history in this place; it's mine, too."

On another occasion, our fifth-graders made an annual visit to the Metropolitan Museum of Art in New York City. Each student had spent several weeks researching an artist of his or her choice whose work was on display at the museum. In addition to learning facts about the artist's life and times, each had explored the artist's style by adapting it in the art room. Each had given an oral report about his or her chosen artist to children in other classes. Now, the fifth-graders were ready to meet at the Met those original works of art that they had imagined for so long. Following a prepared schedule, we arrived at the museum and went immediately to the restaurant to fortify ourselves for the hunt. As the artists' works were located throughout the museum, we had countless galleries to explore before our expedition could be concluded: American Paintings and Sculpture, European Paintings, Modern Art, and as always, Impressionist Paintings. For three hours we wended our way from gallery to gallery, our students crackling with anticipation. Whenever one discovered the treasure he or she was seeking, we all stopped to hear the story of a modern child meeting a bygone artist within the wonderful world of a painting. The child gazed for a while, then took his or her place before the painting in the crowded gallery and began to speak. We never knew what we would hear, for the information that the child had gathered up to this point was only part of the story, learned at a distance. Now, in one another's presence, both the child and the painting came alive. It was not unusual to hear, "I love this painting. The artist sees things the same way I do;" or, "Artists like to leave you wondering." Whatever words came out, the children spoke with authority. At one point, a boy who had just talked about Rembrandt's "Self Portrait" accompanied me down the hall toward the gallery of Impressionist Paintings.

"Thank you, Robert! You did a wonderful job telling everyone about Rembrandt's portrait of himself. They really listened to you."

"I was glad to see him. I don't know if he was glad to see me. His eyes looked right through me."

"Well, perhaps he saw in you the boy he once was."

"His face was the brightest part of the picture. The rest was pretty dark. Other portraits by Rembrandt are the same way. Faces and hands show up."

"Faces and hands tell a story about a person, don't you think?" No answer. I glanced at Robert. He seemed bemused. Had Rembrandt been unwilling to make friends with this boy?

We entered the Impressionists' gallery. Robert glanced around the large room full of sunny impressions of everyday life. "I think some people just live darkly and other people give light to everything."

We hastened over to a Renoir painting before which one of his classmates was standing. Everyone waited to hear what she had to say.

"I love Renoir's painting because the two girls are playing the piano. They are having fun. I play the piano too, and I know just how they feel."

As we drove home from New York that day, I thought about Robert, wondering whether he had changed his mind about Rembrandt. I thought about the comments children had made when they stood in front of their favorite paintings. Yes, they had shown their audiences how knowledgeable a fifth-grader could be about a work of art done years ago. Yes, they had shown the natural poise of people who are accustomed to speaking before a group. Yes, they had loved the attention. But to me, what came across most of all was their keen sense of rapport with an old friend who had created a beautiful thing. One fifth grade student described the experience in a dream that took place after our visit.

> I had an odd dream. It was about meeting my artist, Thomas Cole. At first I was a little bit shy, but then I told him how much I knew about him, so I felt more confident. Then I asked him questions, such as how he felt when his ship was attacked by pirates. He said that he was worried. Then we made a new version of "The Titan's Goblet," the painting that I studied and made a copy of. Afterwards, we went to the Catskills together. Then I told him that some

of his pictures were in the Metropolitan Museum of Art. He was really happy. Then I woke up.

Student

I am convinced that children bear within their souls the image of their Creator. This image is their wisdom, the source of their life and breath and spirit. This is what drives them to create and to transform. These connections are epiphanies that we want children to experience: moments when they discover their essential selves within the forms that art presents to them. Here, in the words of one of the children who visited her artist in the Metropolitan Museum, we find transformation exquisitely described. This child has found her own spirit in the spirit of the dancer.

Degas Ballerina

Standing still,
Afraid,
Mute,
A trance of wonder,
A beam of light
Shining upon an everlasting pose.

Student

Years ago, I frequented the Boston Museum of Fine Art while engaged in a research project. To reach my work location, I had to pass through the gallery containing ancient Egyptian sculptures. There, monumental stone funerary figures stood, their features and forms frozen in timeless frontality. I always felt a chill as I walked past their staring almond eyes. The guard who stood at the entrance of the gallery bore an uncanny resemblance to the figures whose space he protected.

Then there was the boy. The boy was neither young nor old—about twelve, I surmised. Often, he came into the gallery alone, stopped in front of one of the great statues, pulled a stone from his pocket and placed it carefully between the feet of the figure. The boy's manner was reverent. He always bowed his head and mumbled something that I could not decipher. Then, without another word, he would back away, turn, and leave the gallery. One day, I asked the watchful guard, "What do you think that boy was all about?"

"Beats me. You can't tell what kids are up to nowadays—maybe communicating with the dead."

"How often does he come?"

"He's here every day after school laying a stone between the feet of that statue."

"What happens to the stone?" I asked.

The guard shrugged. "I wait 'til the place closes before I take it off. You can't have things like that lying around."

"What do you do with it?"

"Me? Oh, I take it home and add it to the border of my garden. His stones look pretty good in a row. My wife says they make the flowers grow."

Art, drama, and music are natural playgrounds for young children. As the school's art teacher for many years, I witnessed daily the flexibility with which children interweave their own perspectives with those of others. In the light of this wisdom, I introduced a classic art project. On the big table in the center of the room I set a number of familiar kitchen implements: spoon, fork, vegetable peeler, sieve, bowl, saucepan, etc. Each child had a large sheet of black paper and some colored chalk. I asked each one to choose one object, return to his or her place, pick up a piece of chalk, and draw the outermost contour of that object onto the black paper. The outline had to be large, unbroken, off-center, and at an angle. No erasures. Then, each child was instructed to return the first object to the table and chose another. The second outline had to be drawn in another color and had to intersect the first. No line should drift off the edge of the black paper. Then, each child was asked to choose another object and another color, and add the third outline to the previous ones. As the process developed, these intersecting lines formed new, smaller shapes. Finally, I asked the children to pause and take a look at the composite form that they had created by intersecting the shapes of five different kitchen implements. Then they outlined with white chalk the whole new form that floated on the black paper. The children were instructed to fill in the smaller shapes with different colors. The final chalk pictures sparkled like stained glass windows on a sunny day.

Once a year, I required the oldest children to do this particular project—not so much to enhance their skills as to give them a visual metaphor of what happens when individual shapes work together, producing a result that is greater than any of its separate parts. Needless to say, the process required of them a certain amount of faith to overcome their jitters.

"What happened to the spoon I drew? It's cut in two!"

"The peeler is too big. It messed up my bowl."

"Why can't I erase the red fork? It's too bright!"

"If I color in all the little shapes the big ones won't show any more."

Gradually, the tone of their voices changed. "Hey, look at this!"

"Yes, look! You have connected separate shapes and made the whole composition more beautiful than any of its parts. Walk around and take a look at everyone's pictures."

I particularly remember one child's song of praise. "It's like an orchestra. When you put them all together they make music."

"And who is the conductor?" I asked.

"Me!"

Transformation, plain and simple. Children live it every day, in one way or another. This particular art project required them to follow directions closely and move beyond the familiar and particular into new territory. They discovered that they, like the individual shapes, held within themselves possibilities heretofore unrealized. The project illustrates how—when one trusts—authority and creativity harmonize to produce something new. In effect, the teacher is saying, "Trust me, I know you can do it!" and the child responds, "If you say so, I think I can."

—⁓—

Children are usually responsive when given an opportunity to make music. After all, they have heard music since they were in the womb, assuming a mother's heart-beat is musical. I believe that its rhythm permeates the mind and memory long before birth.

One of the school parents, a concert violinist, once told me of the advice she gave each of her children long ago when they professed an interest in learning how to play the violin. "Do you wish to create a beautiful sound? Don't assume that it will come from the instrument at the touch of the bow. The kind of sound that you're thinking of takes years of practice to produce. It will emerge in time, but only after you have earned it. So don't tell me that you want to play the violin unless you are willing to give up other activities in order to practice every day." Her children listened to the sound of her voice and decided accordingly. Those who play the violin today make beautiful music.

Children who are given the chance to play in an orchestra know what such discipline means. They have learned how to listen to one another and how to join together with others to achieve the sound that their conductor awaits. Some orchestra programs offer children the only real discipline they know. The conductors of such orchestras often applaud the extraordinary dedication of their young players. One such conductor claims that the children in his orchestra have learned something even more important than the music; they have learned how to commit to something beyond themselves. Furthermore, the academic reports of these children reflect an improvement in their management of time, their concentration, their retention, and their overall achievement.

Let us focus for a moment on what transformation requires: the beauty that issues from the orchestration of various sounds, the beauty that comes from the combination of various shapes—such beauty is not created without a struggle. Individual parts must give up a certain amount of their autonomy in order to fuse with, or balance or enhance another. Think of a mobile hanging in the air—a superb example of composite grace. Yet each of its parts has very different character and shape. Many adjustments have to be made. Likewise, we need often to adjust or to sacrifice in order to achieve harmony.

—◦◦◦—

Diversity took many forms at Princeton Junior School. From the very beginning, it aroused issues that could not be put to rest. One year, when the school was still operating in the basement of the Lutheran Church on Cedar Lane, we decided to combine the celebration of Hanukah and Christmas in a "holiday assembly". The cantor from the Jewish synagogue began the program by playing and singing "Dreidel, Dreidel" on his guitar, while spinning a dreidel on the floor throughout the verses. Charmed, the children very quickly picked up the words and sang with him. Following the cantor, the pastor of the Lutheran Church told the story of the birth of Jesus in Bethlehem without the help of a guitar or dreidel. Although he told the story well, it came to a sudden end when a kindergartener raised his hand and asked, "If the three kings brought Jesus so many presents and all the angels and shepherds loved him so much, why did he get killed when he was a man?" This child's question was one that pointed to the paradox of a figure who was killed for embodying the wisdom that transcends all of our differences.

The cantor leaned toward the pastor with a twinkle in his eye: "Go for it!"

Dealing with diversity required of me a wisdom beyond my ken and I had to plumb my depths. What I discovered there was a plea for help: My letter to parents in some ways reflects the transformation that I was experiencing myself:

Dear parents of Grade IV students,

Grade IV is a varied class in which each student has much to offer to the others. However, at times, their differences seem more important to them than the common ground on which they all stand. They wish to resolve their struggle and transform themselves into a team headed for a common goal: academic excellence in a nurturing environment. I urge you to help your children tackle the challenge that is deeply rooted in the school's mission: to coexist happily together in a community that is both diverse and demanding. Each of your children has expressed the desire to cooperate with and respond to one another as individuals and co-learners. We have identified two professionals who are highly experienced with the issues and opportunities of diversity. They have agreed to help us all with this important lesson in life.

I believe that we all wish for the same outcome: that our children learn fully and joyfully as a unified class at Princeton Junior School. When, with our support, our fourth-graders learn the lesson of tolerance and transformation that diversity teaches, how much better their world at PJS and beyond will be!

J.

To underestimate the value of diversity is to deprive children of the opportunity to learn one of life's primary lessons: how to get along with people who are different. The future well-being of all of us depends upon our ability to listen to one another, to understand our differences, and to find out how alike we are in many ways. "The more we care, the more we share, in our school, our Princeton Junior School!"

Even if you don't like this person or that person, you still cannot be mean to them. All of the teachers put a lot of pressure on making sure that we treat everyone fairly. And the students did, most of the time.

Alumna

Princeton Junior School was intended to be a safe world for children. Yet there were times when prejudices tripped them and caused them to stumble. One day I looked up to find two seething children staring back at me.

"Hello, Aaron and Hanni! You look upset—what's happening?"

Words rushed into the void so fast that I sprang to close the door. "Now, take a breath and sit down. Let's talk quietly." I took a breath and sat down. They did not.

"She's mean to me all the time. She won't answer me when I—"

"That's not true! I did answer you when we were talking about Ellis Island—"

"Yeah, sure, that was in class! I'm talking about out of class, like in the hall when I asked you—"

"You didn't *ask* me anything. You told me you thought my family tree was rotten." Hanni's piercing blue eyes swept around to meet mine. "Then he went and tore the corner off my great-grandfather's photograph."

At first I couldn't imagine what she was talking about, but then I recalled the class's recent genealogy project. In the hall outside their classroom were pinned posters depicting every child's family, from the present day back as far as he or she had been able to get information. The children had worked on their family trees for days, bringing in photos of babies and pets as well as ancestors. The project was a precursor to the study of immigration.

"What? Aaron, why would you do a thing like that?"

"She did worse to me!" wailed Aaron. "She told me I don't belong on the wall—not on any wall."

My heart sank. "Where did you get such ideas? I can't imagine you both treating each other this way! You've always been such good friends."

"Not anymore," they said in unison.

Rage that boils in the cauldron of hurt feelings can scald the worst. The true friendship that had existed between this boy and girl seemed to have vanished into thin air. What on earth could have happened? Then I thought about what Hanni had said concerning the photograph of her great-grandfather. My thoughts threaded back to the playground of my childhood as I viewed the two children before me. She was a blue-eyed, blonde child of German descent, and he was a brown-eyed, dark-haired child of Jewish descent. My heart sank. "Can you take a minute to tell me about your families?"

Hanni began, "My family is German. Many of my cousins still live in Germany but my parents came to the United States before I was born."

Aaron burst in, "But what she doesn't tell you is how her great-grandfather treated my people. They were living in Germany at the same time he was. My great-grandparents never got out. They were gassed. But my grandparents did, and they came here to live."

"How do your parents feel, Aaron?" I asked.

"They tell me not to play with Hanni because of what her great-grandfather did to my father's family."

"How do you know!" cried Hanni, full force. Again she turned to me. "I asked my dad whether that was true and he just said to stay away from Aaron because it would bring up a lot of bad feelings. I'm doing just what he said and it brings up bad feelings just the same."

Forced separation from a close friend can feel awful, I thought. "So this is your decision? To wreck your friendship in order to punish each other for something neither of you did?" They both looked miserable. It was dismissal time and I had to let them go. That night, I prayed for them as I had prayed for myself long ago when I had been stoned by some classmates on the way home from school for being Protestant. I didn't even protest at the time.

The truce prevailed and the rest of the year passed by with no further battles between Hanni and Aaron. Could my words have had an effect? No—there had been a conciliator more powerful than words. In the winter, a troupe of Irish folk step dancers from a nearby town came to the school. No older than our students, the colorful dancers leapt along a wooden platform, their shiny black shoes tapping to the lively music. The pairs were so synchronized that even their ringlets and ribbons bounced in rhythm. We were all spellbound. Later that spring, the school held its annual talent show. Anyone who wished to perform was encouraged to do so, regardless of skill. I supported this occasion, for the audience always applauded each performer's effort, right down to the most humble demonstration of "Chopsticks" on the piano. On that day, about halfway through the program, a familiar Irish dance tune summoned two dancers to the platform. Clad in colorful costumes, the boy and girl stepped out hand in hand, their toes and heels chattering together like two magpies on a telephone wire. Could it be? The sight of this transfigured couple so happily in tune with one another took my breath away. When they swirled to a finish, the applause was deafening.

Later, I found Aaron and Hanni sitting on a bench, unlacing their boots. I exclaimed, "It was wonderful! How did you do it?"

"We just did!" They went on to explain. After the troupe visited the school, Aaron and Hanni had signed up separately for Irish dance lessons on Saturday mornings. Their parents were unaware of their reunion. Six weeks of dancing stamped out their fear and animosity.

In this epiphany, the wisdom of Aaron and Hanni overstepped centuries of discord.

Throughout the world, infants are no strangers to the process of immigration. From the moment of their conception, they voyage physically from an inner to an outer world. They are surrounded by a fluid that buoys their daily transformations until they reach their port of entry into a new homeland. While they may not remember the place from which they came, they are inherently equipped for the challenges of their new life. Seeing, suckling, sneezing, snoozing—all come naturally to healthy newborns who land on friendly shores. With open arms, they greet the world. Grasping, greeting, and growing all follow in due course as young children, relying on inner wisdom as well as outer encouragement, move from cove to cove. I believe that this is what God created them to do.

In our society, very young children leave home for a few hours a day to go to school. It was always my prayer that the children who traveled so expectantly into Princeton Junior School's harbor would find exactly what they intuitively sought: a safe haven where their souls would flourish. I hoped that once they reached the port of entry, they would continue to immigrate, relying on their wisdom to move naturally through the places where family and school cultures merge, and creatively in the places where family and school cultures clash. I hoped that the children from dense urban neighborhoods would consider the school's rural lifestyle to be an adventure. I hoped that children from abroad—for whom our language was foreign and strange—would learn to communicate through play at first, with language following. I saw that my prayer was answered when I walked around the school and watched children gamely tossing themselves across known borders into unfamiliar territories. Sometimes they landed hard. We referred to these leaps into new homelands as miracles rather than mistakes, for such feats were the consequences of the children's instinctive drive to grow further.

> We are going on the Oregon Trail
> To find a new place to live
> Everyone is sad but excited
> A long time to travel
> On the way many sights to see
> But when the journey has ended
> Our hearts are filled with joy!

Student

New students were sojourners for a while only. Our job was to welcome and encourage them, to recognize and celebrate their natural resources. These would be their life support as they continued on their way from stage to stage. It was of great importance that their natural affinity for immigration lead them to connect with others. From the outset, we adhered to the Golden Rule as children from a wide variety of backgrounds interacted with one another. They were usually colorblind in their search for playmates and friends. "Why are you brown?" was an inquiry born out of curiosity rather than criticism.

In the experience of school children, more consequential than places or programs or means of transportation are their interactions with people along the way. The average child's desire to connect will overcome any number of odds if he or she has good traveling companions. Mastering the art of getting along with others—whether they are siblings, neighbors, classmates, or teammates—is crucial for healthy growth in today's world of global interaction.

Children are born to be in relationship with others and to thereby become fully human. In his book *God Has a Dream*, Desmond Tutu writes, "The world is going to have to learn the fundamental lesson that we are made for harmony, for interdependence. If we are ever truly to prosper, it will only be together." Look at our world scene: it is an international network tangled with victims of injustice and violence. Children need to grow up capable of loosening knots, having learned early from people of different backgrounds, cultures, languages, and beliefs. They will be capable of deep compassion and connection. My prayer for our children is that they will know through their connections with others the true meaning of Paul the Apostle's words: "And now faith, hope, and love abide, these three; and the greatest of these is love" (I Corinthians 13:13, The New Oxford Annotated Bible, Third Edition, New Revised Standard Version with the Apocrypha, p.286 NT).

"Who are we here, together?" To find the answer is the task of every parent, teacher, and student. As immigrants on both temporal and spiritual journeys, our children come to school with God-given inner resources that transcend other learned forms of wisdom. We grown-ups must help them to honor this gift in others as well as in themselves. How else can we prepare them to travel to new places, meet and greet new people, and above all, make new connections that are lasting and loving?

> I miss you and Princeton Junior School greatly, and I miss all the friends I made there . . . I really think PJS was a great place for me to start school in the United States because I always felt so comfortable and always knew that if I ever needed help, someone would help me. I am so glad I went there because if I had gone to another school . . . I would never have been able to do well on the SSAT tests and feel secure. Please say hi to everybody for me and tell them that I miss them. Thank you so much for everything you ever helped me with (which is a lot). I have really improved since I came to America.
>
> Alumna

Since our children are too young to travel independently, they must learn from their classmates who come from other parts of the world. Children from abroad, for whom our language is foreign and strange, adjust to their new surroundings and learn our vernacular within a few months—largely through play. They learn democracy by experience rather than by rote. As one student wrote, "At PJS everyone is friendly and it builds confidence in everyone. You learn a lot but still have fun. You get to meet people from all over the world."

Should we not look upon play as a necessary process for teachers and children alike? Should not the play principle be the *modus operandi* of early childhood education? If play stimulates a child's imagination, concentration, and sense of justice, if play challenges a child to reach beyond his or her boundaries and take the risks that learning requires, then why not allow the power of play to infuse academic subjects? A perfect example of such integration occurred when two of our teachers decided to teach the social studies unit on immigration to second and third grade children by means of a play. In the first phase of the process, every child was encouraged to collaborate with his or her own family to create a family tree. Posters began to appear in the hallway. We marveled at their variety: thin trees, fat trees, short trees, long trees—some with colorful photographs of babies and grandparents, others with clusters of aunts, uncles, and cousins. A few had very little on their branches, for some children simply did not know much about their origins. Each child presented his or her family tree to the others. One second-grader introduced us to her family by commenting on different people in the photographs. After naming her siblings, parents, cousins, aunts, and uncles, and giving their birth dates, she became more descriptive.

> I didn't know I had so many aunts and uncles. My uncle Ricardo found my aunt in Guatemala. He looked everywhere for her. They got married and he brought her to the United States. Then they went back and my aunt had a baby. Then he came to America and she stayed in Guatemala. He had a visa to work here. He showed it to everyone. After some years, he went back and got her and the baby and brought them here. The baby was a little girl. Then two brothers were born.
>
> Student

This story, while short and sweet, confirmed the extraordinary perseverance of our school's custodian. Over the years, several of his family—men, women, and children—strengthened and enriched Princeton Junior School. Another one of the family's children explained: "This picture is of my grandmother. Her name was the same as mine. She dressed up in her Guatemalan costumes every day. We have another picture of her on the little refrigerator at home."

"Did you ever meet her?"

"No, she died and I never got to know her. She stayed in Guatemala. When my mom talks about her I see water coming out of her eyes. I cry with her. It makes me sad to think that old people die. I never got to know them."

"Does the photograph help?"

"Yes, I can know her a little now because I have a picture of her in my head."

"Pictures help us to imagine people we have never met, or places we have never been to."

"On my dad's side, I have an uncle who died. When he was dying in the hospital, they took a photograph of him in his bed, smiling like he wasn't really sick. My dad is very sad now. I am too."

"Do you speak Spanish at home?"

"I do but I can't read or write in Spanish. This uncle here, (pointing to the family tree), is teaching me how to speak Spanish better and I am teaching him English."

"Have you ever thought about going to Guatemala?"

"I want to learn more about Guatemala. I want to visit my family there. The volcano near their farm hasn't erupted yet. But I want to live in America where there are not so many volcanoes." Her deep-brown eyes reflected no trace of the looming cloud that currently threatens her family's security. I was grateful for the hope I found there. This child will shine through the shadow.

In the second phase of the immigration unit, the children visited Ellis Island.

> [We] took the ferry to the island. When we got there we saw the baggage room and the staircase. Maddy and I went up to the balcony where they got inspected by the doctors. I took pictures of the belongings that belonged to the immigrants when they came to America. We also saw

the statue of Annie Moore. She was the first person to step onto Ellis Island . . . I also think I ate too much candy on the way back! I had a great time at Ellis Island.

Student

They became fascinated by the stories of families who crossed the ocean to find a new life in America. Their teachers asked them whether they would like to create a play about immigrants who came to America long ago. At the children's enthusiastic response, their teacher of art, drama, and dance was invited to help them develop their play. They did this during the following weeks by improvising over and over until they developed the characters, dialogue, scenery, costumes, and music that they felt would be best able to express their story. Finally, the *Immigration Play* was ready to be performed.

It was evening and The Commons wrapped its large audience in shadows. When a spotlight washed the central platform, we watched an Irish family on the eve of their departure, all dancing to country music. With warm hugs and prayers, they bid good-bye to their old mother who would remain behind. Next, we watched them crowding onto the dock with other families, to be weighed and herded aboard like sheep driven by a strident stevedore. In the next scene—an extraordinary mélange of boat, sea, and sky fabricated out of painted cardboard—the lusty crowd sang its way across the ocean toward the welcoming beam of beautiful Liberty. She was dressed in their favorite color: green. The chains around her ankles were broken. There were shouts of joy. The following scene showed their landing at Ellis Island, a field of desks and doctors. One by one, the newcomers submitted to a rigorous bureaucratic process. Protocol involved examination of papers, bodies, and baggage.

> People bunched up together
> Being inspected one by one
> Passing money down
> Sometimes being sent back
> Relieved to pass through
> Happy to meet their loved ones
> Immigrants waiting to be called Americans.

It was here in the play that the children's wishes came true. Regardless of how congested or lame or penniless the Irish immigrants were, they talked their way into their examiners' hearts. None had to be sent back. The play ended in a wild celebration among the immigrants and their awaiting relatives. Even the doctors joined in the line dance. What better way for children to take into account the trials and tribulations of their ancestors! To this day, they remember the play they created.

The challenge facing any school for children is to balance two worlds: the boundless inner world of imagination and play, and the more restricted outer world of academic discipline and social relations. Freedom and responsibility must go hand in hand as our young immigrants travel forward, bearing the best of the old world as they enter the new. Whatever balance they learn at school will serve them well on the road.

> Ma says we must move, to America
> Pa says life will be better, in America
> Ma says there is more food, in America
> Pa says we will go by ship, to America
> Ma says there is freedom, in America
> Pa says we will be safe, in America
> Ma says we will have jobs, in America
> I say let us go, let us go, to America!

Student

———ᴡᴡ———

It takes only a look at the bird feeder outside the window to see how frantic competition can be. The contest among dozens of winged rivals is instinctive, sharp, and shimmering. Is it the same for us? Whether the prize we snatch satisfies the body, mind, heart, or soul, it puts out the flame of hunger—at least for a while. So we compete for it. Ever since we peopled the earth, we have competed for water, food, territory, money, and mate. On the other hand, research suggests that cooperation is a basic human characteristic that has led us to form communities to survive. Many ancient war games have evolved into team sports.

A school should allow both competition and co-operation to walk hand in hand. From its beginning, Princeton Junior School has encouraged children to share toys, ideas and experiences with other people whose ages and needs were the same. I have often wondered whether learning to share diminishes an innate drive to compete with others. For some, yes. Some children learn instead to compete with themselves, to better their best. For these, sharing means collaboration, behaving intelligently and respectfully toward one another in the common search for knowledge. Sharing knowledge bears fruit of another kind. People who learn to cooperate during childhood become hardy—able to transform rivalry into resolution and hunger into harmony. Everyone has a better chance of winning.

—⁓—

In good education, privilege has little do with money or power. Rather, privilege is the freedom to learn, to share, and to grow with people of all kinds.

> Sometimes we have good times and sometimes we have bad times. Sometimes we have to be mad. There are good times to play. There are not good times to play—for a reason—like when you have to study for a big test. You should try to do your best at all times.
>
> Student

This comment reflects a late-coming student's struggle. Recommended by her church, she arrived at Princeton Junior School bruised by family circumstances and neglected by urban education. When she first came, she labeled herself as dumb in relation to her classmates. Her moods were exhausting. In time she swallowed her doubts and took advantage of every opportunity to develop both her basic academic skills and her self-confidence—as evidenced by her steady upward learning curve. Despite her deprivation, she persevered and enriched our school community. For this child, doing her best at all times was the ultimate test. She shared none of the advantages of some of her classmates—yet she worked hard to catch up, sometimes without any support from home. Teachers gave up their lunch hours to tutor her. During her fifth grade year, she applied to a fine school in Pennsylvania. She was a successful candidate but for her residency in New Jersey, which led to her rejection. Undaunted, she returned to the Trenton public school, clung to her church, graduated, and earned full scholarships to two local colleges. As I watched her sashay toward the podium to receive her high school diploma along with thousands of others in the Trenton State Arena, I wept like the mother of the bride. I had seen how her wisdom had nearly been defeated by the hopelessness of a broken family in an impoverished city. It had been my privilege to see how a child with so little support had beaten the system.

Then there is the child whose athletic talent is tested by the pressures of competitive sports. When my grandson Myles was four years old, he sometimes accompanied his father to the squash courts. Once in a while, when his father played in one court with another adult, Myles played by himself in the adjacent court. Flinging himself to and fro in an effort to keep up with the squash ball that he had whacked, the little boy fell in love with the game. His father listened to Myles's plea to learn and readily gave him some rudimentary instruction. As they practiced together, Myles loved the sounds, the speed, and the surprises of the sport. Above all, he loved the companionship that his father offered him. Now, six years later, Myles ranks among the best players of his age in the country.

As time went by, Myles became a competitive player, moving forward beyond the level of his peers. Recently, I attended one of Myles's squash matches, in which he was pitted against a more experienced player. Separated from the game by a clear lucite wall, I could see and feel the action as if I were in the court myself. The boys' energy was electric: the static of ball-to-wall, the squeak of sneakers, the whistle of breath all quickened my pulse as I watched them spin and strike the little black ball. Their rallies moved so quickly that they had to rely on the piercing voice of the referee for the score. Myles's energy flared and flagged accordingly. I couldn't help but think that there might be a lot more at stake than the physical skill demanded by the game. Each boy's fierce effort to beat the other seemed to me as ancient and instinctual as any effort known to man. In some deep, primal way, did not their survival depend upon overcoming the opponent? I doubt whether such a thought even crossed Myles's mind. He had been reminded all too often that the match was "only a game." Despite such promptings, he battled valiantly in this particular match, making many a fine shot—but the game began to slip away from him, and he lost in the end. He shook hands with the winner and came off the court somewhat dazed.

I joined the others in congratulating Myles for a game well played. I felt that in addition to his battle in the court, he had been at war with his own mounting dread of failure. He was the younger of the two players. The other boy was seeded first in the tournament. Myles had played as well as he could, despite the odds. This took courage. Myles won in a way that truly counts, as was demonstrated by his enthusiasm for another game with the same boy a few hours later—this time just for the heck of it.

Driving home with his father after the match, Myles at first wailed that he wanted to quit playing squash altogether. By the time he reached home several hours later, he said that he wanted to continue. I wonder whether his change of mind was due to his love for squash, his innate competitive spirit, or his desire to please his father. Children this age are often the pawns of their parents' projections. I once witnessed a hockey game in which the twelve-year-old goalie all of a sudden tore off his leg pads and helmet, threw down his hockey stick, and walked off the ice, shouting, "I hate this game! I always hated it! I never want to play it again! I don't care what my Dad says!" He, like many children who are manipulated by parents, coaches, or teachers can stand it only so long until their wisdom explodes.

To lose despite doing one's best is a disappointment difficult to manage at any age, for it is hard to regard defeat as a learning experience. Myles, along with countless other children, has had to learn to forgive himself, to judge himself not as a failure, but as a courageous player in the process of growing up.

FAITH

Fight doubting yourself;
After you do it you will be proud,
If you do not make it a big deal.
Tough things—don't give up on them.
High in courage is what you want to be.

Student

The student who wrote this and Myles have never met one another, yet in this poem, the wisdom of one child was speaking to the needs of another. The writer perceived that the way to retrieve one's confidence is to have faith in oneself. Thus one becomes a winner.

Myles is learning to observe the way other boys play, to note their strengths and weaknesses, and to adjust his own shots accordingly when competing with them. He must not allow the scoreboard to impede his trust in himself. When future situations arise—in sport, in social relations, in academic enterprise—that pit him against competitors who are beyond his skill, or set standards for competence that he cannot yet meet, his wisdom will help him stand his ground.

Self-knowledge lights the path to leadership. Winning and losing are both part of the game of life; Myles is learning to enter and leave the court with his head high. I praise his parents, who, knowing that Myles competes with boys beyond his chronological and emotional age, continually remind him of his truly great moments during the course of play. "You played the best ever, and won some very good points. That's what you need to remember!"

Think of how simple and yet how complex a ball is. Think how we take for granted movement, agility, and anticipation. Think of those split-second decisions we make on an ongoing basis during a game. So much goes into the development of an athlete that has nothing to do with props or gimmicks—the challenge comes from within.

Above all, this pursuit needs to be fun. We need to walk away wanting more.

Teacher

———ᴦᴠᴠ———

At school, our approach to the education of children was progressive. Creativity, confidence, and academic competence characterized our students as they transferred to other schools, both here and abroad. As for evaluation and assessment by means of tests, the children knew that the teachers and the curriculum were being tested along with each of them. If students did poorly on one particular part of a test, the teacher knew that they needed further exposure and experience. In one case I dressed up in a top hat as the Great Grammarian and tackled a class of students who had failed their grammar tests. I assigned to each of them a part of speech, or a punctuation mark. We spent the afternoon dramatizing exclamatory sentences. The children chose to be nouns, pronouns, active and passive verbs, prepositions, and organized themselves into subjects, predicates, and dangling participles. When the next test came around, they all achieved an A+. Practice tests before final tests often helped the children to transform anxiety into strategy. They were encouraged to compete with themselves and to better their best.

———ᴦᴠᴠ———

One universal challenge for teachers is to evaluate a child's progress in such a way that the child is *understood to the core*. All too often, our efforts at clarity, simplicity, and accuracy result in bland, broad, and prosaic reports that give little definition of the child's uniqueness. A child's personal transformation, so essential to learning, can hardly be described merely as "improvement" or "achievement." Nor can his or her struggle simply be dismissed as "distraction" or "lack of confidence." I have advised teachers to use words that describe each child's one-of-a-kind character, as well as his or her manner of learning, self-knowledge, and awareness of others. Every child is gifted in some way; talent is not limited to the violin or broad jump. The teacher must somehow capture the essential child during the learning process, and then communicate as much. One has to believe that the child *is* the most important person in the parents' world. If this is not the case, then the teacher's respect for the child can be extremely helpful. The sanctity of the individual is preserved.

Regarding communication, teaching/administrating is a performing art. When we communicate, it must be in a positive way, identifying the good in all situations. Negativity does not convey love or understanding. My colleague always reminded me: "It's not what you say but how you say it." In our communication with one another and with parents, we tried to be partners, not judges. So often we are reluctant to expose our difficulties for fear of being judged as weak! We should not fear asking for help. We have all been in the same boat.

When our School opened its doors to parents and visitors, we had a prime opportunity to share our philosophy and practices with current and prospective families. We hoped they would view the learning environment of the School as a world in which children were deeply influenced by beauty, order, and, most important of all, connection. In such an environment children could search for and discover their own inner wisdom as well as the wisdom conveyed by their educators. In a pep-talk to faculty and staff as they expressed some apprehension about such events, I urged,

> "Hopefully, the educational experience that visitors have with you should correspond as closely as possible to the educational experience that we offer their children every day. Please create in your teaching spaces a clear and thought-provoking picture of the educational process for which you are responsible and accountable. Your teaching brings deep satisfaction to children. Miracles occur on your watch. You have much to be proud of. So strut your stuff."

J.

Recently I ran across a letter that I wrote to one of our single parents about her child's inability to perform the required academic work of his class.

> Today Jamal and I talked for a while. I told him that he is regarded by all as an intelligent, resourceful young man, with true potential for academic advancement, and yet his work habits, social behavior, and general attitude have fallen far short of our expectations of him as a fourth-grader—particularly one who has so much going for him. In fact, he has not yet accomplished the necessary work to graduate to Grade V in June. His teachers have repeatedly spoken to him over the year and have done everything possible to give him opportunities to turn himself around. Believe me, we all want him to succeed.
>
> I asked Jamal whether he could pinpoint the problem underlying his lack of motivation. He told me about his grandmother's situation. Yes, when someone you love is lying in a coma, it is heartbreaking and distracting. In addition, he told me that he wasn't trying. I asked him if he wanted to continue at this school next year on the merit scholarship. He said he did. I told him that he would have to work over the summer to finish his fourth grade curriculum and be ready for fifth grade. He said he wants to do this. We will mail you information about our summer tutoring program. I know it will be helpful, and I urge you and Jamal to make it a top priority. Thank you.
>
> J.

In Jamal's case, we were dealing with a child whose school problem stemmed from long exposure to suffering at home where his grandmother lay dying. His apprehension regarding his grandmother kept him from being able to concentrate. He was not the only child who lost a parent or grandparent during the course of the school year. As in all such situations, we had to simply wait until the child could put the pieces back together again. He needed all the help we could give him.

He was able to move on to Grade V the following year, having spent the summer catching up.

Occasionally, time must be suspended in order to let a child's wisdom rise to the surface. Jamal was wise. He said he wanted to keep his merit scholarship and to catch up, and he did, in time, when he could.

Occasionally, we hold our breaths when a child's wisdom reaches beyond the self to provide for another. Sylvia graduated from Princeton Junior School, leaving behind a younger sister. Recently, as the recession tightened her family's purse strings, she wrote the following letter to Princeton Junior School:

> With the economy taking such a shift in the past few years, my parents were presented with some tough choices in order to keep me and my younger sister in the private school system. I saw they were struggling because they could afford to keep one of us in private school, but both would be difficult. I told my parents that I would be willing to leave my school to ensure that my little sister would be able to continue on at PJS and receive the same strong foundation I did. I knew I was already prepared, thanks to PJS, and would never want her to miss out on the same exceptional education.
>
> The strong foundation that PJS built for me (and many others) enabled me to continue on to be a confident and successful student. My mom reminds me that I was such a shy child when I started in kindergarten at PJS, and my teacher told her she would be amazed at my progress. I now know that my teacher was correct, and if it had not been for the education, love, and support I received during my years at PJS, I would not be the strong student and leader among my peers that I am able to be today.
>
> Thankfully, we are both still in our schools and doing very well. The greatest part is that my teachers and all the staff at PJS are still so encouraging and supportive of me to this day. For all of this, I am truly grateful.

Sylvia's letter reveals an authority that I recognize as wisdom. She is confident, but not complacent; she is self-denying, but not self-defeating. For the benefit of her sister, she is willing to sacrifice her own winnings.

Leadership assumes many forms. In Sylvia's case, leadership takes the form of service. Her character, courage, and compassion—energized by the spirit of wisdom—call out the best in others. It is no wonder that Sylvia has been elected to positions of leadership in her current school. Also, it is no wonder that she and her sister continue to attend the schools they were in before the economic shift. Where there is wisdom, there is a way.

From its beginning, our school followed the concept of Servant Leadership—a collaborative, collegial decision-making process designed to strengthen trust among faculty, staff, The Board, and parents. The common purpose of such shared leadership was to inspire children to learn deeply and to care for one another in the process. I used to list all the C words relating to our goals: community, character, competition, creativity, competence, curiosity, courage, companionship, cooperation, connection, communication, compassion, consciousness.

One year, I gathered fifth-graders in my office to talk about important matters. Their status as the oldest and wisest class in the school had quite gone to their heads. I wondered how aware they were of their responsibilities regarding the school community as a whole. We talked about different styles of leadership, and how they, as the graduating class, could exemplify the values of the school community in the way they interacted with the children who held them in such high esteem. They decided to focus on the various services that they could perform on a regular basis. Yellow sashes with "Hi-Five" lettered in black across the front were their badges of leadership and responsibility. They were worn with pride, as the students confirmed:

> Hi-Five is a group of fifth-graders helping out, giving younger
> children the chance to reach their important goals in learning.
> Playing and helping gives us a chance to learn also.

The jobs we have are serving pizza, reading to the little kids, watching the little kids at recess, admissions—which is showing people around the school—and cleaning up the school.

I have to make sure that other and younger kids follow the rules. Also, I need to make sure that the kids are safe and comfortable at school.

Hi-Five is a good way to learn responsibility and have fun.

"Hi" means the highest grade and "Five" means fifth grade. I think it is a good thing to do because I like to help other people.

I think helping out makes a difference in our school. I really enjoy it.

We also help the teachers because a lot of other children don't follow the school rules and if we tell them how to behave, maybe they will also start telling other people how to behave.

We really enjoy doing the work.

Hi-Five means that you are a guide for your fellow students. You are a bit like a teacher, a friend, and maybe a second parent.

I like being a Hi-Five because I like to help out with little kids and greet people at the door in the morning.

Grade V Students

Leadership can go astray at times. Once a group of boys formed a club during several weeks of playground recess. Dedicated to the pursuit of their common interest, marbles, they recruited only the best players with the best marbles. Their site was a flat, hardened mud ring. What started out as a relatively simple game that many could understand and enjoy became an exclusive competition controlled by only a few skilled players. Lagging, positioning, knuckling down, shooting—all became subject to the spontaneous rules of the anointed lead player. Whether players agreed in advance to play "for fair" or "for keeps" was also a burning issue at the beginning of each match.

As time went by, I heard increasing complaints about the "marble masters." They were not allowing anyone else to use their ring. It reminded me of the winter when some children who had built an igloo didn't want anyone else to play in it during subsequent recesses. "They'll *ruin* it!" As a marbles player in my own school days, I could well understand the addiction to perfection, but I could not condone an activity that was supervised by a privileged minority. When I spoke to the masters about their opportunity for true leadership, they reluctantly agreed to open their club to everyone, as long as all players would be careful of the ring. I bought a dozen bags of marbles. In the spirit of their new-found personae, the marble masters surrendered. They even taught the younger ones how to knuckle down and shoot.

—⚉—

No matter how you describe them, cliques are malignant. They can spread quickly, uncontrollably and destructively, particularly in an organism as vulnerable as a school family that relies upon mutual cooperation among its members. Although cliques were a rarity at our school, we were not immune to them. As usual, I found children to be more receptive to healing than their elders.

There it was, the clique, composed of four girls who stood glaring down at me. The clique festered and fumed while I slowly removed my reading glasses to gain some distance and time. The clique was accompanied by its captive—the girl with the braids standing by the door, who seemed acutely ill at ease. The clique clearly had the cohesiveness and intensity of its kind, but I wasn't sure of its purpose.

"Why are you here when you could be outside on this beautiful spring day? Why don't you all sit down so that I don't have to stand up." The clique did so, reluctantly. "Thank you. Now tell me what's troubling you this time." I knew what the trouble was by the way the clique sat—as far away as possible from the girl with the braids who began to cry.

"Nora thinks we don't like her because we won't let her into our play but we've worked on it for a long time and we know all the parts and she would just be coming in not knowing—"

Nora burst in: "Then why did you let Lucy in? She didn't know the parts either and you let her in!"

"Lucy's different. She's been in our plays before so she can remember how we do things."

"You always say that, but then why—"

"Why? Because you're not, you're just not like—"

"Not like what?" I interrupted. "Not like you? You're smart; she's smart. You play soccer; she plays soccer. You're nine; she's nine—"

"But this is different! She's different. *She's* the problem." The clique obviously had a big problem getting the words out. The main reason Nora was a problem for the clique was that she excelled academically.

"Nora, can you tell me what ails them?"

"They won't let me be in any of their things—like what they play at recess. And today I got a note in *her* writing that said I would be terminated."

I looked at the clique's impassive expression. "I was just practicing my handwriting."

In the clique's opinion, Nora was a weak, timid, ineffectual wimp. Nora had become just that, considering the power that the clique had to affect other people's attitudes toward her. I took a sheet of paper and placed a series of dots on it with a magic marker. The dots—all except one—made an incomplete circle. The last dot was placed at a distance in the corner of the paper. I addressed the clique. "Pretend this dot is you, over here by yourself. How do you feel?"

"You say it's me but you really mean *her*."

"Tell me how it feels to *you*, please."

"It feels bad—but I can make the others come my way, no problem."

"You know something? *You* are the clique responsible for what I believe to be a big problem. Unless you can figure out a way to close the circle that this school stands for, you will no longer be welcome in this school. Do you understand what I'm telling you?"

"Yes, Mrs. McIntyre." I dismissed them.

The clique dissolved.

—~~—

One way that the children built a bridge to another school was a practice interview. The fifth-graders who were graduating in June came to my office one by one to be interviewed. I had worked as an admissions officer in an earlier chapter of my life, so I knew what schools might be interested in knowing about prospective students. I also knew that with few exceptions, the average ten- or eleven-year-old, although self-confident, had little experience depicting his or her persona in a twenty-minute conversation with a total stranger.

First, the handshake. (*Don't pull away. Don't wipe your hand on your pants.*)

"Hello, Alice/Elias! Welcome to Howard School! Have a seat!" (*Sit up straight. Take a deep breath. Look him straight in the eye. He's not going to eat you.*)

"Well, now, have you had your tour of the buildings and grounds? What was your impression of this place? Did your guide answer your questions to your satisfaction?" (*Listen closely and answer only the question asked. He doesn't need to know what other campuses you have toured.*)

"Tell me something about yourself—what you want to learn . . ." (*Have you thought about who you are and what you hope to learn? Let's talk about it.*)

And so our practice interview proceeded; I asked questions regarding the child's attitudes and interests, and the child displayed as much self-knowledge as was called for. At the end of the practice, I would read back to my interviewee the very sentences that he or she had used. It was always a pleasant surprise to hear how well the child knew the person he or she was talking about.

—~~—

Our greatest challenge has been to preserve children's wisdom while at the same time preparing them for the inevitable complexity of the outside world. The world of the school should not be such a perfect hothouse that children perish when exposed to the elements. We had to find ways to help children first become accountable and responsible for the basic skills they learned in school—and then to apply such knowledge to their everyday life outside the school. In a program called "Gather 'Round" which was inspired and implemented by one of our parents, the first through fifth grades were given time to reflect upon what it takes to build a healthy community at school and beyond.

Sadly, children are in danger of losing touch with their wisdom as the years go by and life experience dulls their memory of heaven. Whatever wisdom they may have been born with is all too often taught or bought out of them by our culture. Exploiting their natural resources can lead to an erosion of the soul.

Perfectionism is a golden opportunity for fear. Take, for example, the girl who believes that she must earn love by being perfect. She hesitates to take risks for fear she will be criticized for her mistakes. Learning requires certain risks. Or the boy who tears up his whole poem because he cannot rhyme the last line. He forfeits a mile of imagination for an inch of effect. And what about the immaculate mother who, having confined her toddler to his playpen, wonders why he is bowlegged? When we lived in New York City, I told our pediatrician that I was dismayed by the amount of grime our two small children consumed while playing in Central Park every day. His comment offered no consolation. "Two spoonfuls a day'll keep the doctor away." Later, when I informed him that we were moving out of the city, he remarked, "You're giving up the chance to teach your children life's most important lesson: how to get along with other people in a small space."

In the city, does immunity from disease come naturally to children who eat dirt? In school, does immunity from perfectionism come naturally to children who take risks and make mistakes? Mistakes are lessons in disguise. We should be allowed to make them as we grow. When I was in the sixth grade, my teacher chose me to set an example for the rest of the class. She required me to behave in accordance with her will—academically, socially and emotionally. Her expectations unnerved me to the extent that I vomited on the way to school every day. After several months, an immobilizing bilious attack removed me from her clutches for the rest of the year. What a relief.

The perfectionist often deems self-improvement to be of greater value than self-awareness. If one is incessantly monitoring one's conduct, one cannot appreciate the vicissitudes of the maturation process. We need to learn primarily through real-life experiences if we are ever to interact with others frankly, confidently and empathetically. Interacting in this way gives us the best chances for improvement.

Perfectionism sometimes takes a curious turn, as I found out one day in the school. I was asked by one of our teachers to observe her class during a math lesson. I agreed to pay particular attention to two students who continually distracted others from their work. From my vantage point at the rear of the room, I could see the two offenders carrying out their mission to perfection: biting off pencil erasers, grimacing, passing notes, both oblivious to the lesson being presented.

"Mrs. McIntyre! What are you doing in our classroom?" whispered my immediate neighbor, a boy whose exemplary behavior had won him the status of a seat near the windows. He leaned toward me and with grave assurance, continued, "I know why you are here. I bet my teacher asked to you do something about certain people who never stop bothering us. I can tell you who they are."

He may have been correct, but since correcting others seemed to be more to his liking than solving math problems, I whispered back, "No thanks, Luke. I'm here to enjoy watching how you and your class do math." That silenced him for a moment or two. Then,

"Mrs. McIntyre, I've made up a great new rule. Do you want to hear it?"

A new rule? This boy already knew and followed plenty of rules. "Not now, Luke. Later. Let's listen to your teacher talk about borrowing and carrying."

"I already know about that. I want to tell you my new rule that I made up yesterday."

Before I could prevent it, the rule came through, *sotto voce*. "I won't look at my *you-know-what* any more and I won't allow other people to look at my *you-know-what*, either."

Luke's new rule hung in the void as I swallowed my chuckle. "That sounds to me like a pretty good rule to follow. Now I'm going to move to another place, if you don't mind." Who was distracting whom? I mused as I retreated from the poster child and found a new place to observe the two recalcitrants who were tilting their chairs in the front row.

That wasn't the end of it. The following day, a first-grader ran down to my office with dreadful news: the toilet was overflowing in the boys' bathroom and poop was streaming out and did I have a plunger? "Of course, every headmistress has a plunger somewhere," I growled as I tackled the clutter in the utility closet. There it was, along with mops in a small container labeled "TOILET TROUBLE." I grabbed the plunger in one hand, a mop in the other, dashed to the boys' bathroom, and kicked open the door.

"Hello, Mrs. McIntyre," the young man standing at the urinal called me. "It's in the last stall on the left. Someone stuffed a paper towel into it."

I realized that I hadn't knocked on the door—a violation of bathroom rule number one. "Oh, dear, it's you! Don't worry, Luke. I've just come to fix the toilet. I won't look at your *you-know-what*."

As I was plunging away in the last stall on the left, Luke's acquittal drifted back from the other side of the room: "It's okay if *you* want to look, Mrs. McIntyre. You're the principal."

PART III: BECOMING

Almighty God,
Sun behind all suns,
Soul behind all souls,
Show us in everything we touch and
In everyone we meet
The continued assurance of thy presence round us,
Lest ever we should think thee absent.
In all things thou art there.
In every friend we have
The sunshine of thy presence is shown forth.
In every enemy that seems to cross our path,
Thou art there within the cloud to challenge us to love.
Show us the glory in the grey.
Awake for us thy presence in the very storm
Till all our joys are seen as thee
And all our trivial tasks emerge as sacraments
In the universal temple of thy love.

George MacLeod

Occasionally, I see in the lives of children configurations of intense light and shadow—as in *chiaroscuro*. Could the jolt from total darkness to glaring light at birth have instilled this pattern? Whatever the cause, the effect is dramatic. In this gestalt, children swim in a black-and-white medium, either buoyed by fearless hope or engulfed by hopeless fear. When I speak of *chiaroscuro* in the lives of children, I do not mean a static state of inner or outer darkness. Rather, I refer to children's natural reaction of delight or despair in response to the rise and fall of life's current. When children access their wisdom, they trust that there is light within and around them always, and that they will find a cure for the darkness.

It is the same for us adults, only we are older and less trusting. *Chiaroscuro* moments are familiar to each of us, given the twists and turns of life. The tension created by such contrasts can pull us away from our center. We need to remind ourselves and our children that without the interplay of light and shadow, we could not perceive form at all. We live in a state of continual gradation as we try to ease the strain caused by *chiaroscuro*. MacLeod's plea, "Show us the glory in the gray," well portrays our need for God to be present to create, shape, and highlight the form of our existence. "In Him we live and move and have our being" is wisdom's cure for the stress of *chiaroscuro*. (Acts 17:28, New International Version, Bible.)

It happened during the swine flu pandemic of 2009. Julie's call came through on my cell phone while I was in the lobby of a movie theatre. "Mom, can you and Dick come up right away to help me out? We've all had the flu one after another. First it was Georgie, then Olivia, then me—I've been home for a week—and now Amy! She took care of us all and now she's in the hospital with it! She's *really* sick. They don't know whether she'll make it. I've got to go back to work tomorrow so I can't be here to take her place . . . Please come!"

I was stunned by the anguish in her voice. Was she panicking? All I could think of saying at that moment was, "Hold on tight, Julie! You've got to *believe* that Amy will pull through! We'll get there as fast as we can."

We left immediately. Twelve hours later, Dick and I were holding sway over Amy's domain, transporting, cooking, nurturing, and monitoring children during the hours Julie was away teaching. Taking Amy's place gave us a wonderful chance to get to know our grandchildren better. That they sorely missed her and worried about her was evident in the tension they felt as they went about their daily routines. She had lived with and loved them ever since they were born.

Amy was indeed very sick. While she had been caring for the others, she had totally exhausted herself. Swine flu bored its way into her whole body and ravaged her. Comatose for days, she lay in the hospital's intensive care unit, suspended between life and death. High fever, respiratory failure, kidney failure, and countless other complications snuffed the spirit out of her—or so it seemed. We waited for some sign of recovery, but none came. Amy's partner and a very few others were allowed to see her. No children, of course. Olivia and Georgie had a message for her, but no way to deliver it.

"Pray, whether you believe in prayer or not. You've got to *believe* that Amy will live," I told Julie. "Don't allow yourself to think otherwise!" We prayed without ceasing. Julie became adamant that the children somehow give their message to Amy before it was too late. Dick contacted a retired doctor who had been the former chief of orthopedic surgery at Massachusetts General Hospital. He advised Dick to telephone the hospital, identify himself as the priest representing the family of a patient in the ICU, and ask to be connected with the head nurse. Done. Dick conveyed the children's message to a nurse with deaf ears. He waited until the next shift and called again. This time, he spoke with a nurse who believed in the wisdom of children. She took down the words that Olivia and Georgie wanted Amy to hear. From that moment on, the nurse often whispered into Amy's ear, "Olivia and Georgie have a message for you: 'Amy, we love you and we miss you! Please don't die! Come back and take care of us!'" The nurse wrote the children's plea on a piece of paper and taped it to Amy's ventilator. She passed the message on to other nurses who repeated it throughout the nights. Those words were uttered again and again until at last—with the doctor guessing that death was only an hour away—Amy opened her eyes.

Who knows how deeply the children's mantra kindled Amy's spirit and transformed her? For those of us who witnessed her recovery, it was nothing short of a miracle. Now, back at work, she has no memory of her stay in the hospital and still wonders what all the fuss was about. At her doctor's request, she visited the medical staff in the ICU, to show them the remarkable effect of their care. True, they had done their job well, but I think they knew what triggered Amy's healing.

—~~~—

For many years of the school's life, I taught drama. The classes were lively. Children explored structure, sequence, and symbol as they improvised stories old and new. Not only did the stories have power in themselves; they also provided a context for play, aesthetic development, critical thinking, empathy, cooperation, communication, moral and spiritual values, and knowledge of self. I encouraged parents and teachers to read stories aloud to children, to use stories to teach children what was important, and to recognize that they, along with the children, were engaged every day in the story of their lives. Over the course of various projects, I could tell whose imagination came out of a box and whose imagination was fresh. It was all I could do not to judge the boxed children, for they killed many a spirit. To coax them out of the box became my greatest motivation, particularly since such an escape often produced uncontrolled exuberance on the part of the escapee. I spent a lot of time trying to catch up with the runaway, but it was well worth the effort.

One year, some children wanted to engage in drama during their free time. I consented on condition that this time, they make up their own story instead of dramatizing one written by someone else. During the first of twenty sessions, I asked them for suggestions. As usual, they had more schemes than there was time for, everything from romances to murder mysteries. Everybody talked and nobody listened, so I asked them to write their ideas down on a piece of paper, give them to me, and wait until the following session to be apprised of whatever ideas took the lead. The children skidded into the second session with ears flapping. I informed them that I had read all their notes and that there was certainly a story somewhere in the air waiting to be captured and tamed. According to a number of their notes, the story should contain a royal family. Also, the story should have a virtually unsolvable problem. According to several notes, the solution to the problem should come as a great surprise at the end.

This cluster of ideas was a beginning. The children grabbed at the bait. First, they delineated the castle in which the royal family would live; the moat, drawbridge, walls, turrets, and keep were all placed in an imagined landscape. Since no props were allowed, everyone had to memorize the form and placement of various castle structures so players wouldn't walk through walls or into the moat as they played the story.

Second, the children had to create characters to launch the story. Although they didn't know yet where the story might lead, they settled on a king, a queen, a prince, and princess. Four children volunteered to start the story. The first scene took place in the throne room. The king and queen were arguing loudly. The prince and princess wanted to go outside to play, but couldn't get their parents' permission. During the subsequent replays by a number of children, it became apparent that the king was an exceedingly grumpy individual who could never be satisfied. As hard as his wife and children tried, they could not make him laugh or even smile.

By the third session, the king's grumpy temperament was a problem for courtiers and sages alike. No one could persuade the king to change. His bad moods affected not only the court, but the entire kingdom. The queen (who was a good deal smarter than the king) developed a bleeding ulcer. The prince and princess, never allowed to play outside, became lethargic. Courtiers bickered amongst themselves and sages fled to their caves in the landscape. Even the guards gave up keeping watch and slept at their posts. Something had to be done if the kingdom was to survive.

By the fourth session, the story about the grumpy king had reached such an emotional pitch that the class asked for a break in order to figure out how to solve the problem they had created. We stopped the play. I lingered on the sidelines while the children came up with one idea after another. The challenge was how to bring a king's spirit to life. One child suggested a war. Another thought a massive fire might get his attention. The idea of a fairy godmother with a magic wand was voted down. Finally, a child who loved playing the smart queen said, "Let's have the queen announce to all the king's subjects that there is going to be a contest at the palace on a certain date. Whoever performs something that makes the king smile or laugh will be the winner." Everyone thought that this idea was a good one as long as there was a big prize for the winner. For the rest of the session, the children argued about what would constitute the perfect prize. At last, they decided that the winner should be given the chance to be king for a day. Despite one child's protest that the king might consider such a prize as a serious threat to his authority, the smart queen's suggestion won the day. That the king might slip back into grumpiness was a risk they were willing to take.

By the sixth session, some children had spent time dreaming up performances that might bring a smile to the lips of the grumpy king. Some performances involved a magician, a clown, or a jester. Others involved a dancer, a drummer, or a juggler. Still others involved mystical creatures such as gazelles, winged horses, or dragons. Over the course of many sessions, these children rehearsed their scenarios again and again.

By the twelfth session, the class was ready to go back to the original story that had been put aside for a while. The king was as grumpy as ever. The queen, ignoring his protests, sent heralds to every corner of the kingdom to announce the royal contest that was to take place at the palace in a month. People were excited. When the great day dawned, the line of entertainers approaching the castle gate was a mile long.

In the thirteenth session, the castle's throne room was converted into an arena for the royal contest. The courtiers were dressed in their finest attire (no costumes, but elaborate bowing and scraping and doffing of imaginary hats). The queen barked orders to pages, who scurried in every direction. The guards buffed their armor and stood at the door. The prince and princess posed charmingly at the king's feet. The king, gloomier than ever, slumped on his throne and shot accusing glances at his wife. The crowd in the royal arena was electric with hope that the day had finally come for the kingdom to be relieved of its problem.

Sessions fourteen through nineteen consisted of scenarios by all the performers who aspired to make the king laugh and forfeit his throne for a day. Although every act drew roars of approval from the crowd, not one succeeded in dislodging the king from his usual dismal demeanor. He yawned, he groaned, he shook his head causing each successive performer to withdraw in dismay. I became worried that we had only one session to go and still no one had come up with a solution to the problem. Someone must come up with an idea. I looked in desperation at the boy who was playing the king, but he only shrugged.

To my surprise, the twentieth session revealed a denouement that the children had worked out among themselves without telling me. The final performance was about to take place in the arena. From his high throne, the king scowled down at an acrobat who bowed low before him. The acrobat rolled out his mat and performed a series of spectacular stunts. These drew no more than a grimace from the king, who waved to the guards to show the man out. Paying no heed to the guards, the acrobat rolled up his mat, faced the king, and boldly posed a question.

"Your Royal Highness, have you ever turned a somersault?"

"A somersault? Of course not," retorted the king. "Why would a person in my position stoop so low?"

"I just wondered. Somersaults are fun. They charge up the brain and make you smart."

The king bristled. "I am already very smart."

"Then perhaps you're afraid of turning a somersault. I suppose you wouldn't dare to try one." The acrobat turned to leave.

"What do you mean, I wouldn't dare? I can accomplish anything I wish. After all, I am the king." His Royal Highness shifted uncomfortably on his throne.

The acrobat turned around and once more faced the king. "Your Lofty Highness, if that is so, would you let me show you how to accomplish a somersault?"

"If you insist upon making a fool of yourself, I won't object. But get on with it, and then get out."

The acrobat rolled out his mat with a flourish. "If you please, Your Majesty, come join me!" With a smile, the acrobat gestured to the king to come down from the throne. At first the king hesitated, his eyes sweeping around the room. Then, with exaggerated nonchalance, he did what he was told.

"Now, simply do as I do." The acrobat squatted in front of the mat and placed his hands a foot apart. Much to everyone's astonishment, the king sighed heavily and did likewise.

"Now, place your head upside down between your hands, like this." The acrobat bent over and placed his head upside down between his hands.

The king bellowed, "I can't be bothered to do such a ridiculous thing! Be off with you, you fool!"

"But, Supreme Highness, you are so close! I know you can do it! You will feel new life flowing through your veins!"

The acrobat's upside down appeal brought a cheer from the crowd. They began to clap and chant: "You can do it! You can do it!"

The king was startled. Frowning all the while, he carefully removed his crown and handed it to a page. Then he stooped over and placed his head upside down between his hands, imitating the acrobat's position. Thunderous applause.

The acrobat quickly turned a somersault and sprang to his feet. "Come along, Your Highness! Kick up your heels! The end is in sight! You'll be happy and bright!" The crowd became silent.

The king, with a huge grunt, ever so slowly raised his behind up into the air and gave a little kick. Nothing happened. The crowd held its breath. He gave a bigger kick. Still nothing happened. Finally, he gave such a kick that his body turned a perfect somersault. The crowd roared, the queen danced a jig, the prince and princess jumped for joy.

What a surprise! There sat the king bolt upright on the mat with his legs straight out in front. At first he simply stared into space, then his mouth twitched into a smile, then he began to laugh. Soon he was laughing so hard that tears tumbled down his cheeks.

Within moments, a resounding shout went out across the land: "Long live the king!" And so he did. He lived happily ever after and so did everybody else.

You may wonder why I tell this particular story in such detail. To be sure, I have no script—only a memory of *The Grumpy King*. Yet the lessons I learned from the children during the development of this play will remain in my heart forever. I learned that when left to their own devices, children will create stories that encompass essential matters of human concern. In the case of *The Grumpy King*, a person of great power and authority was trapped by his unhappiness. No one could persuade him otherwise. His depression undermined the entire realm over which he had control. His bad moods seemed an unsolvable problem; people lamented, animals limped, crops lay fallow. Finally, a playful act—a somersault—gave the king a way to recover his spirits.

His subjects became whole as well. That the children chose *play* to win the day was no surprise.

It was not only the children's story that impressed me during those drama sessions. The manner in which they dealt with individual challenges was impressive. For example, they had to think of a way to include all sixteen children in the play. The king and his family amounted to four characters only. His wife and children had no success in cheering him up, so somehow the problem had to be solved by the rest of the players. They, in turn, wanted their roles to be more than spear-bearers; they wanted to be show-stoppers! The girl who often chose to play the queen was wise to suggest a royal contest that would feature everybody as a star performer. The unique and compelling act that each player produced made the king's intransigence even more deplorable. The children helped one another create distinctive scenarios by highlighting one another's dialogue, pantomime, and pace. Only once did the spell break when two girls fought over who was to be the leading lady in their skit. They became so absorbed in their struggle that I had to intervene. Did they think that the king would be amused by a catfight? No. Why not let the leading lady have a double, a mirror image who would reflect her every action perfectly? Their willingness to forgive and start afresh resulted in a spectacular skit in which the two girls reflected one another's movements so accurately as to portray a perfect butterfly. Everyone was mesmerized except the king, who stared fixedly at a spot on the ceiling. I am still moved by the girls' readiness to forgive one another and begin again.

Another lesson that I learned from children during the making of the play had to do with faith. The children demonstrated the presence of wisdom in their eagerness to heal the king. They believed from the beginning that the royal problem would be solved. Somehow, they knew that the grumpy king was both the source of the problem and the solution. The king was a weak, lonely man who could neither give nor receive love. His subjects were profoundly in need of his support, for he was their leader and representative—their symbol. Likewise, the king needed the support of his subjects in order to realize his leadership, authority, and sovereignty.

The vital connection between the king and his realm had been severed. The children's solution involved the whole community coming together in an effort to relieve the king of whatever was impeding his and their happiness. They needed the king to be transformed so that they could be renewed. *Everyone* was rejected by the king: his family, his courtiers and sages, his subjects. In the royal contest, *everyone* tried to cheer him up. Although they were rejected by the king, they received hearty support from one another. The more troubling the king's situation, the more determined the children were to find a way through to the other side. At last, wisdom, disguised as an acrobat, engaged him in a truly playful act. He shed his crown, knelt down, and rediscovered himself as both a child and a king. The community's reborn king personified their recovery. In this play, I felt the children were depicting the drama of the soul.

It was our practice to remind children that almost every story has a beginning, a middle, and an end—and that their life-story was just beginning; the characters and the plot awaited their call. What happened next would depend on how wisely they learned and applied their basic skills to their daily lives with creative imagination. They eventually learned that the end of one story leads to the beginning of another. This is what education is all about.

We encouraged children to take time to develop their own story, never losing sight of those timeless essentials: wonder, work, and wisdom. It was no surprise that many of their stories began with "Once upon a time" and ended with "happily ever after."

———~~~———

Our hope is that by the time they graduate, the children have progressed from the core to the final chamber of Princeton Junior School's nautilus. While they are still works in progress, they have learned to read, to write, to conceptualize and solve problems in math and to follow the scientific method. They have learned the languages of music, art, and drama as well as English and elementary Spanish. They have learned the arts of public speaking and of conversation. They have learned to conduct research using the invaluable resources of the library and the internet. They have learned sportsmanship. They have learned about how people lived, governed, journeyed, and sought justice throughout the history of this country. They have plumbed their depths and discovered their essential selves. They have loved to learn and learned to love.

I continually give thanks for what children have taught me about their wisdom, their creativity that connects them to others and empowers them to transform, and their transcendence that connects them with those who are "out of bounds," such as Cezanne, Woodrow Wilson, and Amy. In the sometimes choppy currents of school and family life, their wisdom helps them to solve problems and resolve conflicts, and to express their passion for healing and justice in ingenuous, powerful ways. These things come naturally to children when they are encouraged to access and play with their wisdom. I pray to God that we won't school their wisdom out of them. If we do, there will be a millstone around our necks. If we allow it to flourish, they will indeed cheer up the world.

In my family, special occasions were traditionally accompanied by a bagpiper. Processions at family weddings, funerals, and anniversaries often marched to the poignant strains of the pipe. In the school family, the ceremony at the end of each year—the graduation of *every* child from one level to the next—was launched by a bagpiper. An impressive figure, he would appear in full regalia at the entrance of the school, his melodies greeting the throng of well-wishers who gathered to celebrate each child's accomplishments. Once we were settled on Fackler Road, the whole school—children, teachers, staff members, trustees, and I—would assemble on the circle for the procession. The piper would set forth, kilt and ribbons swinging to the rhythm of his purposeful stride. I marched behind him, followed by my beloved staff who carried flags and banners bearing the names of the school, the state, and the nation. Then came the long, colorful procession of children with their teachers, the youngest class foremost, and the eldest class last of all, dressed in white.

The piper would walk the circle once and then veer off to the left, droning alongside the school's south boundary. Leaving the schoolhouse far behind, he would lead his lively followers up a hill toward their school garden. The foliage in every bed waved to the passing children as if to call out, "Thank you for your tender care throughout the spring. Now it's your turn to bear fruit!" The procession would then turn from the garden to flank the northern boundary, everyone by this time breathless with excitement and anticipation. The piper would plunge down the sledding slope, past the gourds on the play yard fence, and into the birch allée planted by students when we first arrived at Fackler Road. Through this leafy tunnel the throng would pass until it emerged on the other side of the meadow, facing the labyrinth at the edge of the woodland. Who knows how often folk have walked this mysterious maze so meticulously created by Grade IV? Only its mossy paths can give the answer. From the labyrinth, the piper would lead the procession across the big field back to the schoolhouse, arriving at last in the courtyard outside The Commons, There, framed by a mass of yellow roses cultivated by the children, he would pivot and pipe the oncoming procession to their seats, one class after another until the last Grade V settled down in front of the crowd. The graduation ritual has never changed. Every child in the school is named and thanked for his or her work and play throughout the year.

The graduation procession marked both an end and a beginning. While walking the bounds of the school, we were all, in effect, straddling both the past and the future. We were in a special moment in the midst of time and space. Whereas Grade V represented the longest past, the three-year-olds represented the longest future. In the Princeton University Parade, the younger ones follow in the footsteps of the ones who have gone before, but in our graduation procession, the older ones follow the younger ones. Why? Practically speaking, the youngest children go first because if they followed the taller ones and got too far behind, they wouldn't see or hear the piper well and would become distracted. The little ones need to feel the pulse from the beginning of the procession. True, the older children come of age and leave the school to go out into the world, but the younger ones are really the authorities when it comes to living in the present with wonder, trust, and courage.

—◆◆—

Butterflies flying by, being very silent, drinking nectar in their own special way.
Their wings spread beautifully, flapping so tenderly,
Oh, beautiful is the butterfly flying by.

Student

The monarch butterfly is bound to act in accordance with its instinct, its wisdom, as it transforms from stage to stage, whereas we humans, while acting upon our natural impulse to transform, are relatively free to create or destroy. Our wisdom leads us to create, but unfortunately, in the process of growth, we can lose sight of this image of God within ourselves. We become spiritually blinded. Fearfully, we stumble in the dark. I am convinced that at these times, our hunger for restoration corresponds to the powerful longing of our wisdom to reconnect, renew, restore, recreate. We are invited to return to the light of our wisdom. Such an experience I call an epiphany—a gift of infinite love for which I am deeply thankful.

As butterflies in the larval and pupal stages follow their natural instincts, so children in the early stages of education consciously access their wisdom in addition to acquiring skill and knowledge. Instinctively, a butterfly emerges from the chrysalis and spreads its wings in the sunshine so that the wings' solar cells can absorb the energy of the sun and the butterfly can fly thousands of miles away. Similarly, our children emerge from a school where they have plumbed their depths and spread their wings in the warmth of their Creator so that they may fly away.

Graduation is a time to be happy and sad. I am happy because I am moving on to the next stage of my life. I'm going to do well in a place where I will have different choices. I am sad that I have to graduate because I grew up at this school. I will miss the teachers, the activities, the classes, and the building. I will miss the loving community. This school is a big part of my early life. This school holds good and sad memories of the many years I have been here. I remember show-and-tell, splash day, and my first lonely day at this school. This school lets me know that I can be who I want to be and that I have more knowledge than I think I have. I will visit whenever I can because I care. Thanks to this school my life has improved. Early memories of this school will always stay in my heart . . . The rising sun is a symbol for me because it is what has happened to me. It is me."

Student

Above all, I pray that children come to appreciate their vast capacity for transformation through creating, healing, and growing. I pray that they perceive their wisdom to be a gift God's infinite love, a gift to be shared with others. I pray that they believe every moment of life to be precious. I pray that they have the courage to fly, joyfully, high in the sky.

I leave you now with my words to the children of Princeton Junior School when I retired.

As I ripen, I shall cherish "what from thee I have learned" during my years in this school:
How to play—with tools, with words, with ideas
How to trust
How to connect
How to make believe
How to be transformed
How to wonder
How to build and make
How to make do
How to let go
How to forgive
How to appreciate the difference of others
How to help one another
How to be fair
How to love
Thank you, dearest, dearest children.

ALUMNAE,I REMEMBRANCES

1.

"At the Junior School, the teachers struck a balance between pushing each individual to excel and creating a community through cooperative learning. This meant that as a weak math student, I was paired with one of my stronger peers. It also meant that as a second-grader, I went to the fourth grade for spelling. As a fifth-grader, I lead a reading group for first-graders; I was so proud to have that responsibility. It felt good to use what I knew to help someone else, and I thrive on that feeling today.

"Each of my teachers was exceptional in a different way. I'll never forget the day I invited Mrs. McIntyre, the headmistress, to lunch at my house, and she came! (I was four.) Mrs. Robins encouraged me to set a goal and see it through—I finished every book by Beatrix Potter by the end of first grade. Mrs. Gorman taught me to write poetry. At age seven I promised to dedicate my first book to her, and I intend to keep that promise. In February of this year, I published my first short story. Mrs. Skey had the motto, "Results, Not Excuses," and she taught me determination by making me write an essay on why I thought I couldn't learn math—it was called "The Wall." Our teachers encouraged us to reach as far as we could. I had fun at the Junior School, but I didn't feel like a child; I felt like a member of a society. My ideas were valued and taken seriously.

"I think my best advice for kids out there is to find what you love and dedicate yourself to it. If you work hard at something you are passionate about, not only will that pursuit take you far in life, it also will help you weather all the tough times. Love the guitar? Play all the time, no matter what anybody says, and find other kids who like to play, too. You won't be lonely and you won't be bored; you'll have something to be proud of."

2.

"In looking back on my years at PJS, I realized that many of my accomplishments at my present school stem from a strong foundation of learning at PJS.

"When I first came to my present school, I was placed in advanced math. I did not realize it at the time, but in fifth grade at PJS, I was actually learning at a seventh-grade level. While I continue to do well in math, history may just be my favorite subject. I was very proud when I won the year-end history prize in sixth grade, and I remembered how PJS set me up for a good ideal school experience with this subject. There were no grades then to motivate the students—just an eagerness to learn. If we were studying the silk trade in social studies, we hatched silk worms in science and then went on to art for a creative project on the same topic. This kind of immersion in a subject developed a passion for learning that has never left me . . . Another one of my favorite subjects is science. I believe the reason I excel at science is because the PJS science program taught me to explore and discover new things. Mrs. Zeppenfeld is truly an artist when it comes to inspiring students to love learning, because she let us go with the flow, make a mess, discover how to make mistakes and dig our own way out, and to feel an integral part of the natural world. I will never forget the monarch butterfly project and the river explorations, where we would get wet and dirty and it didn't matter.

"Public speaking is another one of my favorite subjects. This is mostly due to the inspirational oral presentation projects assigned at PJS, such as the Metropolitan Art Museum presentation where we studied an artist, created an artistic interpretation of his or her work, went to the Met to see the work in person, and then gave an oral presentation to the other grades. A background of public speaking in a familiar and comfortable environment at a young age has helped me in all my subjects in my present school because I have the confidence to voice my opinions without fear of making mistakes.

"Confidence is the key word when it comes to describing my lower school years at PJS. I gained the confidence to make my own choices, to take leadership positions, to relate to both peers and adults, and most importantly, to try new things. By learning through exploration and discovery at Princeton Junior School, I achieved a level of confidence that has carried me through middle school and will continue to be by my side, like a good friend, throughout my academic life."

3.

"During my one and a half years at Princeton Junior School I have realized many things. I have become a more confident and wiser person.

"First, I have discovered myself as a person. I have realized I can do well no matter what. I don't have to worry about being the most popular or the best at anything. I have even become a better friend and student because of all the positive influences laid before me. I can be more sportsmanlike and let go, realizing it's just a game. I am more laid back and not uptight.

"I used to walk into school not desiring to learn and expecting the worst because of bullies and peer pressure, but now I look forward to school and its advantages. I have a hunger to learn that has completely taken me over in full force. Now I read three books or more a month and get lost in a book whenever I get a chance.

"If Mrs. McIntyre and Mrs. Craven hadn't had a passion for teaching, this school wouldn't have been created. I attribute my success to Mrs. McIntyre and Mrs. Craven because they created a great environment for learning. I now have a more promising future."

4.

"To Mrs. Boruch, teacher of Grade V: Where do I start? The Boruch Math Tips really paid off. Whenever I have a math test, I still get out my quadrille notebook. The math here is very advanced and ahead of most schools, but I already know a lot of the things from class at PJS. Worldly Wise vocabulary also paid off. I use a vocabulary word occasionally. In history, I know most of the things we are learning. In English, I am ahead of the gang. Fifth grade was one of the best years of my life, and I can thank you for giving it to me.

"PS: I still listen to B. B. King."

5.

"Another thing that PJS really helped me with was writing. I had always loved to write but never gotten the chance. In fourth grade, with Mrs. Moore, we had a writer's workshop, where all you do is writing. I loved it. Even thought I complained sometimes, I did like it. I made many books that year, and I still read them sometimes for fun. In fifth grade, my teacher, Mrs. Boruch, liked us to go outside in the rain, snow, or sunshine and listen for what we heard. Then we would come inside and write it down and then compare it to what everyone else heard . . . All this writing has really helped me, because writing really is a big part of your grade as you get older. For your SSAT, you have to write a really good essay and put up a big defense for what you think is true about the statement you are given, so this really helped me a lot."

6.

"We played Red Rover and created an excellently wonderful time that has drawn me to team sports ever since in attempts to recreate it. Just this summer I was fortunate enough to go to the Royal Henley Regatta to row with Dartmouth's women's crew team. Thank you, Dede, for starting the passion so long ago!

"What I remember most about PJS is what a fantastically fun time I had learning. In first grade, I distinctly recall cracking up over books we read in a group with Mrs. Robins, from *Winnie-the-Pooh* to *A Cricket in Times Square*. I recall the wonder of each of us students as we individually constructed our own circuits with a battery, wire, and small light bulb—I felt as smart as Thomas Edison. Such academic curiosity and confidence has been invaluable, and PJS carefully, firmly established it when I was there . . .

"Learning mathematic concepts in the classroom was so fascinating to me that I recall laughing out loud when I discovered how high one could count on an abacus with so few beads—and add, and multiply, and divide. It was mind-boggling."[7].

"I began Princeton Junior School in kindergarten and continued through fourth grade. What I took away from PJS was not just memories of a great community. When I began at PJS I had an eagerness to learn and make friends. Another very important thing that I took away from PJS was creativity. I am a singer and a songwriter, and I believe that what planted that seed of creativity was PJS, not only through the arts program, but also through the encouragement I was given to jump into my interests and pursue my dreams. Just as important to me was that I made lifelong friends at PJS. We still look back at our PJS experiences today. They are experiences that I wouldn't trade for anything."

8.

This poem was a gift to me upon my retirement.

> I know the place where once this rose stood tall.
> Freely she took the soil of herself
> To help along the bees, the bugs, and all.
> She led and she inspired everyone else;
> Within her presence others learned to be
> A caring lot of helpful growers, too.
> She readied earth and planted many seeds
> That still today do strive to rise and bloom,
> And even as she chooses t'end her reign
> To step aside and rest her loving face,
> That which she's tilled sits ready evermore
> T'show future buds the light in their own ways.
> And those that know her will forever know
> All that she's done to help this world to grow.

TRIBUTES

> There are different kinds of gifts, but the same Spirit distributes them. There are different kinds of service, but the same Lord. There are different kinds of working, but in all of them and in everyone it is the same God at work.
>
> As it is, there are many parts, but one body. The eye cannot say to the hand, "I don't need you!" And the head cannot say to the feet, "I don't need you!" On the contrary, those parts of the body that seem to be weaker are indispensable, and the parts that we think are less honorable we treat with special honor . . . God has put the body together . . . there should be no division in the body, but that its parts should have equal concern for each other. If one part suffers, every part suffers with it; if one part is honored, every part rejoices with it. *(1 Corinthians 12:4-6, 20-26 NIV, Bible)*

I give thanks and praise to all of you whose Wisdom and courage brought Princeton Junior School to life. The words of this book cannot possibly describe the miracles that you have wrought. I have purposely avoided referring to you by name or even describing your extraordinary creativity in detail, for my goal has been to focus on children. Having said that, I must add that the reason our children have been so eager to share their Wisdom is and always will be because they are loved, nurtured, encouraged and challenged by *you*.

(The following names belong to those of you who were with me before I retired in 2005.)

Trustees

Teachers

Elisabeth Bennett
Jean Bessette
Martha Bolster
Karen Boruch
Phyllis Boulton
Stephanie Bower
Racquel Brewer
Gloriann Burton
Sarah Chamlin
Marina Choufrine
Sally Chrisman
Marilyn Ciafone
Linda Clark
Lorrie Costanzo
Helen Craven
Jennifer DeGregory
Devon Delaney
Sarah Dixon
Jean Duff
Louise Dunham
Dotty Eiger
Marian Ferrara
Dianne Finger
Melinda Flatley
Karen Frelinghuysen
Elisabeth Fuccello
Marie Garber
Sandi Godfrey
Lee Goodwin
Frannie Gorman
Jennifer Graya
Judy Hill
Mimi Howe
Nancy Hughes
Gloria Hunter
Beth Inouye

Barbara Janssen
Renee Johann
Debbie Keller
Elena Koly
Elisabeth Lansing
Peggy Linke
Wendy Lomasarro
Mary Lott
Maria Lundy
Eileen Marin
Jason Micheli
Christina B. Moore
Susan Netterfield
Debbie O'Hare
Sahoko Okabayashi
Beatriz Orlanski
Rashmi Patel
Deborah Pedraza
Anne Pfieffer
George Poli
Nancy Robins
Deborah Robbins
Sandra Rosenthal
Cathy Royal
Cynthia Sage
Ada Schneider
Cathy Schnitzler
Carol Schonfeld
Leanne Seabright
Lori Shally
Lidia Sikora
Denise Singer
Judith Sinner
Peggy Skemer
Sally Skey
Julie Smith

ACKNOWLEDGMENTS

Princeton Junior School has been blessed with an architecture that enhances the quality of life of its individuals as well as the values and mission of its community. The school has been blessed as well with an evolving educational landscape that transforms the children who cultivate and care for it. For extraordinary foresight and creativity, I thank Mark B. Thompson, Architect, Nancy Takahashi, Landscape Architect, Henry and Susan Pikaart Bristol, Architects.

———

I thank the women of my literary peer group, whose insights and suggestions have been exceedingly helpful to me as I developed this book: Sally Branon, Irene Lynch, Meg Pinto, Janet Stern, Maggie Sullivan, and Letitia Ufford.

CPSIA information can be obtained at www.ICGtesting.com
Printed in the USA
BVOW070446100713

325481BV00001B/2/P